ACTIVISM IN THE PUBLIC SPHERE

Activism in the Public Sphere
Exploring the discourse of political participation

WAYNE CLARK
Department of Human Sciences
Buckinghamshire Chilterns University College

LONDON AND NEW YORK

First published 2000 by Ashgate Publishing

Reissued 2018 by Routledge
2 Park Square, Milton Park, Abingdon, Oxon OX14 4RN
711 Third Avenue, New York, NY 10017, USA

Routledge is an imprint of the Taylor & Francis Group, an informa business

Copyright © Wayne Clark 2000

All rights reserved. No part of this book may be reprinted or reproduced or utilised in any form or by any electronic, mechanical, or other means, now known or hereafter invented, including photocopying and recording, or in any information storage or retrieval system, without permission in writing from the publishers.

Notice:
Product or corporate names may be trademarks or registered trademarks, and are used only for identification and explanation without intent to infringe.

Publisher's Note
The publisher has gone to great lengths to ensure the quality of this reprint but points out that some imperfections in the original copies may be apparent.

Disclaimer
The publisher has made every effort to trace copyright holders and welcomes correspondence from those they have been unable to contact.

A Library of Congress record exists under LC control number: 00109572

ISBN 13: 978-1-138-72867-7 (hbk)
ISBN 13: 978-1-138-72863-9 (pbk)
ISBN 13: 978-1-315-19042-6 (ebk)

Contents

Acknowledgements   *vi*

1. Introduction   1
2. Investigating Political Participation in Britain   16
3. The Public Sphere, Discourse and Political Participation   42
4. Methodology and Research Design   71
5. Case Studies   89
6. Structures of Political Participation   98
7. Mapping a Typology of Political Participation and Activism   114
8. Analysing the Process of Political Participation   139
9. Conclusions   172

Bibliography   *193*
Name Index   *203*

Acknowledgements

There are a number of people I would like to take the opportunity to thank. First and foremost, I must express gratitude to my doctoral supervisors at the University of Luton for their constant support and advice during the past three years: Dr Usman Khan and Dr Peter McLaverty. I would also like to extend acknowledgement to Professor Michael Rustin for his frequent and valuable insights. Without the advice of my supervisors, I may well have overlooked important theoretical and practical questions. I would also like to thank all members of the Labour Party, Amnesty International, the Exodus collective and various Tenants' and Residents' Associations to whom I have spoken during the course of this research. Your time and patience has been highly appreciated, and without your contribution this research would not have been possible. In addition, I would like to extend special thanks to the Communications Department of Amnesty International UK for contributing to the smooth progress of my interviews with members of Amnesty International. Acknowledgement must also be given to the various local Constituency Party workers within the Labour Party who have taken part in this research, but have preferred to remain anonymous. Finally, I would like to express my gratitude to my parents and brother. Without their continued support and enthusiasm this book would never have been completed.

1 Introduction

The politically active citizen provides a compelling symbol of democracy in action. Potent images such as the urban unrest inspired by the global anti-capitalist protests of 1999 or the continuing direct action against genetically modified food in Britain serve to remind us of the power of the politically motivated citizen. Underlying these images is a long-standing commitment amongst theorists of radical democracy to the potential role that involvement in political life can play in developing a stronger sense of citizenship and consequently a more politically vocal public. The direct involvement of citizens in political life is invariably seen as a fundamental part of a democratic polity.

Yet, in liberal democracies such as Britain, political involvement is a multi-faceted phenomenon with many disparate forms. Not all examples of political activism will necessarily represent a challenge to state power or global multinational exploitation, for example. Similarly, one cannot necessarily assume that all forms of citizen action will occur outside of state structures. Indeed, local state initiatives designed to encourage greater involvement amongst the public are a fundamental part of contemporary policy debates within British local government. It is also important to be aware of the changing nature of political participation. For instance, the proliferation of 'social movements' during the 1970s and 1980s has recently been supplemented by the advent of so-called 'do-it-yourself' or direct action politics epitomised by groups such as Reclaim the Streets. At the same time, we have witnessed the rise of large-scale campaigning groups such as Amnesty International and Greenpeace which, in many respects, represent a challenge to the position of established vehicles of political action such as political parties. However, in the rush to identify 'new' forms of political activism, we should perhaps be wary of overlooking those seemingly mundane forms of political activity that occur on a daily basis within well-established political forums. It would also be naïve to ignore the fact that involvement in political and public affairs remains a minority pursuit in Western liberal democracies. The vast majority of people tend to have little or no direct contact with political bodies, and it is only a committed few who undertake regular and sustained participation in the political sphere.

With these comments in mind, the question arises of whether it is still possible to talk of a generic form of political activism that is underpinned by democratic ideals. Indeed, one might pose the question of what exactly is meant by the term 'active'? And how significant are contemporary forms of voluntary political activism within processes of democratisation and political deliberation? This book aims to explore these themes by examining the ways in which citizens of varying levels of political activity understand and interpret their own political action. Drawing upon fieldwork conducted within several political organisations, the book examines the nature of contemporary political participation through the development of a typology of activism. Furthermore, the book aims to critically analyse the deliberative role played by those forms of activism to be found within the political spaces of civil society. The data presented in this book was collected within a spectrum of institutions, each of which has a specific organisational and membership structure. They are made up of the British Labour Party, the British section of Amnesty International, two Tenants' Associations, one Residents' Association and a radical collective known as Exodus. However, before turning to a more detailed discussion of the aims of the book I will consider exactly what is meant by the term 'political participation'.

Defining Political Participation

The realm of political participation connects citizens with the democratic process. This book will seek to examine this relationship in detail, and to ascertain how and why citizens engage with political life. But what exactly do we mean by 'political participation'? It is a term that embodies a vast range of diverse activities, and a watertight definition therefore often remains elusive. Nonetheless, Parry *et al* (1992, p. 16) have sought to define the term as 'taking part in the processes of formulation, passage and implementation of public policies'. For analytical purposes, it is thus possible to view participation as a form of activity that involves citizens undertaking some level of involvement in political life beyond the basic act of voting. Although it would be naïve to understate the role of electoral voting as the most basic unit of participation, there is growing interest amongst political scientists in those forms of participation that take place beyond the ballot box. The political participation of citizens therefore represents a layer of activity that supplements the established representative political mechanisms associated with liberal democracy.

For the purposes of this study, I also follow Parry *et al* (1992) by viewing participation primarily as a form of action rather than as the exchange of political opinions that does not necessarily translate into activity. This is not to deny the importance of such stocks of informal political discussion that take place throughout the population. However, political debate that occurs on an everyday basis exists at a level below the forms of citizen participation that will be explored in this book. I also exclude individual acts of participation such as complaints to a local council or wearing an Amnesty International badge. Such acts are undoubtedly important aspects of the participatory repertoire, but in this book I focus on political activity that is mediated by structures of participation. The key aim of this book is to examine the nature of political practice that takes place within the public sphere, and I adopt the starting point that political agency is primarily negotiated in and through those structures that mediate political participation. For this reason, I focus on citizens who have decided to become involved in participatory bodies at the level of membership.

As I have already noted, it is also important to acknowledge that the field of citizen participation contains a wide and diverse spectrum of activities. Some of these forms of action might be easily classified as 'political', whilst others may not be conducive to such a label. The decision to join the Labour Party, for instance, cannot be easily equated with membership of the Royal Society for the Protection of Birds, despite the fact that both acts could be convincingly seen to operate within the domain of citizen participation. The question of what actually constitutes 'the political' raises perennial philosophical ambiguities. Inevitably, any definition of the term 'political' will be selective, and the line that divides the 'political' from the 'non-political' is constantly changing and is invariably subject to contention. Difficulties associated with attempting to demarcate what can be defined as 'political' can also be detected in recent discussions about the appropriate focus of political science. Stoker (1995, pp. 4-5) highlights the drift away from a narrow understanding of political science as the study of the formal institutions of government toward the idea that 'politics' can be viewed primarily as a generic type of process. Leftwich (1984b) consequently argues that 'political' activity occurs throughout society and can take place in any form of social encounter where there is 'conflict and co-operation….[which]….reflects and indeed influences the structure of society' (Stoker, 1995, p. 5).

Yet it is important to retain the idea that activity that takes place within certain social locations has more efficacy and influence than action that occurs within less privileged political arenas. This is particularly relevant to those structures through which citizens are able to contribute to political discussion and debate. By viewing any form of social interaction as inherently political we tend to divest citizen involvement in political structures of its significance as an index of the type of democracy we have. As Beetham (1996, p. 46) observes, the extension of the definition of the 'political' into the realms of everyday life may foster a preoccupation with the minutia of those spaces at the expense of the wider forces that shape such activity. Those deliberative processes that are structured around an implicit claim to legitimacy and authority clearly have a unique character within liberal democracy, and the bodies that sustain the political participation of citizens provide a point of mediation between citizens and such decision-making processes.

Locating Political Participation: Voluntary Participation and Civil Society

This leads us into a consideration of where we might locate the forms of political participation to which I have referred. Certainly, it is difficult to talk about political participation or the political life of citizens without making reference to the capacity and attributes of civil society. This concept has been defined in a number of ways, but is generally seen as the nexus of organisations that exist outside of the state and sustain voluntary citizen mobilisation. This is a concept that has inspired a great deal of theorising in recent years. In the past decade there has been a growing interest in the potential for invigorating the capacities of civil society, and it is increasingly common for theorists of democracy to advocate a concept of politics that is distinct from institutions of the state. According to writers such as Keane (1988), this arena of citizen participation represents a dynamic and vibrant space in which citizens can potentially interact in an egalitarian manner. This turn toward the capacities of civil society has implications for understandings of the current composition of political participation. If civil society represents the primary source of vitality within contemporary political life then close attention needs to be paid to the forms of political practice that emerge within these spaces.

The definition that one ascribes to the concept of the 'political' is also relevant to understanding civil society. Burns *et al* (1994, pp. 274-277) distinguish membership organisations such as Tenants' Associations or national campaigning groups from informal voluntary organisations such as local swimming clubs for the disabled. The latter operate on the basis of freely given labour that does not have an overtly political agenda. Gyford

(1991, pp. 128-141) has similarly identified the informal sector and the voluntary sector as two closely related sources of citizen participation built around the principle of a body of people who join together for the betterment of an aspect of their local community. Nonetheless, it has historically been argued that the opportunity to develop skills and competencies within such 'social' voluntary associations plays a key role in prompting more overtly political participation (Olsen, 1972, p. 318; Verba and Nie, 1972, p. 186).

However, in this book I have focused specifically on the political dimension of citizen participation. These are the spaces in which citizens can potentially interact with issues of general concern and through which they can articulate their own interests. The quality of democracy depends, at least in part, on the capacities of these political structures of citizen participation because they provide a key role of linkage and mediation between citizens and the wider democratic process. However, I also contend in Chapters Two and Three that one cannot artificially separate civil society out from state structures when attempting to conceptualise the context of political participation. Rather, I argue that the structures that comprise the political arena are located in the continuum that stretches between institutions of the local state and the terrain of civil society. This 'public sphere' is the milieu in which citizens are able to mobilise in a political manner by engaging in acts of participation. In this book, I seek to analyse a range of political institutions that represent the scope of this spectrum.

Civil society is also distinctive for being most closely associated with those bodies that operate on the basis of voluntary participation from citizens. In contemporary liberal democracies there is a tangible assumption that citizens should not be required to participate in the structures that comprise political life in the sense used throughout this book. Although one might perhaps be able to detect a palpable informal social pressure to vote in national elections in the UK for example, there is little sense that citizens might need to take part in political activity beyond the act of voting. The notion that individuals should contribute to the political process in a compulsory manner would seem an anathema to dominant understandings of what constitutes a democratic system of government. In advanced liberal democracies, formal political 'rights' protect the right of citizens to engage in political activity, but the overriding emphasis is on voluntary mobilisation. Political participation is widely seen as an option, and certainly not a duty associated with being a citizen.

Inevitably, these general points have important implications for the nature of contemporary political activity and for our understandings of what actually constitutes political participation. The participatory acts that most citizens are able to undertake will tend to have an indirect influence on decisions taken within the policy making process. It may also mean, as Parry et al (1992, p. 7) observe, that a large portion of political participation is reactive in the sense that it responds to agendas or decisions taken by those in authority. The majority of citizens thus fail to take a direct role in the production of political goods, and remain what Burns et al (1994, p. 267) refer to as 'consumers' of politics. Political involvement is therefore far from a duty, as was the case in classic models of democracy associated with the Greek system of government (Held, 1987, pp. 13-35). The Athenian model of political life was defined by the direct participation of the citizenry in decision-making, a practice that was seen to encourage a sense of civic virtue and public duty. In the liberal democratic system of government, voluntary participation is the overriding norm within the structures of political participation. Consequently, those who take part in politics do so as and when they see fit. In this book, I take up this idea of voluntary mobilisation as a fundamental defining feature of political activity of citizens and critically examine the implications for the nature of contemporary democracy. Perhaps the most obvious starting point for such an analysis is to examine the levels and composition of voluntary political activity.

Patterns of Political Participation: Who, in What Ways and How Much?

In Chapter Two I present an overview of existing data with regard to the composition of patterns of participation. It will be shown that it is a sizable minority of the adult population who choose to become involved in politics on a regular basis, and it will be demonstrated that there is a correlation between access to valuable social resources and a propensity to take part in political life. In short, involvement in public and political affairs remains limited in most Western liberal democracies (Parry et al, 1992; Dalton, 1988). There is also strong evidence to suggest that 'habitual activists' populate the realm of political participation. Existing research into, for example, school governorship, Neighbourhood Forums and the British Labour Party shows that those who put themselves forward for the more intense levels of participation are often likely to be already active within a range of groups throughout the wider community. Furthermore, those who are heavily involved in political life are unlikely to be representative of the wider population. Those individuals with access to valuable social resources are more likely to participate in an intense manner. The importance of these findings was stressed by the recent Final Report of the Commission for Local Democracy which noted that '[D]emocracy will always be limited if it does not seek to ensure the widest involvement' (Commission for Local Democracy, 1995, p. 32). Miller and Dickson (1996, p. 25) subsequently claim that there is 'a situation of haves and have nots in relation to the general question of belonging and interest in local and national politics'.

We can therefore say with some certainty that despite the continued theoretical interest in the question of citizen involvement, the reality of political participation has often been the cause for some disquiet. It is not uncommon to encounter the argument that we live in an 'anti-political' age that is defined by an ever-widening detachment from participation in political activity (Mulgan, 1994). We are frequently told that political apathy and alienation are rife and that this is reflected in low levels of citizen involvement in politics. However, recent experimentation in the area of citizen participation has indicated that members of the public are willing to take part in decision-making when they are offered a key role in the democratic process (Coote and Lenaghan, 1997). In terms of voluntary participation, it is too simplistic to assume that citizens are necessarily apathetic without first investigating the question of how actual experiences of political participation affect the decision to become involved. This is a theme that will run throughout the book as I attempt to collate the experience of those who have actually taken part in some aspect of political life and consider the implications for questions of political motivation and experience. The fact that a majority of citizens are not directly involved in political life makes voluntary participation in political structures a particularly interesting area of study. Those people who take part within political parties, for instance, on a regular basis and engage in direct face-to-face participation are especially unusual within liberal democracies.

Theorising Political Participation

The image of an Athenian city-state comprised of citizens deliberating over issues of public concern thus seems rather distant. As Walzer (1992, p. 92) notes, '[P]olitics rarely engages the full attention of the citizens who are supposed to be it's chief protagonists'. This is particularly relevant when we note that behind much of the survey analysis of levels of participation is a strong theoretical tradition that invariably links the participation of citizens in politics with notions of 'democracy'. It has been widely argued that an integral part of a democratic polity is the ability to be able to contribute to the determination of social and political goals. At the heart of such thinking is a commitment to the value of an inclusive and political realm in which citizens are able to exercise some form of deliberation over public affairs. The guiding principle of this line of thought is the idea that citizens should be able to take advantage of 'a rightful share in the process of government' (Held, 1987, p. 291).

From this perspective, involvement in political processes is invariably perceived as 'developmental' in the sense that it encourages a greater sense of civic efficacy and an appreciation of the value of participation. Democracy, in this sense, is seen not as the protection or pursuit of private interests but crucially as the exercise of 'the public use of reason', as Bohman (1996, p. 2) puts it. One of the most influential recent trends in this area relates to the notion of discursive or deliberative democracy, or the idea that citizens should play a pivotal role in a policy making process that sustains rational argumentation and considered political interaction. Yet others might argue that these seemingly low levels of participation are actually quite acceptable. Those working in the realist tradition associated with the work of Schumpeter (1952) would view high levels of participation as a damaging influence upon the process of government. In this view of democracy there should be a strict 'division of labour' between citizens and the government (Held, 1987, pp. 164-187). The involvement of citizens in political life should then be restricted to periodic participation in elections in which political institutions are provided with the authority to act free from interference.

Clearly, discussions based around levels of political participation can only take us so far. For instance, one cannot easily make generalisations about the degree of political activity in relation to the past because there is little tangible historical data to which such statements can be compared. To describe current levels of participation as 'high' or 'low' is therefore something of a misnomer. A more productive route is to shift the focus of the debate toward qualitative analysis of the actual nature of those forms of participation that take place. The central issue then becomes the quality and process of this political activity. It should also be clear from the preceding discussion that the theoretical approach that one adopts to the nature of democracy shapes understandings of the potential role of political participation. In this book I appropriate the critical communications theory of Jürgen Habermas to interpret the nature of political participation. I will return to this theme shortly.

The Concept of 'Activism'

Any discussion around the question of political participation will eventually make reference to the idea of 'activism'. A main aim of this book is to explore exactly what is meant by this term. However, it is possible at this stage to note that political theorists and policy analysts have often evoked the term in a normative manner. Traditionally, activism has been seen as a 'constraint' upon the power of political elites. Cochrane (1996, p. 212), for instance, suggests that activism is an essential component of a vibrant polity: '[L]ocal democracy is not something that can be guaranteed, and it will only be achieved through the campaigning of a changing set of activists on a range of issues in the framework of a positive commitment from the institutions of local government'. Seyd and Whiteley (1992, p. 1) similarly suggest that the political activity of Labour Party members 'helps to keep democratic politics alive in Britain'. Woliver (1993) is indicative of a similar approach when she equates activism with grass roots dissent formed at the community level to challenge perceived injustices. Central to this conception of activism is the ability of citizens to hold government and policy makers to account, a practice that Hill (1994, p. 26) fittingly refers to as 'claims for local activism'.

Given that political participation is beset by a series of apparent inequalities, these positive interpretations of 'activism' have not always been reflected amongst policy practitioners. Recent years have seen a growing critique of voluntary forms of participation, and a number of political institutions have subsequently begun to develop new mechanisms that might allow them to reach out to citizens without relying upon existing bands of engaged citizens. In response to the perceived shortcomings of voluntary participation, there is growing interest amongst local authorities across Europe in developing innovative mechanisms of public involvement (Stewart, 1995; 1996; 1997; Khan, 1999). Implicit in these developments is a growing interest in the development of a more deliberative political process. Integral to this experimentation is a growing assumption that conventional methods of involving the public often fail to fulfill the requirements of a democratic polity.

Political institutions that exist outside of the state have also been keen to develop new methods of communicating with their members, and indeed with the wider public. The Labour Party, for instance, has cultivated a number of internal structures that are intended to enable the leadership to reach beyond existing active Party members to the broader electorate. This shift in membership policy has been presented as a move toward enhancing internal democracy, but the crtique of traditional activism is clear. Tony

Blair has argued that the Party has 'altered our structures and organisation to remove the damaging domination of small groups of activists that almost wrecked the party' (Blair, 1996). The introduction of One Member One Vote in 1993 and the current development of initiatives such as Policy Forums represent a significant shift away from traditional activist driven structures of the recent past. Mandelson and Liddle (1996, p. 216) confidently state that 'even if the activists of the past wanted to reassert themselves the new structure of the party would not permit them to take back control'.

Although these structures differ greatly in aims and agenda, they nonetheless share an affinity with the idea that formal mechanisms are increasingly needed in order to overcome the perceived shortcomings associated with voluntary participation. The move toward new political structures of the kind outlined above reflects an implicit assumption that there is something inherently limited about the nature of the activity in which the most politically active citizens engage. Yet this movement against voluntary activism does not sit easily with traditional views of the value of those citizens who take a heightened role in political life. 'Activism' has been widely perceived as a crucial component of maintaining public debate about political issues, and is consequently seen by many as an important underpinning to democracy in Britain. Despite this conundrum, there is currently only limited primary research that has attempted to acquire grounded assessments of the actual forms of involvement that inhabit the voluntary structures of political participation. This book aims to fill this gap by critically examining the question of what actually happens when citizens take part in participatory activity. We know a great deal about who takes part in political life and how much participation takes place, but our knowledge of how this political activity actually occurs is less detailed. In order to adopt such an approach it is necessary to develop a theoretical perspective that will allow us to relate the real world of participation to broader normative conceptions of democracy.

Participation and Political Discourse: Habermas and the Public Sphere

Perhaps the most widely discussed work in this area is provided by the German sociologist and philosopher Jürgen Habermas (cf. McCarthy, 1984; Ray, 1993; Outhewaite, 1994; Horster, 1992; Brand, 1990). His extensive theoretical framework attempts to connect modes of existing political participation to wider processes of rationalisation by arguing that participation 'should not be considered as a value in itself but related to the conditions in which it occurs' (Outhewaite, 1994, p. 3). This type of approach is especially important if we are to relate theoretical concerns about the nature of democracy to the actual practice of political participation. Drawing upon his Marxist roots, Habermas directs our attention toward wider structural changes that he argues have eroded the strength of debate within the political structures of advanced capitalist liberal democracies. At the heart of Habermas' work is a normative concern with exposing the conditions that disrupt rational and meaningful political debate. Underlying this is the potential for the opening up of forums of public discourse to sustain what Habermas defines as 'communicative action'. In short, this represents the ideal of socially coordinated action that is built upon less distorted political arrangements in which the force of an open argument holds sway. This is ultimately seen as the source of rational public debate, and Habermas argues that this democratising tendency needs to take the institutional form of a participatory 'public sphere'. This term refers to a space, or a multiplicity of interconnected spaces, in which citizens are able to discursively interact in order to discuss and shape the development of public policies (Habermas, 1989a; Habermas, 1992c; Habermas, 1996b, pp. 329-374).

A key question that continues to plague those interested in these themes might be put in this way: are existing avenues of political participation likely to facilitate the tendencies that Habermas identifies? Do the most basic units of democracy to be found in the arenas of political activity offer an appropriate basis within which a communicatively structured public sphere can be reinvigorated? Or, in view of the inequalities afflicting the realm of voluntary political participation, does the internal nature of civil society preclude the development of rational and open forms of public discourse? These questions are of prime importance in the context of current debates about the role of political participation in developing rational and deliberative forms of politics. These themes also raise the question of the respective role that structures of the state and civil society can play in facilitating increased deomcratisation within advanced capitalist societies. In Chapter Three, I explore the work of Habermas in more detail. More specifically, I pose the question of whether political structures must remain outside of the state and the policy making process if they are to develop the communicative tendencies identified by Habermas. In order to begin to address these broad questions, we clearly need to relate such theoretical concerns to the real world of participation. This is the overriding aim of the book.

Although existing analysis tells us a great deal about who takes part in politics and how many people choose to do so, the question of what it actually means to participate in different facets of political life remains somewhat ambiguous. For instance, attempts to consider why some participants become heavily involved in political structures whilst other participants refrain from doing so have often been conducted with only limited reference to the actual practice of political participation. The heart of this book builds upon existing data by investigating the 'real world' of voluntary political activity and subsequently addressing a number of fundamental concerns about the current state of democracy in Britain. The main aim of the book is to analyse the different forms of participation that develop across a range of participatory structures, and to consider the relationship between this spectrum of participation and the specific structures within which such political activity develops. The book seeks to examine from a critical perspective the process of taking part in a range of political institutions, and to address the question of how people experience different forms of political participation. I therefore shift the prevailing focus of discussion from the composition and levels of political participation to question of *how* citizens participate in political life. This has enabled the book to reflect critically upon the types of political culture that inhabit the participatory realm that exists beyond electoral turnout.

Guiding this inquiry is an interest in accounting for the factors that shape the dominant traits of voluntary political participation in Britain today. With this book I therefore aim to provide some insight into the question of how and why certain forms of political participation become institutionalised within the structures that sustain political activity. Rather than focus on factors that remain distant from the actual conditions within which political activity takes place, such as psychological disposition or individual assessments of costs and benefits, I seek to locate my analysis within the practice of political participation itself. A central argument of this work is that the testimonies of those who participate in political life provides the most insightful method of developing an understanding of how and why voluntary political participation becomes patterned in particular ways.

Overview of the Fieldwork

This book sets out the findings that have emerged from a comparative study carried out in the South East of England. The fieldwork utilises a range of predominantly qualitative methodologies including semi-structured interviews, non-participant observation and documentary analysis. Using the data I have collected from approximately sixty interviews within the aforementioned organisations, I intend to illustrate a range of experiences of political participation. The book also seeks to analyse the membership policies of the various organisations, and the interviews with participants are therefore supplemented by a number of interviews with relevant organisational staff members, including Tenants Housing Officers, Labour Party Constituency Secretaries and Campaigns Department staff at Amnesty International UK. The fieldwork also entailed observing a range of internal committee and membership meetings. Where necessary, I also undertook analysis of relevant documents such as internal surveys, minutes of meetings, constitutions, membership reports and such like.

Each of the bodies studied in the course of this book was included as a result of its specific individual structural and organisational make up. The Tenants' and Residents' Associations, for instance, represent a traditional and long-established mechanism of state-citizen dialogue that is often based upon high levels of intense involvement. Amnesty International, on the other hand, relies upon a large-scale membership structure with the optional opportunity for participation in a network of local campaigning groups. Whereas the former is based upon small-scale local participation, the latter relies upon more 'business' oriented modes of membership mobilisation that have a national focus (Jordan and Maloney, 1997). The Labour Party has recently been embroiled in a major process of internal restructuring in which the role and position of members within the Party has been subject to substantial change. Finally, Exodus is an example of the 'do-it-yourself' politics closely associated with youth culture that has proliferated over the past decade. Although these four structures of political activity have distinct aims and internal structures, when taken together they represent a spectrum of citizen activity that raises common questions regarding the nature of political participation within liberal democracy. Of particular interest to this book is the style and structure of these groups, and the potential effects of these factors on the differing types of participation that members engage in. Although I will provide some level of background detail on each body in Chapter Four, it may be worth stressing that this investigation is not intended as a historical study.

There are several assumptions that have guided this study from the outset. Firstly, the analysis of cultures of political participation can tell us a great deal about the boundaries and limits of what Nancy Fraser (1992) refers to as 'actually existing democracy'. By investigating the real conditions of political participation we are able to assess the room available to citizens for political discussion and debate within the voluntary structures of liberal democracy. The present study adopts the premise that the nature of political participation and political discourse are crucial indicators of the quality of contemporary democracy. The question of how people participate in political life is therefore equally as important as the question of which issues attract public attention or how many people may choose to participate. Secondly, I argue that existing analysis of political participation has provided little understanding of what it actually means to take part in political life. The concept of 'activism', for instance, remains a fairly abstract category that is defined primarily by the amount of participation that people undertake. There is currently only limited understanding of how participants experience different forms of political activity. Consequently, we know little about how and why political participation takes the forms that it does within different bodies. Thirdly, I assert that the best way to gain a more detailed understanding of these processes of political involvement is to talk at length to those who have experienced it, rather than continuing to rely on research strategies that remain distanced from the actual conditions of political participation. This requires a process of reflecting upon the experiences and impressions of a cross-section of those who take part in political life, ranging from the most intensely active to the participants with minimal involvement.

By drawing upon the testimonies of respondents I attempt to contribute to a growing interest in analysing the process of taking part in political participation. In recent years, the interest in measurable policy outcomes of participation has been complimented by analytical interest in the experience of political participation itself. As Parry *et al* (1993, p. 29) note, the 'experience of participation, not only the results but of the process itself, is crucial to the vitality of democracy itself'. This, then, is a central problem that the book addresses. I have deliberately made only passing comment on the ideological and policy agendas of the organisations investigated in the course of this study. This is not to deny the importance of the issues to which these groups address themselves. Rather, I have specifically attempted to focus on the internal workings of these groups. The findings of this book suggest that the experiences of these processes are crucial in understanding broader patterns of voluntary participation within liberal democracy.

Plan of the Book

The first half of the book is intended to provide a rationale for the overall research programme. Following this introductory chapter, I include two related chapters. These sections outline the empirical and theoretical background informing this research respectively. In Chapter Two, I examine previous findings with regard to the composition of patterns of political participation in Britain. I also consider the range of approaches that have been taken by political scientists to the question of citizen mobilisation. In Chapter Three, I provide an outline of the theoretical perspective that I have adopted in my analysis of the findings. This chapter outlines the work of Habermas in greater detail and examines the ways in which I use this theoretical perspective to interpret the nature of political participation.

The second half of the book presents an analysis of the findings generated by fieldwork. The data is organised and presented thematically rather than by case study. This has been done in order to draw out clearly the main themes that have emerged from the primary data, and to enable comparisons to be made between the participation that takes place within each organisation. In Chapter Five, I analyse the membership policies of these participatory structures, and consider the role that members play within each group. In Chapter Six, I present a typology of the forms of political participation that take place within these institutions. This allows me to explore the nature of 'activism' across the various organisations. In Chapter Seven, I then examine in more detail the actual process of taking part in political life, and consider the question of how and why certain forms of political activity and discourse become institutionalised within structures of political participation. In the final chapter, I draw conclusions from the research material, and reflect upon some of the major issues arising out of the analysis of political participation provided by this study.

2 Investigating Political Participation in Britain

The theme of political participation has enjoyed a growing popularity amongst political scientists in the past decade. In recent years, the focus of much of this analysis has shifted from relatively abstract discussions about the relationship between democracy and participation toward the empirical reality of political activity to be found in Britain. This has produced a large amount of analysis of levels of citizen involvement in political life and attempts to map the socio-demographic composition of such participation. In consequence, there has been extensive discussion about the patterns of voluntary participation to be found in the realm of citizen politics.

This chapter has two main aims. My first objective is to examine the insights that are currently available from existing research into the make-up of voluntary political participation. Three main questions have guided this survey of the literature that explores the composition of political participation. Firstly, it is important to consider the various ways in which people have been shown to take part in political life. This, in turn, requires some attention being given to the various structures that sustain political participation. Secondly, we need to ask questions about the actual composition of political participation within Britain. Who takes part? How often do they take part? How much participation occurs in Britain in the 1990s? Thirdly, we can draw upon the limited available data in order to begin to explore the internal dynamics of political participation. This allows us to undertake an initial examination of what actually takes place within sites of participation.

The second aim of the present chapter is to consider the various ways in which political scientists have approached the question of political participation. In recent decades, there has been much discussion in the available literature about the question of why people choose to take part in political life. While there is only limited coherence in this literature, a number of detailed models have been developed in order to account for the mobilisation of citizens. I will contend that whilst these accounts of participation point to important areas for analysis, key aspects of political participation have been largely overlooked. In particular, I argue that the data examined in this chapter raises a whole series of largely unanswered questions about the ways in which people experience the process of taking part in political participation. There has subsequently been little consideration of how and why certain forms of political activity develop within different political structures. As a result, I assert that greater attention needs to be given to the discursive nature of the political activity of citizens. Such an approach also needs to pay close attention to the interplay between wider forces influencing the political public sphere and the nature of citizen political activity. This in turn raises deeper theoretical questions about the limits and capacities of voluntary political participation within the political public sphere of advanced liberal democracy. These theoretical points will be taken up in more detail in Chapter Three.

Addressing these two main aims will provide us with a clearer picture of the patterns of participation in Britain today. In this chapter, I explore this data in detail and consider both the implications and limitations of the available literature. It will be shown that although the composition of political participation is a complex phenomenon, a number of general observations can be made. In particular, I will demonstrate that political participation remains a minority preference in Britain, with the most well resourced socio-demographic groups tending to take the most prominent role in political life. Given that voluntary political participation is beset by inequalities of influence, it becomes particularly important to develop a clear understanding of the nature of 'activism'. It will be argued that whilst the existing literature provides a number of valuable insights into the composition of political participation, it tends to interpret the concept of activism in rather narrow terms as the amount and frequency of participation undertaken by citizens. I argue that there is consequently considerable scope for developing analysis that is more sensitive to the qualitative dimensions of political participation.

Structures of Participation

The term 'political participation' covers an extremely wide range of activities, and encompasses a broad spectrum of organisations. It has already been noted in Chapter One that it is too simplistic to talk about people 'taking part' in political life in a generic sense. It is therefore important to recognise that political participation cannot be realistically perceived as a unified realm of activity. Both Parry *et al* (1992) and Dalton

(1988) have taken up this point, and have developed a number of general categories into which individual acts of participation can be placed. These range from collective or communal group participation through party political and campaigning activity to direct or protest participation (Parry *et al*, 1992, pp. 233-237).

In recent years there has been much discussion about the changing face of the involvement of citizens in political life. One area where this has been most evident is in the widespread use of the terms 'social movement' and 'new social movement'. Sociological theorists have asserted that these entities have become increasingly prevalent within citizen politics during the past three decades or so. These terms refer to loose, informal constellations of political or cultural action that seemingly challenge the conventions of traditional politics, both in terms of the issues addressed and the styles of political organisation adopted (cf. Byrne, 1997; Diani, 1992; Scott, 1990; Boggs, 1986). Within this literature, the growth of such 'social movements' is seen to represent a 'non-reactionary, universalist critique of modernity and modernization [sic] by challenging institutionalized [sic] patterns of technical, economic, political, and cultural rationality' (Offe, 1990, p. 233).

However, ambiguities persist as to what actually constitutes a 'social movement' (Byrne, 1997, p. 10-25). Tonge (1994), for instance, proposes that 'pressure movement' is a more appropriate term to define political activity such as the British anti-Poll Tax protests of the 1980s. There has also been discussion about the ambiguous overlap between the 'political' and the 'cultural' within these movements (Cohen, 1993). Further difficulties exist over the question of whether individual organisations or more informal, dispersed networks actually qualify as a 'movement'. Does Amnesty International, for instance, represent a form of human rights 'social movement'? It is also unclear to what extent the 'new social movements' are genuinely constitutive of 'new' forms of political action (Tucker, 1991). These terms associated with 'social movements' are often used in an indiscriminate manner to refer to a diverse collection of political participation, stretching from large-scale pressure groups through to direct forms of action such as road protests. It is beyond the scope of this book to fully engage with this extensive literature. Suffice is to say that these problems of definition tend to negate the usefulness of the concept for the purposes of this book. Nonetheless, these themes do raise a number of important points about the capacities of the voluntary political action that inhabits civil society to facilitate strong channels of public discourse. I will return to this theme in more detail in the next Chapter when I discuss the work of Habermas.

The literature surrounding the concept of 'social movement' is also accurate to point out that the sphere of citizen participation is currently experiencing the expansion of increasingly unorthodox activities. It is commonly argued that we are in the midst of the decline of established forums of participation and the rise of innovative forms of activity that challenge conventional norms of political organisation and activity. There are two key areas to which I wish to draw attention. Firstly, the past thirty years has witnessed the dramatic rise of single-issue pressure groups such as Greenpeace, Friends of the Earth, the Campaign for Nuclear Disarmament and Amnesty International. In 1971, Friends of the Earth had only 1,000 members in Britain, but by the end of the 1980s the figure had risen to 140,000 and the figure currently stands at around 200,000 (Byrne, 1997, p. 3). The British section of Amnesty International had a membership of 117,000 in 1993 (Amnesty International UK, 1994, p. 14), but by 1996, this figure had risen to 127,000 (*The Independent* 29th March 1996). The membership of the youth section of Amnesty International UK has also risen sharply from 1,300 in 1988 to 15,000 in 1995 (*The Independent* 17th February 1997). Greenpeace has around 400,000 individual members in Britain (NCVO, 1998). A second characteristic of the changing nature of political participation can be found in the growth of increasingly direct forms of political action during the 1990s. McKay (1996, p. 1) argues that a diverse network of civil disobedience has emerged that is built around 'cultures of resistance'. Groups such as The Land Is Ours and Reclaim The Streets are associated with the recent proliferation of what has been referred to as the 'do it yourself' political culture (McKay, 1998a). This has been defined as 'a youth-centred and -directed cluster of interests and practices around green radicalism, direct action politics, new musical sounds and experiences' (McKay, 1998b, p. 2).

A common theme that unites these two facets of contemporary political participation is the notion that traditional structures such as the political party are being sidelined as the main vehicles for organising political activity. In this vein, Jordan and Maloney (1997, p. 178) suggest that 'alternative organisations are emerging as would-be surrogates for [political] parties'. There is clearly some evidence to support this claim. In the early 1950s the Labour Party achieved membership levels of over one million (Seyd and Whiteley, 1992, p. 16), but by 1985 the figure had dropped to 313,099 (Seyd and Whiteley, 1992, p. 16). Despite the upturn in membership prior to the 1997 British General Election, more recent reports suggest that national membership rates may have dropped dramatically to about 385,000 since Labour's victory in the 1997 General Election (MacAskill, 1998). In a similar vein, Whiteley *et al* (1994, p. 226) argue that within the Conservative Party there is 'clear evidence of a decline in both activism and the strength of attachment to the party amongst remaining members'. In 1994, it was estimated that the Liberal Democratic Party had only about 100,000 members (Webb, 1994, p. 113). With these figures in mind, Whiteley *et al* (1994, p. 220) echo a commonly voiced book when they suggest that 'the whole British party system is in serious decline at the grass-roots level'.

Although single-issue campaign groups have seen a dramatic upturn in membership levels in recent decades, it is important to remember that current figures do not show a vast difference between the membership levels of political parties and such groups. It is therefore still a relatively small section of the British population who choose to join these various organisations. There is also a danger that the search for 'new' forms of radical or spontaneous forms of political action can overlook the continuing influence of established structures of political participation. Undoubtedly, the legitimacy and validity of political parties is subject to some challenge. Political parties have found themselves subject to increasing pressures including weakening public legitimacy, the aforementioned proliferation of single-issue pressure groups and the growth of increasingly assertive publics at the local level (Gyford, 1991, pp. 32-51). Nonetheless, the political party remains a key institution within the democratic process. One should also perhaps be cautious in equating single-issue campaign groups such as Amnesty International with the notion of 'unconventional' political behaviour. These types of organisations are increasingly regarded as an established feature of the political process. One should also be wary of labelling all groups of this type as representative of a single category of participation. For instance, Amnesty International consciously adopts less direct methods of campaigning than Greenpeace. Similarly, Amnesty International offers its members a more participatory role within its internal structure than Greenpeace.

With this in mind, it is apparent that analysis of political participation must pay close attention to the intricacies of the various structures through which citizens are able to articulate political views and interests. Given that I have questioned the appropriateness of 'social movement' theory in analysing the rapidly changing phenomenon of voluntary political participation, it is necessary to explore the dialectical relationship between citizens and specific political organisations in a closer manner. For example, in attempting to gain a clearer picture of the nature of political participation it is important to consider the types of membership that different types of groups actively seek. Jordan and Maloney (1997, p. 119) go so far as to claim that 'well-organized [sic] groups get the members they seek'. Amnesty International and Greenpeace, for instance, put a lot of effort into attracting members through direct marketing techniques. Jordan and Maloney (1997) describe Amnesty International as a 'memberless group' in that the hierarchy of Amnesty International UK 'want to limit their [member's] participation to sending in cash to support campaigns selected by the organisation – supporters should be seen and not be heard' (Jordan and Maloney, 1997, p. 188). They add that 'the elite or policy entrepreneur controls the policy agenda while the volunteers do the depoliticized [sic] mundane work' (Jordan and Maloney, 1997, p. 188). It is concluded that Amnesty International UK is indicative of what can be described as a 'protest business', in the sense that the organisation adopts business practices in order to primarily secure funds from its members rather than provide forums for members to take part in internal policy processes (Jordan and Maloney, 1997, p. 122). These comments are perceptive in highlighting the spread of campaign organisations structured around minimal forms of membership involvement. But this is not necessarily an image that officials within Amnesty International UK would accept. In Chapters Five and Six I will consider the implications of these factors for the membership policy and the nature of membership activism respectively.

Some have argued that the British Labour Party has cultivated a similar internal structure in the past few years. For example, Webb (1994) has observed that the major British political parties have been forced to adopt increasingly centralised and standardised internal structures in order to adapt to rapidly changing political environments. Recent findings have shown that those Labour Party members who have joined since 1994 are far less participatory than their so-called 'Old Labour' counterparts (Seyd and Whiteley, 1998). This data shows that about one fifth of the new members had delivered Party leaflets on three or more occasions, but the figure was almost forty per cent for the more established members. Almost two thirds of the new members had never delivered leaflets, but the figure was far lower at forty three per cent for long standing members. The survey also reports that those who had joined before 1994 were nearly four times more likely than recent recruits to participate in Party fund-raising events. Seyd and Whiteley conclude that the Labour Party has cultivated a substantial body of 'imaginary participants' who donate money to the Party but do little else.

Yet organisations such as the Labour Party and Amnesty International clearly still need members who are willing to undertake tasks within the organisation on a regular basis. The Labour Party, for instance, requires members to canvass in local constituencies at election times.

Similarly, Amnesty International relies on local group members to run campaigns in localities. It also needs individual members to write letters or take part in campaigns organised through specialist networks or its Urgent Action scheme. The point to consider here is that the membership structures and the membership policies set up by specific organisations may have a strong influence on the nature of political participation that takes place within that group. The specific character of this interaction remains largely overlooked in the existing literature. I take up this point in more detail during the discussion of my findings when I explore the dialectical relationship that exists between the political action of participants and the structures within which their political activity occurs.

Any survey of the realm of political participation must also recognise that opportunities for citizen participation do not always originate outside institutions of the state. The political public sphere to which I have referred encompasses local state structures that are engaged in efforts to involve local people in decision-making processes. As Croft and Beresford (1992, p. 20) point out, participation is a concept that enjoys episodic popularity within the areas of local government and social policy. The attempt to involve local people in the provision and implementation of council services is one of the most significant trends in local government during the past two decades. During the 1980s, a number of 'new left' local authorities undertook programmes of decentralisation in an attempt to devolve power down to the community level (Burns *et al*, 1994; McLaverty, 1996). A range of structures were introduced including Neighbourhood Forums in Islington and Sheffield (Burns *et al*, 1994, pp. 180-201; Khan, 1990) and Neighbourhood Committees in Tower Hamlets (Burns *et al*, 1994, pp. 202-218). Of course, structures for user consultation have been a staple part of the relationship between council tenants and housing departments for many years, and Tenants' Associations have a long history within the world of citizen participation (Goodland, 1994). In the 1990s, local authorities have once again become interested in methods of public consultation and participation. Hill (1994, p. 25) has subsequently referred to a 'return to the grass roots' within the changing orthodoxy of the local policy arena.

Even this cursory glance at the British political landscape has shown that citizen involvement in political life is an extremely complex and diverse arena. The arena for policy formation and political decision-making is filled with a wide range of interest groups, intermediacy organisations, pressure groups and structures of state-citizen dialogue. It would, of course, be close to impossible to provide a complete audit of the political structures that inhabit the continuum that I have argued stretches from the state and across civil society. Perhaps the most productive strategy is therefore to investigate a range of structures that reflects the spectrum of participation to be found in Britain, and this is the approach that I take up in this book.

Patterns of Political Participation

Recent years have seen the emergence of a small cluster of studies that explore the make-up of the involvement of citizens in political life. This statistical survey based data is particularly useful for uncovering what might be defined as the social and political patterns of participation. Not surprisingly, the existing data on the make up of political participation is fairly complex. Nonetheless, a series of notable trends have been identified. I will begin by examining the levels of participation that take place in Britain.

Amounts of Participation: How Active are British Citizens?

In contemporary liberal democracies the propensity to take part in political life is evident amongst a minority of the British population. As Byrne (1997, p. 3) puts it 'political activism of all types is a minority sport in Britain'. The figures are quite striking. According to Parry *et al* (1992, p. 49), three quarters of the population can be considered to be 'passive' in the sense that they fail to take part in political life beyond the basic act of voting, and for these citizens 'politics is largely a spectator sport'. For the vast majority of the population, participation in the political process remains limited to voting and sporadic forms of limited mobilisation such as contacting a local councillor. One in four of the population are willing to 'stand up and try quite hard to be counted' (Parry *et al*, 1992, p. 228), and it is concluded that less than one quarter of the British population 'sustain the citizenry's role in political life' (Parry *et al*, 1992, p. 228). Parry *et al* (1994, pp. 228-229) conclude that just one and a half per cent of their overall survey respondents can lay claim to the label of 'complete activism' in the sense that they are involved in the widest possible range of political activities. Similarly, Dalton (1988, p. 47) demonstrates that less than one in ten of those who participate regularly in Britain take part in a variety of acts across the spectrum of participation. According to Parry *et al* (1992, p. 228), these citizens are the 'true gladiators in the political games'. Unlike most people, these citizens are willing to 'fight their causes with all the participatory weapons at their disposal' (Parry *et al*, 1992, p. 237).

Socio-demographic Patterns: Who Takes Part in Political Life?

Any survey of political participation will show that there is more to understanding the composition of political participation than the question of how many people are willing to take part in political life. It is also necessary to ask exactly who inhabits the arenas of participation, and indeed who does not choose to take part in politics. If those who show a propensity to take part in political life are from a narrow socio-demographic band then it may be possible to argue that certain groups are excluded from contributing to the political arena. As Parry *et al* (1992, p. 6) observe:

> ....it can be important in a democracy to know how far the opportunities to participate are seized fairly evenly by people across the broad spectrum of society or whether the most intense political activists tend to be overwhelmingly drawn from one stratum of society....conversely, it may be a matter of concern if there exists an 'underclass' of people who are economically and socially disadvantaged and who also fail to make their own mark on the nation's agenda through political action.

Although the evidence is far from comprehensive, by analysing existing survey based research it is possible to make a number of observations about the social, economic and demographic background of those who contribute to political activity.

The first observation that emerges from this analysis is the distinctive profile of those who tend to not participate beyond voting. According to Parry *et al* (1992), these people are low on various personal resources such as educational attainment and income. Over one half have no qualifications, and a disproportionate number are to be found in the poorest quarter of the population. Consequently, Parry *et al* (1992, pp. 124-135) observe that the working classes are underrepresented in all aspects of political life. In addition, a large proportion of these inactive citizens are young people aged between 18 and 29.

A number of significant trends also emerge from analysis of those who do undertake some form of participation. It might be logical to assume that the members of political parties would be closely aligned with the composition of the voters of particular parties. However, it is immediately apparent from recent analysis of the Labour Party that the general body of the membership is somewhat different to voters (Seyd and Whiteley, 1992, pp. 38-40). The main differences centre around the fact that membership tends to be drawn from middle class professionals and from those with above average incomes, whereas electoral support is characterised by the inclusion of working class manual workers and those with a below average income. Almost half of the membership is considered to be 'salariat' in the sense used by the British Election Study as lecturers, teachers, social workers, doctors and solicitors. The figure is only fourteen per cent for Labour Party voters. The manual working class forms about one quarter of the membership but comprise a substantially larger slice of Labour's electoral base at fifty seven per cent. Drawing upon similar analysis of the British Conservative Party (Whiteley *et al*, 1994, pp. 42-44; pp. 51-52), we can say with some certainty that certain socio-demographic groups are underrepresented within the membership of the major British political parties. This tends to comprise the young, the working class and women, although the differences are often fairly subtle (Fisher, 1996, p. 147).

These findings have been reinforced by analysis of large-scale campaigning groups. It has been shown by Jordan and Maloney (1997, pp. 112-113) that almost half of Friends of the Earth members come from managerial, professional or senior administrative occupations, whilst in Amnesty International UK the figure is slightly higher at fifty two per cent. Over a quarter of British Amnesty International members and more than a third of the Friends of the Earth membership in Britain have a degree (Jordan and Maloney, 1997, p. 111). Jordan and Maloney (1997, p. 121) consequently describe the average Amnesty International member in Britain as well educated, middle class with a professional occupation from a relatively affluent household.

The question of the demographic make-up of those displaying a propensity towards extensive involvement in the political sphere has been an issue of concern for analysts of citizen participation for a number of years. Parry *et al* (1992, p. 416) argue that 'the quality of a democracy is adversely affected....when those who are most active are highly unrepresentative of the population as a whole'. The notion that there are significant social and cultural biases at work within the sphere of political participation is reinforced by the analysis of those who play the most pronounced role in political life. For instance, a recent study of voluntary school governors concluded that governing bodies 'may be far from representative of the population of as a whole' (Brehony, 1992, p. 208). Taken in conjunction with other research into school governorship, Brehony (1992, p. 209) makes a general statement to the effect that 'the majority of governors are from professional and managerial or executive backgrounds'.

This image of the realm of political participation being peopled by an unrepresentative band of citizens is supported by analysis of local government participatory initiatives. In their overview of participation in public services, Boaden et al (1982, p. 179) noted that 'the middle class participate more frequently in the issues involved in local service provision'. When public institutions attempt to encourage participation from the wider community it is often the case that 'those who participate tend to be overwhelmingly, but not exclusively, middle class, better educated, long-term residents well established in their community' (Boaden et al, 1982, p. 14). Similar findings are evident in a recent study of Neighbourhood Forums (Khan, 1990). It is noted that 'in general participants are drawn from a narrow band of largely middle class, middle aged and more established individuals, with groups such as women with family responsibilities, the young, disabled, and ethnic minorities largely underrepresented' (Khan, 1990, p. 84). The most active participants tended to come from 'the more settled and secure elements of the community' (Khan, 1990, p. 15). The question of race was also found to be an issue in analysis of Neighbourhood Forums in Islington. Burns et al (1994, p. 191) found that black and ethnic minority Forum members are only half as likely to attend meetings as white members. This type of data is reinforced by a recent White Paper on local government which laments the fact that as a body councillors do not reflect the make-up of the local community within which they are based (DETR, 1998). In Britain, only a quarter of councillors are female, and ethnic minorities are also strongly underrepresented. On the other hand, those aged over 45 are over represented.

The trend for those who are active in the political sphere to be drawn from highly resourced sections of the population appears to be substantiated by Parry et al (1992, p. 234). They observe that almost fifty per cent of 'complete activists' have undertaken some form of higher education. The average figure in the survey was only sixteen and a half per cent. Parry et al (1992, p. 69) consequently state that 'degree-holders are not only an educational elite, but they are also a participatory elite'. In terms of wealth, nearly half of the 'complete activists' qualify as a member of the richest quarter of the population. Parry et al (1992, p. 236) also describe middle age as 'the golden age of participation'. It was also found that the majority of heavily involved members of Neighbourhood Forums tend to be of retirement age (Burns et al, 1994, p. 236). These findings are not particularly surprising in the context of broader composition of political participation in Britain. Fitzgerald (1984, p. 105) states that the involvement of citizens in political life 'is very much a middle-class sport'.

Habitual Activism?

Once the existing data is investigated in greater detail it becomes clear that a key component of contemporary forms of political participation is a tendency for small numbers of people to be involved in a form of serial participation. These citizens are involved in a variety of different modes of participation, rather than sepecialising in one particular aspect of the participatory repertoire. These citizens might therefore be defined as 'habitual' participators. Andrews (1992) has explored this notion of habitual participation in her analysis of lifetime socialists. She has developed a social-psychological model of lifelong socialist activism built upon life history analysis, and argues that such individuals develop a 'habit of responding' to political issues. She notes that:

> Activism is not merely something which the respondents do, or even a part of them. It is them. During their long, accumulated years of engagement, they have come to define themselves through their activism (Andrews, 1992, p. 234).

Andrews goes on to note that 'participants do see themselves as makers of history, not as individuals, but as members of political organisations' (Andrews, 1992, p. 308). However, the focus in this analysis is very much on those members of the Labour Party who might be classified as 'active'. There is a tendency to equate Party membership with the most heavily involved participants. There is consequently little data that examines why those who are less involved in the Party do not become heavily involved in a similar manner. There is also little attempt to consider how the full range of Party members perceive the more involved members, and indeed the potential effects of their experiences upon their own involvement in the Party. One can also argue that the social-psychological focus of this study means that the context within which Labour Party activism is placed is primarily historical in character. The actual political mechanisms within which participation takes place remain largely absent from such analysis. In the next chapter, I will develop a theoretical framework that allows us to connect political participation with the structures through which it is mediated.

Parry *et al* (1992, p. 234) have correlated the levels of group membership across various modes of participation, and found that almost one half of the so-called 'complete activists' had four or more ties to other groups. The average for the survey population in Parry *et al*'s study was only fourteen per cent. In contrast, those who fail to participate beyond voting are likely to have very little linkage to established organisations. The majority of this section of the population are members of, at most, one organisation. According to Parry *et al* (1992) the most politically active citizens undertake more collective actions and contacting activity than even those who specialise in such activities. Parry *et al* (1992, p. 231) consequently observe that '[T]he complete activists may be fewer in number but they certainly get around'. From this perspective, 'activists' are seen to have a high level of attachment to a multiple number of groups, and are likely to 'pursue their goals across the participatory landscape' (Parry *et al*, 1992, p. 236). Those citizens who take an active role in political life are therefore likely to be integrated into existing participatory structures, and are likely to have a personal network of group affiliations. The tendency for certain individuals to compile a large amount of group membership is reinforced by other relevant research. Jordan and Maloney (1997, pp. 119-120) report that there is a high level of overlapping membership between Amnesty International, Greenpeace and Friends of the Earth. Almost one in five members of Amnesty International are also members of Friends of the Earth, whilst thirteen per cent of the Friends of the Earth membership are members of Amnesty International. Almost one third of Friends of the Earth members are also in Greenpeace, and the figure stands at over one third of the Amnesty International membership. Of course, being a member of a number of groups does not necessarily imply that one becomes involved in that organisation to any great degree. However, more detailed findings suggest that it is often the case that active participators are likely to be heavily involved in other bodies. For instance, in their study of Labour Party membership Seyd and Whiteley (1992) discovered a trend for active Party members to be simultaneously involved in a range of internal and external forms of political participation:

> Some people appear to be involved both in a number of Party and outside interest groups, suggesting that there is a 'network' of highly active people within the Party who are clearly involved in many kinds of political campaigns as well as in the Party organisation (Seyd and Whiteley, 1992, p. 93).

In a similar vein, recent analysis of voluntary school governors suggests that certain governors are also involved within a range of other bodies (Brehony, 1992). It is noted that 'what comes across very strongly….is their [the Chair's] deep involvement in a variety of voluntary activities in civil society as well as in local politics' (Brehony, 1992, p. 211).

Inevitably, data of this type has raised concerns over the democratic credentials of prevailing patterns of public involvement. For instance, Puddifoot (1996, p. 353) refers to an Achilles heel of local participation, namely the dilemma of 'how much those who claim to speak for or represent the views of the community actually reflect the views of the wider residential population'. Similarly, Burns *et al* (1994, p. 223) note that '[O]ne of the objections most commonly voiced to the idea of extending participatory forms of democracy is that only some people participate, they are often quite unrepresentative of those they purport to speak for'. Dalton (1988, p. 71) raises a similar concern that 'the politically active may become even more influential while the less active see their influence wane'. Parry *et al* (1992, p. 432) similarly observe that rises in the levels of participation may simply serve to 'amplify the already louder voice of the advantaged in British society'.

Accounting for Political Participation

Rational Choice Theory

The suggestion that it is a substantial minority of the population who take part in political life inevitably raises the question of why some people participate whilst others remain reluctant to enter the political realm. Perhaps the most common account of citizen mobilisation is the rational choice model. This interpretation of political participation argues that the individual calculation of the costs and benefits of involvement in politics predicts the likelihood of participation taking place. Put crudely, the rational choice model argues that if the benefits of taking part in political activity are seen to outweigh the potential costs, then mobilisation is more likely to occur. Rational choice theory is most closely associated with the work of Olson (1965) who classically argues that 'rational, self-interested individuals will not act to achieve their common or group interests' (Olson, 1965, p. 2). Individuals are therefore seen to be able to participate successfully within political groups if there are sufficient incentives from which the individual can benefit.

Two main types of incentives have been identified, namely outcome and process. The former sees participation as a route to achieving individual aims within the organisation in question. The benefits for participants may simply be an improvement in the individual's social or economic position. Participation is then likely to represent a form of self-interest. In political parties, for instance, 'activism can be regarded as an investment which must be made if the individual has ambitions to develop a future career in politics' (Seyd and Whiteley, 1996b, p. 219). It may also be the case that there are more obvious social benefits, in the sense of developing a credibility or 'reputation' within social networks. The process incentives are more closely related to the experience of participation itself. It is argued that political participation occurs as a consequence of the opportunity to interact with like-minded people within political structures. From this perspective, the benefits of participation can be 'soft' or non-material, and may take the form of individual feelings of solidarity, collective worth or social value. Consequently, the rational choice model implies that only irrational or truly altruistic people will take part in political life on a frequent basis. Olson (1965) therefore predicted that very few individuals would decide to become involved in public interest groups.

Although rational choice theory has been applied to participation in the Labour Party (Seyd and Whiteley, 1992; Seyd and Whiteley, 1996b) and the Conservative Party (Whiteley et al, 1994), the theory is susceptible to persuasive criticisms. By focusing exclusively upon individual calculations of the potential costs and benefits of political mobilisation, the theory transposes economic models onto the act of political participation. It can thus be regarded as a predominantly instrumental view of citizen participation in the sense that it employs narrow economic reasoning to account for mobilisation. Critics such as Dryzek (1990) have subsequently suggested that rational choice theory draws upon a culturally specific understanding of rationality and action that is particular to capitalist ideology. Rational choice theory thus marginalises other dimensions of rationality that are not necessarily structured around calculations of costs and benefits. I will discuss the implications of these persuasive criticisms for the question of how we might interpret political participation in the next chapter when I discuss the work of Habermas.

Rational choice theory can also be criticised for its methodological individualism. The political activity of citizens is seen to stem primarily from the unconstrained mobilisation of self-interested individuals, and sociologists have argued that this approach overlooks the structural limits on individual action (Ward, 1995, pp. 82-87). In their analysis of pressure group participation, Jordan and Maloney (1997, p. 99) go some way to address these shortcomings by noting that 'the explanation of membership has to shift its focus....from that of cognition by the individual to understand the decision in relation to the recruiting activities of the group'. In other words, it is unrealistic to explain political participation without reference to the relationship that exists between participants and the participatory environments within which they take part. This in turn requires that we focus attention on both the experiences of participants and the attitude of political organisations toward their members. It also requires that greater attention is given to the actual process of taking part in political participation and how people experience such activity.

The Resource Mobilisation Thesis

The existing survey data shows that there are clearly a number of strong and persistent inequalities at work within the realm of voluntary political participation. It has been widely argued within the available literature that this empirical data reflects the importance of access to social and cultural resources within the sphere of political participation. The resource mobilisation thesis attempts to account for differing levels of political activity by highlighting the availability and usage of resources throughout society. A range of personal, social, political and economic attributes have been traditionally identified as influencing the distribution of participation through the population. Verba and Nie (1972) classically argue that the capacity of individuals to put valuable social resources to use is directly related to the distribution of political participation. They state that 'the social status of an individual – his job, education and income – determines to a large extent how much he participates' (Verba and Nie, 1972, p. 13). It is argued that these faculties are converted into mobilisation through the development of cognitive 'civic attitudes'. These include 'a sense of efficacy, of psychological involvement in politics and a feeling of obligation to participate' (Verba and Nie, 1972, p. 13). This approach has been influential in shaping understandings of the skewed composition of involvement in political life. Dalton (1988, p. 71), for instance, argues that 'involvement in politics is becoming even more dependent on the skills and resources represented by social status'.

Resource mobilisation theory has also been employed to explain habitual activism. A further strand of this theory suggests that a participant's associational affiliations act as an important resource. Originating in American political studies, this theory argues that the relationship that exists between an individual and political networks can influence levels of participation. Those citizens who are heavily embedded within pre-existing group networks are more likely to be able to convert that particular resource into participation (McCarthy and Zald, 1976). In attempting to account for what makes citizens into regular participators in political activity, Parry et al (1992, pp. 225-227) similarly conclude that group-based resources are pre-eminent.

Recent theoretical work in this area has attempted to tie activism more clearly to existing networks (McAdam and Paulsen, 1993). It is argued that within pre-existing issue networks, certain actors acquire a status of presumptive rights that enable them to become opinion leaders. These individuals are seen by other members of the network as the most experienced and knowledgeable members of the policy community: 'The perception that certain people have a better grasp of an issue and potential alternatives leads to recognition of their key actor status' (McAdam and Paulsen, 1993, p. 248). Snow et al (1980) have also suggested that contact with existing participants can play an important role in accounting for mobilisation. The emphasis in this version of resource mobilisation theory is thus on the organisational or network infrastructures in which individuals are located, rather than on how somebody might simply feel about a particular issue.

Resource mobilisation theory is useful in exploring the question of why political participation fails to reflect the composition of the wider population. However, it would be naïve to draw simplistic boundaries between different socio-demographic sections of the population in relation to the tendency to take part in political life. It is important to note that in certain cases the trend for the most politically engaged citizens being unrepresentative of the wider population is not always replicated. According to the available data, a prime example of this is the Anti-Poll Tax movement. Bagguley (1995, pp. 703-705) claims that anti-poll tax groups in Leeds contained a wide cross section of the local population that were thought by many participants to be broadly representative of local areas. It is therefore important to recognise that participation is a 'multi dimensional' phenomenon (Parry et al, 1992, p. 416). The image of a pyramid with the most politically active at the top and the rest of the population in varying degrees of inactivity below is somewhat misleading. Parry et al (1992) observe that it is perhaps more accurate to conceive of a number of pyramids representing different types of participation within which citizens specialise or, in some cases, move between. However, the potential for movement between these types of participation is only likely to increase within the domain of the 'complete activists'. As we have noted, intense participation of this type remains the domain of a minority of the population.

In summary, we can see that a picture is emerging of how analysts have used the term 'activist' in recent years. This concept is portrayed in rather general terms as those well-resourced individuals who are heavily involved in a number of organisations simultaneously. Although this data clearly indicates the range of inequalities that inhabit the political public sphere, the limits of the data are apparent. We simply do not know enough from this type of empirical analysis about how people take part in political life to provide a thorough examination of the nature of 'activism' in contemporary liberal democracies. A major criticism of existing approaches to political participation is centred upon the suggestion that analysis is often abstracted from the actual conditions within which people take part in political life. This is despite the fact that the limited data that has touched upon the internal nature of political participation has raised a series of key questions. In this book, I adopt a somewhat different approach to the question of political participation. Firstly, greater attention needs to be given to the structures within which participation occurs, and secondly more emphasis needs to be placed on the question of how participants experience the process of being involved in these structures. There is a limited amount of data which partially addressees these themes, and I now turn to a discussion of this research.

The Process of Political Participation

Existing analysis of political action highlights a number of important tendencies within participatory spheres. Firstly, there appears to be a widespread propensity for experienced and frequent participants to dominate proceedings within sites of political participation. In their study of Neighbourhood Forums in Islington, Burns et al (1994, pp. 199-200) report that Forum meetings 'can be dominated by a few confident people....the leaders of the local Tenants' Associations hold sway while other forum members said little'. In his study of Neighbourhood Forums, Khan (1990, p. 17) similarly found that regular participants tend to be 'experienced in the running of meetings' and therefore 'can exclude the inexperienced from fully participating in meetings'. This is also clearly demonstrated in the aforementioned analysis of school governorship. As Brehony (1992, p. 210) notes, 'non participant governors have the formal opportunity to participate but they do not'. Brehony discovered that the contributions offered by female and black governors during meetings were often ignored or even interrupted. O'Mally (1977) presents a remarkably similar picture in the analysis of a local socialist group in Notting Hill in the late 1960s. She refers to:

> ....the workings of the People's Centre being dominated by the shifting movement of cliques, and to the meetings being dominated by the most

confident, those with the loudest voices and the greatest capacity to interrupt and hold the floor.

O'Mally (1977, pp. 164-165) also points to the tendency for attendance at meetings to fail to translate into inclusive participation: 'The licence to speak at meetings was both completely open and yet for many who lacked the confidence and capacity to interrupt, completely closed'. It might be persuasively argued that those with high levels of experience in political life have the knowledge and capability to dominate the process of participation. To some extent, this is supported by the available data. For instance, analysis of school governorship states that governors 'with knowledge and experience of local politics have on the whole been much more able to influence decisions than those who have not' (Brehony, 1992, p. 214). In her analysis of campaigns against Housing Action Trusts in Tower Hamlets, Woodward (1991, p. 54) notes that it is important to acknowledge the importance of 'the processes by which agendas for action are formed'. Woodward observes that:

> ....power is unequally spread. The dominance of particular groups and individuals within that movement will influence attitudes prevalent in that movement as a whole, and these relations of power will be reflected in the agenda of that group (Woodward, 1991, p. 54).

Secondly, existing data also raises the question of the relationships that exists between the most influential participants and other participants. It is noted by an analysis of London Docklands campaign groups that the most active members demonstrated a gate-keeping tendency to initiate and facilitate particular paths of action (Marris, 1987). This gate-keeping role for deciding upon strategies and tactics was underpinned by a mediatory position through which the most heavily embedded participants operate as a link between the local communities of the Docklands and political action opposing re-development. Again, these findings with regard to the relationships that exist between key participants and others remain tentative.

The available literature also points toward a third dimension of voluntary political participation, namely the tendency for forums of political participation to rely upon small clusters of regular participators. According to existing findings, it is common for certain key participants to provide the main source of activity at the centre of organisations. The available data suggests that it is not unusual for voluntary political structures to be built around a core of active participants who are surrounded by members in varying states of relative inactivity. For example, in their study of Labour Party membership Seyd and Whiteley (1992) have shown that only one fifth of the membership spend more than five hours per month on Party activities. Less than one in twenty of the overall sample were distinctive in that they spend over twenty hours per month engaging in such action (Seyd and Whiteley, 1992, p. 88). Although Seyd and Whiteley (1992, p. 88) note that 'there is a lot more work done by Party members than many observers of Labour Party politics suspected', it remains clear that those who spend a large amount of time on Party activities remain in a substantial minority.

When it comes to those members who have become involved in representative activity within the Labour Party itself, Seyd and Whiteley's investigation highlights a further and substantive trend of minority participation. Almost three-quarters had never stood for office within the Party and eighty five per cent had similarly never stood for elected office (Seyd and Whiteley, 1992, p. 93). Only one in twenty members had been a Labour councillor, and only about one in seven had held any office within the Party. Only fifteen per cent of members have represented the Party on an external body (Seyd and Whiteley, 1992, p. 93). It is concluded that these individuals 'might be described as the elite Party activists who are likely to have disproportionate influence over the local Party organisation' (Seyd and Whiteley, 1992, p. 94). Similar findings are evident within analysis of the Conservative Party:

> ....two rather distinct grass-roots Conservative 'parties' exist. One is a party of activists who are involved in campaigning, attending meetings, and running elections; the second is a party of supporters who do not get involved in these activities at all, but do get involved in fairly low-cost things like petitions and giving money to the party (Whiteley *et al*, 1994, pp. 102-103).

Clearly, the party political member who takes on an active role in his or her party is thus in the minority in Britain. The vast majority of party members are predominantly inactive in the sense that they take little part in the day to day administration of local affairs or party campaigning. Fisher (1996, p. 155) subsequently observes that political parties are defined by the fact that 'many members are sleeping members in that they only awake at elections and even then, for some the slumber remains unbroken'.

Similar findings are evident in analysis of single-issue campaigning groups. In their study of the British section of Amnesty International, Jordan and Maloney (1997, pp. 140-141) similarly observe that active members are in a minority. Their findings indicate the existence of four main categories of membership. 'Chequebook supporters' are those who simply subscribe to Amnesty International and thus provide the minimal financial contribution required for membership. These are the least active section of the membership. They are also shown to be less likely to join for the purposes of actually taking part in the activities of the organisation. 'Chequebook activists' are those members who donate additional money to the organisation. The third category is known as 'temporal activists'. These members volunteer their own time for various Amnesty International activities. Finally, Jordan and Maloney argue that there are 'super activists'. These members give more than the minimum in terms of both time and money. Unfortunately Jordan and Maloney do not indicate the size of the overall membership that each of these categories represents. One would assume from the general data presented by Jordan and Maloney that the 'chequebook supporters' and 'chequebook activists' constitute the majority of the membership.

Further data compounds this image of Amnesty International as being structured around a small number of active members and a largely unengaged body of inactive members. A recent investigation has found that only fifteen per cent of British Amnesty International members belong to local groups (Maloney, 1996, p. 10). According to Jordan and Maloney (1997, p. 191), almost three-quarters of the British Amnesty International membership saw the opportunity of being 'politically active' as of little or no importance when originally joining the organisation. An internal Amnesty International UK Report from 1995 shows that the average number of active members who regularly attend group meetings is only fourteen (Amnesty International UK, 1995). Beyond the core of active members there tends to be a periphery of occasional participants who similarly constitute fourteen members on average. However, the average number of 'sleeping members' who only receive the local group's newsletter is far higher at thirty-nine. Of those members who do regularly take part in local group activities, only about a half hold a position of responsibility within the group (Amnesty International UK, 1989). In a similar vein, few individual members actually attend the Annual General Meeting of the British section of Amnesty International despite formal access being available for all members. Active members who are affiliated to a local group appear far more likely to attend the Annual General Meeting, with almost half of groups likely to send a delegation (Amnesty International UK, 1995).

Those who become heavily involved within Amnesty International are also far more likely to remain at the centre of campaigning activity than their less active counterparts. The 'turnover' of membership in local groups is currently fairly static, and over three quarters of members within local groups have been involved for more than one year (Amnesty International UK, 1995). It is worthwhile contrasting this apparent stability amongst the local group membership with the high turnover that occurs within the wider membership of the British section of Amnesty International. According to Jordan and Maloney (1997, pp. 166-169), organisations such as Amnesty International are forced to balance heavy net membership losses and gains on an annual basis. Their data suggests that dropout rates of between thirty and forty per cent are quite normal in large-scale campaigning groups. For instance, over one third of the membership of Friends of the Earth who joined in 1991 failed to rejoin in 1992 (Jordan and Maloney, 1997, p. 166). The average life span of an Amnesty International member is four years, and the 'normal' annual turnover rate of the membership is around forty per cent. Despite the fact that between 1992 and 1993 Amnesty International UK acquired a sixteen per cent overall gain in membership, this had to be achieved against the backdrop of a loss of almost one quarter of the entire membership from the previous year. This translated into a total lapsed membership of over twenty thousand. When compared to the information on local group participation, these figures suggest that those members who become involved within groups are more inclined to remain active within the organisation.

More small-scale investigations have reinforced this idea that a small core of participants tend to be found at the heart of participatory forums. For instance, Nicholson *et al* (1981) highlight the existence of a tight knit group of trade union officials who form the central hub of union activity. By analysing attendance rates it was discovered that:

> ....there is (a) a sizeable core of stewards who attend almost all meetings (b) a majority who miss some but not all, and (c) very few who regularly fail to attend. In short....we have found an activist core of branch officers, committee members, chief shop stewards, and stewards who have active contact across departmental boundaries (Nicholson *et al*, 1981, pp. 122-123).

The aforementioned analysis of school governorship again points to similar findings. Brehony (1992, pp. 209-210) notes that 'it becomes more and more apparent that governing bodies typically consist of a core of activists surrounded by a periphery of governors in varying states of inactivity'. Furthermore, Brehony (1992, p. 210) points to the existence of what he refers to as 'hyper-activists' who are likely to occupy the position of Chair of governors. These governors manage to 'stand out from other members in the core of activists' (Brehony, 1992, p. 210).

In his account of the operation of the four main Action Groups that formed in response to the re-development of London Docklands in the 1970s and early 1980s, Marris (1987, p. 70) observes that 'the core of each group consisted of no more than half a dozen'. Furthermore, within each group 'a professionally trained planner or community worker was the sustaining organizer [sic]'. The activities that enabled these groups to function were reliant upon the efforts of a small number of heavily involved participants. Again echoing previous findings, Marris observes that these individuals were distinguishable by their experience and established position within local organisations and groups. The trend for the most active individuals to be involved in a range of external groups was also repeated in this example. Those most heavily involved in the Action Groups were also 'active' in the Labour Party, trade associations and local community groups (Marris, 1987, p. 71). Marris does not specify the degree of action indicated by the use of this term. Nonetheless, it is clear form the account provided that the active Action Group members were involved in a multiple number of other areas of participation.

It is also worthwhile to note that over one half of the so-called 'complete activists' have a strong and clear belief in the value of taking part in political life. Their levels of 'efficacy' tend to be extremely high. Dalton (1988, p. 50) defines efficacy as '....the feeling that one's political action can affect the political process'. He goes on to assert that 'a feeling of political efficacy motivates individuals to become active in politics, while the absence of efficacy evokes political apathy and withdrawal'. Whereas the most politically active in society appear to have some faith in the value of participation, Parry et al (1992, p. 290) show that 'most people report themselves unmoved by the experience of their action'. For example, almost three-quarters of those who had taken part in party political activity reported that canvassing on behalf of the party made no difference to their view of the value of political participation.

However, Parry et al (1992) go on to observe that those who do actually experience far more positive effects from participation are those who are already active in the political realm. As they put it, 'a strong impact is felt by a very small group of often intensively active people' (Parry et al, 1992, p. 291). Thus, whilst less than one third of those who had undertaken a single act of participation reported that the experience increased their knowledge of the political process, the figure was over half of those who take part frequently (Parry et al, 1992, p. 294). With this in mind, 'it is those who are most interested in politics and, above all, those who most frequently talk about it, who also learn most' (Parry et al, 1992, pp. 294-295). According to existing data, the majority of those who take part in political participation tend to be unimpressed with the experience and are therefore perhaps less likely to return to the political realm. The more active participants, on the other hand, tend to 'have learned to live with the disappointments which are entailed in political life' (Parry et al, 1992, p. 295). I will take up this point in more detail in Chapter Seven when I show how the most involved participants tend to lower their participatory expectations and aims.

Clearly, the data that explores the process of participation indicates that there are a number of important internal dynamics occurring within participatory spheres. It has been suggested that there is currently little understanding of how the actual experience of political activity affects patterns of participation. The role of the conditions within which political activity occurs thus remains rather remote from existing understandings of political participation. In the remainder of this book I will adopt an approach to political participation that builds upon the data presented in this chapter, and attempts to address the limitations of the existing literature.

New Directions for Analysis

This chapter has moved from a general analysis of levels and composition of participation within Britain to a brief examination of what takes place within existing structures of political participation. It has been shown that although the composition of political participation does not always accommodate clear-cut conclusions, there are nonetheless a number of persistent inequalities affecting spheres of voluntary political participation. I have stressed that it is a sizable minority of the population that chooses to engage with the political realm. It has also been shown that it is the most well resourced members of society that are the most likely to participate in political affairs. The latter sections of this chapter have opened up the discussion about the nature of political participation to incorporate the question of how participation proceeds within various structures. However, the findings in this area have been shown to be fragmentary and somewhat limited.

There are two main areas that will allow us to address these various shortcomings. Firstly, attention needs to be paid to methodological issues. The vast majority of research that has been conducted into the question of political participation and activism has been conducted in a statistical manner. The predominance of survey based analysis of the political activity of citizens is useful in providing a picture of the complex composition of political participation. However, the use of quantitative methods of data collection tends to generate an understanding of participation that fails to probe beneath the 'surface' of political action. The emphasis on mass survey based data may well lead to the researcher engaging with the field of participation at a level removed from the internal life of such activity. Survey based analysis of political participation can therefore only go so far in explaining why political activity is shaped in the way that it is. An excessive focus on the levels and the socio-demographic composition of political participation tends to sideline an analytical interest in the process of taking part in political activity. In order to develop our understandings of contemporary forms of political participation, it is therefore necessary to adopt predominantly qualitative methods of investigation. I will discuss these issues in more detail in Chapter Four.

The second aspect of my approach to political participation is to widen the scope of the theoretical debate within which the nature of political participation is explored. The penchant for utilising quantitative methods has tended to limit the capability of political scientists to consider the question of how and why certain aspects of citizen participation develop within the political public sphere. The different types of 'activism' that emerge within structures of voluntary political activity are central to this issue, and I have argued that the existing literature tends to characterise such participation primarily in terms of the factors that can be measured by quantitative data. At the same time, the practice of political participation has rarely been placed within a framework that is based in a broader theoretical awareness of the forces shaping the contours of the political public sphere. By adopting such an approach the focus of analysis can then be shifted from the measurement of political activity toward interpreting different cultures of political participation.

The debate about the skewed composition of participation raises a whole series of broader questions about the role and status of citizen participation within advanced liberal democracy. One might ask exactly what theorists of democracy actually expect from existing political structures? This in turn leads into a broader discussion about the limits and capacity of voluntary political activity that takes place within the political public sphere of advanced liberal democracies. Is participation in increasingly fragmented societies inevitably restricted to the articulation of sectional interests or is there scope for the development of a more inclusive realm of political participation? Within such a discussion, the respective roles that one assigns to institutions of the state and civil society inevitably come to the fore. As Burns *et al* (1994, p. 246) put it: 'Is the creation of a space for open public dialogue and decision-making possible, or is such a space mythical, perhaps precluded by the very nature of the state and civil society themselves?' If we are to address some of these questions then we require a deeper understanding of the nature of different types of political discourse that emerge from the existing structures of the political public sphere, and I take up this aim in the second half of this book.

At this point, our investigation intersects with a number of recent debates over the value of 'public deliberation' or 'deliberative democracy'. These themes raise the question of the nature of discourse that occurs within sites of political participation. In the next chapter, I will explore this theme in more depth and draw upon the work of Jürgen Habermas in order to develop a theoretical and interpretative framework within which to link the 'real world' of political activity to the wider debates I have touched upon. This will also allow the practice of participation to be placed squarely within the structures that mediate political activity, and in turn allow us to reflect upon the relationship that exists between different forms of activism and these structures. It will also enable us to develop the debate around political participation beyond quantitative questions toward a deeper understanding of the internal nature of different forms of political activity. By adopting this approach, I hope to shed some light on the factors that shape voluntary political participation of the types described in this chapter.

3 The Public Sphere, Discourse and Political Participation

The data outlined in the previous chapter raises a whole series of largely unanswered questions about what it means to take part in political life and how participants experience political participation. This, in turn, prompts an interest in the different types of activism that inhabit the realms of voluntary political participation. By exploring these issues the traditional focus on measuring levels of participation and mapping the socio-demographic composition of political activity is supplemented by an interest in examining the actual process of taking part in political participation. The question of how and why certain forms of political participation develop within different political structures then comes to the fore. I have also suggested that existing empirical analysis of the composition of political participation inevitably raises a broader theoretical concern with the role and position of citizen participation within contemporary liberal democracy. In particular, I have raised the question of the extent to which, in advanced capitalist societies, one can identify the potential for the development of open spaces of public debate within the voluntary political structures of civil society.

In recent years, these themes have begun to attract the attention of a wide range of theorists. It is increasingly argued that the negotiation of social and political legitimacy should rely upon strong public discourse in which citizens are able to collectively deliberate over matters of public interest. The nature of political participation consequently comes to the fore. A large body of theory is consequently 'seeking to articulate forms of democracy in which the moment of collective deliberation is highlighted as the very source of political legitimacy' (Blaug, 1996, p. 72). There has been much talk in recent years of the value of 'deliberative democracy' or 'public deliberation' (Bohman, 1996; Fishkin, 1991; Miller, 1993; Dryzek, 1990). Giddens (1994, p. 33), for instance, highlights the importance of a 'public arena in which controversial issues – in principle – can be resolved, or at least handled, through dialogue rather than through pre-established forms of power'. At the heart of this trend is the idea that '[P]olitical equality without deliberation is not of much use, for it amounts to nothing more than power without the opportunity to think about how that power ought to be exercised' (Fishkin, 1991, p. 36).

Underlying much of this work is an assumption that current forms of political debate and participation fail to measure up to these high ideals of deliberation. As Fox and Miller (1995, p. 7) put it '[M]ost of what passes for public conversation is not that at all'. Critics have suggested that our participatory institutions are in reality dominated by 'aggregative, episodic and inflexible forms of decision-making' (Bohman, 1996, p. 1). As we have seen in the preceding chapter, the existing data with regard to political participation gives some credence to this claim. However, there is a wide gap between this desire for a more deliberative democracy and current understandings of actually existing forms of political participation. Despite the development of this normative theorising, the capacity and role of contemporary forms of voluntary political activity remains somewhat unclear. There has been only limited attempt to relate the interest in more deliberative forms of political participation to the political activity that takes place on an everyday basis.

I intend to use this chapter to lay the foundations of a theoretical discussion that allows us to connect these normative and practical concerns. This theoretical framework will consequently provide a set of criteria through which the findings of the research can be interpreted. At the same time, I hope to underline the idea that the nature of political participation and the discursive character of political interaction have a deep significance to our understanding of the state of contemporary democracy. In order to fulfill this task I draw primarily upon the discourse centred concept of society presented by the German philosopher and sociologist Jürgen Habermas.

This complex body of work is informed by the central idea that although advanced capitalist societies have experienced a decline of meaningful public discourse, they nonetheless contain the potential for the reconstruction of critical and rational forms of public communication. At his most incisive, Habermas gives us a reason for continuing to hold onto the principles of radical democracy in an era of continuing philosophical and political scepticism. For the purposes of this investigation, the value of Habermas' work can be traced primarily to the fact that his theoretical project places the issue of political participation and political discourse at the centre of his conceptualisation of democracy. Moreover, both critique and normativity motivate his theoretical work. On the one hand, he displays a 'substantive preoccupation with the way in which enlightenment....turns from a means of liberation into a new source of enslavement' (Outhewaite, 1994, p. 2). On a methodological level, Habermas is therefore concerned with identifying obstacles to political communication that lead to a narrowing and constriction of political discourse, and contribute to the development of what Habermas defines as 'linguistic pathology' (Holub, 1991, p. 8).

On the other hand, Habermas has formed a developmental concern with the practical reconstruction of spaces capable of sustaining rational deliberation. Habermas argues that this radicalisation of the nature of democracy in advanced capitalist society can only take place in the realm of participatory democracy in which citizens are able to deliberate over issues of public concern. According to Habermas, public opinion can potentially act as a source of critical and rational judgement rather than simply as a forum for the expression of periodic preferences or manipulated consent. Habermas suggests that analysis must pay close attention to those political processes that act as sources of legitimacy in advanced liberal democracies, and consider the extent to which state structures of administration are open to the various public forums within which citizens participate. This provides the basis for a 'constitutionally regulated circulation of power' (Habermas, 1996b, p. 354) within political decision-making apparatus and enables the development of informed political debate of a rational character. The respective role that one attributes to state structures and civil society is of some importance in this dynamic, as is the character of political participation.

In this chapter, I have three main aims. Firstly, I introduce several of Habermas' most relevant concepts including communicative and instrumental rationality, the public sphere, the colonisation of the lifeworld, and discourse ethics. I argue that Habermas' account of the relationship between rationality and discourse provides a framework that enables us to categorise the tendencies to be found in the realm of political participation. This subsequently allows for the critical analysis of political practices and the process of political participation. Secondly, I develop a more specific discussion about the position of political participation and civil society within Habermas' theoretical framework. Finally, I examine the ways in which I intend to employ Habermas' work in the remainder of the book.

Jürgen Habermas, Critical Theory and the Frankfurt School Tradition

The work of Habermas is most commonly associated with the Frankfurt Institute for Social Research, or the Frankfurt School (cf. Outhewaite, 1994; Geuss, 1981; Rasmussen, 1990; Love, 1995). This group of philosophers, social scientists and cultural critics was originally established in the late 1920s, and adopted an interdisciplinary neo-Marxist agenda spanning philosophy and the social sciences. The Frankfurt School is best known for developing an agenda built around a 'critical theory' of advanced capitalist societies. Growing out of its Marxist roots, the broad aim of the School has been to develop a critique of social relations that are structured around domination and alienation, and to ultimately provide the tools with which subjects can challenge their oppressive social circumstances. Geuss (1981) argues that Critical Theory can be distinguished from the objectifying stance of the natural sciences by virtue of its reflective character. He notes that it is 'a reflective theory which gives agents a kind of knowledge inherently productive of enlightenment and emancipation' (Geuss, 1981, p. 2). It is not my intention to discuss this heritage in great detail. My more modest aim in this chapter is to map out some observations on how Habermas' theoretical offerings provide an applied basis for interpreting the realities of political interaction and participation in the 1990s.

Whereas the work of the early Frankfurt School led to a predominantly negative interpretation of the possibilities of the Enlightenment era, Habermas argues that it may be possible to revive what he defines to as the normative content of the 'unfinished project' of modernity (Habermas, 1996a). Thus, at the base of Habermas' version of Critical Theory is the reconstructive idea of being able to overcome defects of the era of modernity that produce a 'one-sided' and skewed society. Habermas' contribution to his philosophical heritage can be broadly seen as a hermeneutical development of the Marxist revisionism with which the members of the early Frankfurt School were engaged. In particular, Habermas argues that Marx's theory of labour is inadequate to account for the nature of mass democracy in advanced capitalist societies (Habermas, 1996d, pp. 284-287). Habermas subsequently presents a substantive reconstruction of historical materialism (Love, 1995, pp. 47-51).

Central to this project has been a turn toward a philosophy of the universal underpinnings of communication and discourse. The route that Habermas follows in this revisionist exercise is primarily centred upon a critical assessment of the role of communication as a mediatory component of processes of societal rationalisation. The apparent move away from a traditional Marxist focus upon overtly material factors toward questions of discourse and communication represents a substantial redefinition of Habermas' Marxist roots. As Ray (1993, p. 63) observes, Habermas' theory of discourse is primarily 'a theory of learning capacities, or formal properties of communication, rather than of privileged social locations such as class'.

Redefining Rationality: Intersubjectivity, Communicative Action and Discourse Ethics

Two major epistemological shifts inform this overall development. Firstly, in contrast to the Frankfurt School's predominant emphasis upon what he sees as a 'philosophy of consciousness', Habermas proposes a paradigm shift toward an intersubjective praxis (Crossley, 1996). Intersubjectivity is seen by Habermas as a 'background knowledge' (Habermas, 1984, p. 13) through which it is possible for a reciprocal relationship based upon a shared understanding to flourish. Questioning the monological modes of moral and political discourse identified by Kant, Habermas proposes a subject to subject relation within our interpretation of social interaction: 'the grounding of norms and prescriptions demands the carrying-through of an actual dialogue and in the last instance is not possible monologically' (Habermas, 1992a, p. 68). In this sense, 'moral conversation must be real, not hypothetical' (McKenny, 1991, p. 438). Habermas suggests that this concept of intersubjectivity provides the basis for social action that is reflexive and capable of sustaining extensive argumentation.

Secondly, Habermas advocates a redefinition of the nature of rationality. Habermas' conception of modern reason embodies the possibility that rationality can take a number of distinct forms. In order to justify this move Habermas has extended the hermeneutical direction of the later work of Horkheimer and Adorno by expounding primarily upon the relationship between 'argumentative speech' and reason. Habermas distinguishes between the instrumental or strategic aspects of rationality, and the potential for rationality contained in the everyday practices of communication. The former embodies purposive action which primarily 'realises defined goals under given conditions' (Habermas, 1971, p. 92). In other words it refers to activity in which pre-defined means are used to achieve specific ends, neither of which are open to question. This is broadly defined by Habermas as 'instrumental rationality'.

In *The Theory of Communicative Action* (1984; 1987b) and *Moral Consciousness and Communicative Action* (1989b) Habermas has developed his vision of a broader conception of reason. He argues that existing alongside this strategic orientation is a form of rationality governed primarily by consensual norms that are (however implicitly) recognised by discoursing actors. Rather than resort to an abstract characterisation of rationality Habermas argues that this aspect of language use can actually be found within the 'universal pragmatics' of everyday communication (Habermas, 1979). Habermas (1992b, p. 142) therefore defines this conception of rationality as a 'linguistically embodied reason', or as it is more commonly known 'communicative rationality'. At the heart of this idea is the controversial claim that '[R]eaching understanding is the inherent telos of human speech' (Habermas, 1984, p. 287). Building upon this linguistic turn, Habermas claims that practical discourse takes place when there are no restrictions on deliberation and when the force of the better argument is able to hold sway. This 'ideal speech situation' defines the formal discursive conditions in which claims to legitimacy can be raised and redeemed without being subject to constraint. Discourse can therefore be defined as:

> ....that form of communication....whose structure assures us: that the bracketed validity claims of assertions, recommendations, or warnings are the exclusive object of discussion; that participants, themes, and contributions are not restricted except with reference to the goal of testing the validity claims in question; that no force except that of the better argument is exercised; and that, as a result, all motives except that of the cooperative search for truth are excluded (Habermas, 1975, pp. 107-108).

Only when a discursive interaction is subject to the force of a fully redeemed argument can it be said to be free from manipulation and domination. Kemp (1985, pp. 186-188) identifies four main structural prerequisites of the ideal speech situation. Firstly, participants in a discourse must be able to initiate and perpetuate interaction. This means that everyone must be allowed to raise questions and respond to inquiries. Secondly, all participants must be able to express attitudes and feelings. Thirdly, all of those who take part must be allowed to permit and forbid arguments. Finally, it is necessary for participants to have equal opportunities to provide explanations and interpretations. These four principles also require something of the participants, namely that they be understandable, sincere, appropriate and truthful in their utterances. Put simply, Habermas' discourse centred theory of democracy relies on all parties that may be affected being able to contribute to debate in a free and equal manner. But it also implies that participants are capable of developing a form of 'communicative competence' in which agents are able to both present reasons for their contribution and allow space for others to participate in the same manner. Habermas argues that these 'discourse ethics' are built around 'the central experience of the unconstrained, unifying, consensus-bringing force of argumentative speech, in which participants overcome their merely subjective views' (Habermas, 1984, p. 10). Discourse is not simply about providing opportunities for the expression of a perspective but being able to modify or develop that viewpoint through a genuinely intersubjective exchange in which some form of agreement can be reached.

Habermas (cited in Kemp, 1985, p. 198) thus speaks of the 'anticipation of an ideal speech situation' that operates within the practical discourse of the real world. Crucially, Habermas feels that his model allows him to distinguish between entry into discourse with a goal-oriented approach and an attitude geared toward reaching mutual understanding. This, in turn, implies a contrast between highly rigid discursive frameworks and more open and enabling forms of discourse. Outhewaite (1994, p. 70) identifies the crucial difference between these two sides of rationality outlined by Habermas:

> Unlike the 'cognitive-instrumental' notion of rationality in teleological action, where ideas of the manipulation of, or adaption to, an environment are central, a model of rationality grounded in communication implies an option in favour of 'a wider concept of rationality' oriented to 'argumentative speech'.

It is not my intention here to fully discuss the validity or otherwise of Habermas account of language and communicative action. Nonetheless, it is worth noting that the assertion that mutual understanding represents *the* original and ideal role of language has been subject to substantial critique (Lyotard, 1984, 1988; Keane, 1988, pp. 230-235). Others have suggested that Habermas' heavy reliance on a universalist, rational conception of discourse stifles the more affective or ambiguous character of political identity, argumentation and rationality (Connolly, 1991, pp. 161-163; Myerson, 1994, pp. 40-50; Crossley, 1996, p. 124; Braaten, 1995).

These criticisms carry some weight. By employing terms such as 'ideal' speech and 'consensus' Habermas does indeed draw upon a strongly rationalistic idea of discourse that appears to allow little room for ambiguity. However, it is worth noting that Habermas is often misunderstood as implying that consensus oriented argumentation necessarily leads to an enforced agreement. On the contrary, Habermas actually suggests that conflict is inevitably part of discursive interaction. As Chambers (1995a, p. 240) observes, 'disagreement, like agreement, can be more or less rational depending on the reasons one has'. The only requirement in Habermas' model is that participants are able to justify and redeem their objections via the force of the better argument. Of course, it must be noted that the concept of a discourse free from constraint is clearly an abstract ideal, but this does not remove its value as either a potential guide for action or as a principle of critical evaluation. As Habermas himself puts it, 'it is a critical standard against which every actually realized [sic] consensus can be called into question and checked' (cited in Kemp, 1985, p. 198).

Habermas also implies that his communicative model of reason opens up possibilities for the extension and radicalisation of existing systems of political interaction. Habermas classically argues that this can only be achieved when social relations are organised 'according to the principle that the validity of every norm of political consequence be made dependent on a consensus arrived at in communication free from domination' (Habermas, 1971, p. 284). Habermas values this rational form of 'discursive will formation' because it is intimately related to a greater democratisation of society. It can 'set in motion ways of defining collective goals that merely administrative or power-oriented decisions would lead astray or cripple' (Habermas, 1992a, p. 67). At the heart of Habermas' understanding of the potential of discourse ethics within advanced capitalist society is the idea of the efficacy of rational public discourse.

Habermas can therefore be seen as contributing to the traditions of radical democracy, which suggest that participation can have a developmental effect on those who take part in proceedings. This classical theoretical tradition suggests that participation can have an important educative impact on participants. This is encapsulated by Pateman (1970, p. 105), who notes that we 'learn to participate by participating'. Whereas conventional orthodoxy suggests that such ideals are largely redundant in modern complex societies Habermas implies that communicatively structured discourse can potentially reinvigorate the developmental outcomes of participation (Warren, 1995, pp. 168-172).

The concept of communicative action consequently lies at the core of Habermas' idea of democracy and a rationally organised society. In this sense, the notion of practical discourse can serve as a funnel for establishing legitimacy within political disputes (Chambers, 1995a, p. 234; Cohen and Arato, 1995, pp. 350-351). It is important to note that Habermas is not suggesting that discourse ethics needs to dominate everyday life or that all public institutions can be organised according to the principles of discourse ethics. Rather, the discourse ethic can serve as a level of deliberation to which participants in a discourse can move when there is disagreement or conflict about issues. Discourse should therefore not be viewed as a forum in which neatly bracketed decisions can be taken and then regarded as complete. In the context of debates around the practical construction of a public sphere, discourse needs to be conceived as 'a long term consensus-forming process and not a decision procedure....we must visualize [sic] discourse as the place where collective interpretations are constructed' (Chambers, 1995a, p. 250). This is evident in Habermas' more recent assertions to the effect that democracy is not capable of organising society as a whole. As Calhoun (1992b, p. 37) points out '[T]he routine rational-critical discourse of the public sphere cannot be about everything all at once. Some structuring of attention....must always exist'.

Having mapped out his dual conception of rationality, Habermas has moved on to show how these aspects of reason have become embedded in the social and political institutions of capitalist liberal democracies. This focuses upon processes of selective rationalisation, whereby distorted formations of communication become installed in social and political life. A dominant theme in Habermas' work is the idea that contemporary society is increasingly organised according to instrumental reason, whilst communicative action becomes marginalised as a way of organising social interaction. It thus becomes possible to criticise the developmental tendencies of modernity 'not as an excess, but as a deficit of rationality' (Habermas 1987a, p. 310). Habermas speaks of 'pathologies of modernity' that have been instrumental in ushering in a deformed version of reason, whilst simultaneously putting his faith in the potential of an 'unfinished project' of modernity. Consequently, Forester (1985c, p. 205) observes that '[P]olitically debilitating distortions of communication are political artefacts and not natural necessities'.

Habermas' model thus leaves room for the reformulation of political participation in line with more communicative and rational principles. In this sense, new forms of social, cultural and political organisation may be able to redeem the rational potential encased within modernity. The task of a critical social theory is to be 'critical of the reality of developed societies inasmuch as they do not make full use of the learning potential culturally available to them' (Habermas, 1996e, p. 310). As White (1995b, p. 8) observes, the 'cultural potential of modernity constitutes the critical standpoint from which particular aspects of Western modernization [sic] can be judged negatively'. Much of this discussion proceeds at a fairly abstract level, but it should be clear that at the centre of Habermas' writings is the idea of 'giving new life to ideals of reason and freedom by revealing their false embodiment in....bourgeois Western political institutions' (White, 1995b, p. 4). Central to Habermas' overall project is an effort to relate his thematic categories to the conditions within which political conversations proceed, and to reveal the systematic distortion of political debate. The next stage of our discussion is to consider in more specific terms how Habermas claims this skewed institutionalisation of rationality has come about within the realm of political participation, and how it is perhaps being challenged.

The Public Sphere and Political Participation

At the heart of Habermas' work is an interest in the conditions of rational political debate and discussion within the mass democracies of advanced capitalist society. Much of Habermas' critique of contemporary political structures stems from a concern with the erosion of spaces of participatory democracy and the continuing spread of instrumental rationality as the main co-ordinating principle of political life. Habermas argues that public debate and argument is good for democracy, and it is only through discursive interaction in the public arena that democracy can be played out in any meaningful fashion. As Outhewaite (1996b, p. 8) points out, these avenues of inquiry have led Habermas to both a critique of technocratic ideology and a mapping out of the practical basis for rational public discussion within advanced capitalist society.

In part, this concern stems from his account of the disintegration, and possible reformulation, of a 'public sphere' capable of sustaining participatory democracy and dialogue. In *The Structural Transformation of the Public Sphere* (1989) Habermas classically argues that a vibrant public sphere developed in Britain and Europe during the eighteenth century with the growth of coffee houses, the public press and similar 'discursive' sites. Habermas claims that these arenas enabled informed citizens to interact and discuss public affairs in a deliberative and critical manner. The policies of the administrative state consequently came under the gaze of a critically reasoning public who engaged in increasingly rational forms of discourse. This bourgeois public sphere 'may be conceived above all else as the sphere of private people come together as a public' (Habermas, 1989a, p. 27).

I do not have the room to fully consider the accuracy or otherwise of this account here. Habermas' historical description of the emergence of a public sphere has been subject to wide scrutiny, and a number of criticisms have been made of the overall thesis (Eley, 1992; Fleming, 1995).

Habermas argues that the life of the bourgeois public sphere was short lived. It is suggested that a number of processes, including the gradual interpenetration of the state and society, led to the eventual disintegration, or 'refeudalisation', of the public sphere within the mass democracy of welfare state societies (Thompson, 1993). Consequently, he argues that the space available for public discourse in contemporary society has become limited. Electoral mobilisation and the achievement of short-term ends have become paramount in politics, whilst the spaces available to citizens for rational political discourse have been divested of their influence. As Habermas (1989a, p. 231) puts it, 'organizations [sic] strive for political compromises with the state and with one another, as much as possible to the exclusion of the public'.

Politics therefore becomes 'professionalised'. Consequently, practical public discourse becomes the home of a disempowered, mystified form of communication. Habermas thus argues that the public sphere 'becomes the court before whose public prestige can be displayed – rather than in which public critical debate is carried on' (Habermas, 1989a, p. 201). Rational debate is sidelined and dismantled as 'publicity loses its critical function in favour of a staged display' (Habermas, 1989a, p. 206). According to McCarthy (1989, p. xii), the effects of this process are profound:

> The public sphere of social-welfare-state democracies is….a field of competition among conflicting interests, in which organizations [sic] representing diverse constituencies negotiate and compromise among themselves and with government officials, while excluding the public from their proceedings.

Habermas thus characterises contemporary political structures as part of a 'modern technocratic democracy' (Outhewaite, 1994, p. 2) in which a de-politicised administration holds sway. Habermas argues that these institutions are components of a system of public policy that tends to exclude practical questions from public discussion. This process generates 'inhibiting factors….in the existing arrangements that condition citizens to an unpolitical follower mentality and prevent them from reflecting and being concerned with anything but their own short-term personal interests' (Habermas, 1992c, p. 450). Instrumental reason manifests itself in political activity when effectiveness becomes the measure of the justification of actions. Issues of public concern are reduced from moral and social appropriateness to questions of technical strategy. Political discourse then becomes oriented toward achieving pre-defined ends rather than the working through of practical-moral questions in which all affected parties are able to participate. In short, the political process is defined by instrumentality rather than open deliberation.

Reflecting the wider normative and developmental tone of much of his work, Habermas bemoans the apparent decline of a rational public sphere. Inevitably, the idea of a space capable of sustaining moments of rationally structured public debate has some currency for questions of radical democracy. Fraser (1992, p. 110) comprehensively defines this ideal of the public sphere as:

> ....a theater [sic] in modern societies in which political participation is enacted through the medium of talk. It is the space in which citizens deliberate about their common affairs, hence, an institutional arena of discursive interaction.

In recent years, Habermas has turned his attention to the question of how a similar arena of inclusive public discourse might be revived today. He notes that this would only be possible 'on an altered basis, as a rational reorganization [sic] of social and political power under mutual control of rival organizations [sic] committed to the public sphere in their internal structure as well as in their relations with the state and each other' (Habermas, 1974, p.55). Consequently, Habermas (1992c, pp. 445-446) argues that 'the settling of political questions....depends on the institutionalization [sic] of practices of rational public debate'. It is then necessary to show how it might be possible for 'the public....to set in motion a critical process of public communication through the very organizations [sic] that mediatize [sic] it' (Habermas, 1989a, p. 232). This 'critical publicity' (Habermas, 1989a, p. 249) necessarily entails an expansion and deepening of rational discourse rather than a continued narrowing of public deliberation. Miller (1993, p. 89) highlights the value of Habermas' work in this area:

> ....rather then retreating to a minimal form of liberalism, we can seek to shift democratic practice towards the deliberative ideal, encouraging people not merely to express their political opinions....but to form those opinions through public debate in public settings.

The internal nature of political structures and the types of activity that develop within these spaces are therefore of some importance to the perspective developed by Habermas. The normative dimension of Habermas' work explicitly connects the negotiation of legitimacy with the quality of discourse informing public policy and public debate. Habermas takes us from an abstract critique of the rational potential of modernity to the idea of communicative action as a possible source of democratisation. Taking up Habermas' work on the public sphere, it becomes possible, or indeed necessary, to view contemporary forms of political participation as a phenomenon that is weighted with significance. Of course, it could be suggested that by doing so we are imposing an abstract concept over a range of activities that are in reality simply based upon the mobilisation of particular interests and preferences. However, Habermas shows that if we reduce the realm of political participation to basic questions of interest then we are overlooking the potential role of the political activity of citizens within the development of a critical publicity.

According to Habermas' developmental theorising, participation is not seen as an optional outcome of liberal democratic structures but rather as 'fundamental pressure built into differentiation and complexity as such' (Warren, 1995, p. 169). The normative dimension of Habermas' theorising suggests that both established and emerging forms of political participation can be seen as reflective of broader processes of rationalisation. As Dryzek (1995, p. 103) puts it: 'there is more going on here than an ordinary political clash of particular interests'. This point can be most clearly detected in Habermas' attempt to intertwine the concept of communicative rationality with broader processes of systemic change in advanced capitalist societies.

The Colonisation of the Lifeworld Thesis

In order to account for a number of political, social and cultural changes affecting advanced capitalist liberal democracies, Habermas has developed his colonisation of the lifeworld thesis. Drawing primarily upon his account of communicative rationality, Habermas firstly argues that we need to be aware of the importance of a 'lifeworld' within social communication and action. This lifeworld

> ....stands behind the back of each participant in communication and....provides resources for the resolution of problems of understanding. Members of a social collective normally share a life-world (Habermas, 1992a, pp. 108-109).

The lifeworld can therefore be understood as the basis of social interaction in everyday life. It is a stock of culturally transmitted and linguistically structured patterns of symbolic reproduction that shape tradition, culture and social exchange. As Brand (1990, p. xii) puts it, the lifeworld represents 'the whole ensemble of human relations which is coordinated and reproduced....via the medium of language'. In this sense, the lifeworld can be seen as the natural home of communicative rationality or intersubjective understanding. In order to account for the fragmentation of rationality, Habermas suggests that this lifeworld is increasingly subject to attack. The instrumental forces of the state and capital, known as the system, are seen to be colonising areas of life that have traditionally been negotiated by intersubjective communication. An uncoupling of economic and administrative systems leads to the lifeworld being mediated by the instrumental or strategic interest:

> The encroachment of forms of economic and administrative rationality into life-spheres that in fact obey the independent logic of moral-practical and aesthetic-practical rationality leads to a type of colonization [sic] of the lifeworld. By this I mean the impoverishment of expressive and communicative possibilities which....remain necessary even in complex societies. These are the possibilities that enable individuals to find themselves, to deal with their personal conflicts, and to solve their common problems communally by means of collective will-formation (Habermas, 1984, p. 20).

A number of specific effects of colonisation have been identified, particularly in relation to the involvement of citizens in political processes. Perhaps the most fundamental is the disruption of spaces for political articulation and communication. The fragmentation of the lifeworld manifests itself in the restriction of possibilities for communicative action within political spaces:

> ....politics now takes on a peculiarly negative character. For it is oriented toward the elimination of dysfunctions and the avoidance of risks that threaten the system: not in other words, toward the realization [sic] of practical goals but toward the solution of technical problems (Habermas, 1971, pp. 102-103).

The colonisation of the lifeworld thesis is in many respects an extension of Habermas' account of the disintegration of the public sphere. Habermas states that in the mass democracy of advanced capitalism 'politics has become an affair of a functionally specialized [sic] subsystem' (Habermas, 1996f, p. 359). This assemblage of political activity develops its own internal logic and disconnects from the functions and resources of the lifeworld. As Habermas puts it: 'The public sphere as political, in which complex societies can acquire normative distance from themselves and work out experiences of crisis collectively, takes on a remoteness from the political system' (Habermas 1996f, p. 361). Thus, established avenues of political communication are increasingly incapable of sustaining rational discourse. This process of reification sees the replacement of communicatively structured discourse by instrumentally steered interaction. This is an important point to bear in mind, because once potentially autonomous spheres of political activity become subject to an instrumental logic then that way of conducting political discourse may soon acquire a status as the 'norm'. This point will be developed shortly when thinking about how Habermas aids our methods of analysis.

The erosion of spaces of participatory democracy is fundamental to the colonisation of the lifeworld. However, Habermas' account of these processes should be conceived as making reference to potentialities and tendencies, rather than certainties. As Habermas (1996e, p. 323) himself puts it:

> ….the deformation of the structures of a damaged intersubjectivity are by no means predecided processes that might be distilled from a few global concepts. The analysis of lifeworld pathologies calls for an….investigation of tendencies and contradictions.

With this in mind, it is perhaps not surprising that central to the colonisation thesis is Habermas' identification of resistance to this process. Colonisation produces contradictory effects in which the spread of instrumentality is echoed by the emergence of a potential for more rational and democratic political communication. Habermas (1987b, p. 339) consequently argues that Marx tends to overlook the 'intrinsic evolutionary value' of processes of colonisation. The fragmentation of traditional lifeworlds is a process that leads to the 'opening up' of previously unquestioned cultural assumptions and social norms. Habermas argues that 'the prejudiced background consensus of the life-world is crumbling….the number of cases is increasing in which interaction must be co-ordinated through a consensus reached by the participants themselves' (Habermas 1992a, pp. 184-185). Traditions and conventions become open to a reflexive public scrutiny. This process of rationalisation increases opportunities to set up conditions of political debate in which the force of the 'better argument' can prevail:

> The release of a potential for reason embedded in communicative action is a world-historical process; in the modern period it leads to a rationalization

[sic] of life-worlds, to the differentiation of their symbolic structures, which is expressed above all in the increasing reflexivity of cultural traditions, in processes of individuation, in the generalization [sic] of values, in the increasing prevalence of more abstract and more universal norms, and so on. These are trends which do not imply something good in themselves, but which nevertheless indicate that the prejudiced background consensus of the life-world is crumbling, that the number of cases is increasing in which interaction must be co-ordinated through a consensus reached by the participants themselves (Habermas, 1984, pp. 184-185).

Habermas argues that as lifeworld horizons disintegrate, individuals are forced to discursively negotiate new forms of identity. As Outhewaite (1994, p. 87) puts it:

....the rationalization [sic] process involves processes of structural differentiation towards a hypothetical end state in which cultural traditions are constantly criticized [sic] and renewed, political forms are dependent on formal procedures of justification, and personalities are increasingly autonomous.

In this context of increased reflexivity 'political goals neither depend solely upon tradition, nor arise merely from the will of a charismatic leader, but develop through discussion and debate among the public' (Baxter, 1987, p. 50). Habermas argues that in increasingly complex and diverse societies it is no longer possible to rely on a homogenous background of cultural and moral conviction. Attempts to resolve normative disputes of a moral-practical nature therefore need to occur at the level of an increasingly rationalised discourse. As Chambers (1995a, p. 244) notes, Habermas is suggesting that 'we must construct a consensus; we can no longer appeal to one that is ready made'. In this sense, modernity 'has to create normativity out of itself' (Habermas, 1987a, p. 7). For Habermas, the emergence of 'rationalised lifeworlds' carries with it the growth of spaces in which traditional norms lose their efficacy in favour of rationally motivated discourses. Within complex post-traditional societies, democratic empowerment represents 'the only means of restoring solidarity, authority, and capacities for collective action' (Warren, 1995, p. 169). Therefore, underpinning Habermas' project is a normative interest in fulfilling the largely unrealised vindication of the rational potential of learning capacities released within modernity. The realm of political participation plays a key role in such a process.

Although Habermas points toward the potential for increasingly rationalised lifeworlds, he also acknowledges the crucial role of organised capitalism in processes of social reproduction. He suggests that there is an 'indissoluble tension' (Habermas, 1996d, p. 285) between capitalism and democracy as principles of social integration, and this clash inevitably has consequences for the involvement of citizens in political processes. This relationship between lifeworlds and complex media steered systems creates tensions that lead to the loss of freedom and meaning. These twin principles clash in the political public sphere where the autonomy of the lifeworld is forced to face up to the administrative system. Habermas argues that 'the political participation of citizens takes place under certain structural conditions' (Habermas, 1987b, p. 344). This conflict leads to 'an alienated mode of having a say in matters of public interest' (Habermas, 1987b, p. 393). This is seen by Habermas as the 'reification of communicatively structured domains of action' (Habermas, 1987b, p. 332). As Ray (1993, p. 57) puts it, 'capitalist modernity has involved an over extension of monetary and bureaucratic systems which have inhibited the formation of fluid, decentred, non-authoritarian types of communication'. Habermas sees such reification as a 'pathological deformation of the communicative infrastructure of the lifeworld' (Habermas, 1996e, p. 310). According to Habermas, the political system acts 'selectively through excluding themes and contributions from public discussion' (Habermas, 1996d, p. 286). The political activity of citizens becomes muted and largely ineffective, and consequently 'develop[s] no explosive power' (Habermas, 1996d, p. 291).

Furthermore, Habermas argues that the formal political rights of liberal democracy serve to conceal and nullify the blunted character of political participation in the mass democracies of advanced capitalism. They serve to conceal capitalist interests and consequently legitimate a 'bourgeois participatory ideology' (Love, 1995, p. 54). The formalisation of the category of the 'citizen' leads to 'a segmenting of this role from the decision-making process, a cleansing of political participation from any participatory content' (Habermas, 1996d, p. 290). Habermas argues that these processes lead to 'a neutralization [sic] of the possibilities for political participation opened up by the role of citizen' (Habermas, 1996d, p. 287). We can thus detect in Habermas' work an interest in acquiring 'a grasp of the structures which make some outcomes....more likely than others, which implies a focus....[on] the relationship between social inequalities and the management or regulation of potentially destabilizing [sic] conflicts' (Ray, 1993, p. xii). As such, it has been argued that Habermas shares a Gramscian and Foucaultdian concern with the social construction and management of political consent (Forester, 1985b, p. xi).

It is clear that Habermas feels that the extension of participatory democracy requires the reclaiming of spheres of interaction mediated by instrumental rationality. This provides a potential basis for the development of discourse ethics within political institutions and structures, although Habermas (1996b) has recently argued this can only take on a limited role within society. As he puts it 'political steering can often take only an indirect approach and must....leave intact the modes of operation internal to functional systems and other highly organized [sic] spheres of action' (Habermas, 1996b, p. 372). Nonetheless, Calhoun (1992b, p. 1) makes the point that Habermas' project is trying to recover 'an institutional location for practical reason in public affairs and for the accompanying valid, if often deceptive, claims of formal democracy'. This is inevitably a delicate and precarious process. But what does it actually mean in practice? And which specific political structures does Habermas attribute with the potential for developing rational-critical forms of discourse? Having briefly outlined the thematic background to Habermas' overall project, we can now turn to a more detailed discussion of the Habermas' concern with the possible reconstruction of spaces of political participation.

Locating the Role of Civil Society

In recent years, Habermas has written more explicitly on the possible sources of a reformulation of a communicatively structured public sphere capable of sustaining rational-critical political discourse. Specifically, Habermas has turned to the sphere of civil society in order to locate what he sees as a resistance to colonisation of the lifeworld. In recent times, interest has grown rapidly in the potential development and extension of civil society. As noted in Chapter One, there are a number of competing definitions of what might constitute civil society. A traditional 'liberal' view refers to the privately structured capitalist economy that exists outside of state influence as the basis of civil society (Fraser, 1992, p. 133). Marxists have also located civil society within the economy as constituted through markets in labour and commodities. A more productive definition for our purposes refers to the spectrum of voluntary organisations that exist outside of institutions of the state and the economy. According to Walzer (1995b, p. 7) civil society refers to 'the space of uncoerced human association and also the set of relational networks....that fills that space'. These range from small-scale clubs and associations through to established political parties and large scale pressure groups. It also includes those bodies that might be classified as more novel or innovative in terms of their internal structure.

Since the late 1980s, a rhetoric of civil society has emerged in which the term refers primarily to those organisations in which citizens are able to participate in a direct manner. According to writers such as Keane (1988) these bodies represent a space in which citizens can mobilise and organise in a participatory manner. For some theorists the apparent diversity of civil society betrays a more substantive force at work within this realm. McRobbie (1994, p. 109) highlights the importance of those 'forces of opposition' that emerge from 'the margins, from the realms of pressure groups, associations, voluntary organizations [sic] and other forms of local, grassroots or campaigning groups'. Reflecting the agenda developed by Habermas, it is suggested that these groups and organisations provide a credible basis of participatory activity through which resistance to state encroachment can be mobilised.

As Hall (1995, p. 1) notes, this concept has become popular because civil society is seen as 'the opposite of despotism, a space in which social groups could exist and move – something which exemplified and would ensure softer, more tolerable conditions of existence'. Habermas reflects this theme by arguing that new conflicts, or 'new frictional surfaces' (Habermas, 1987a, p. 357), are frequently emerging across the terrain of civil society. These tensions generate organisations and forms of participation that, through their internal structures, sustain increasingly rationalised discourse. The form taken by such participatory structures is of some significance: 'These are carriers of new learning capacities, proto-public spheres which offer potential solutions to systemic crisis in that they presage more fluid and democratic types of organisation' (Ray, 1993, p. 73). Habermas (1981, p. 33) has argued that these forms of participation contain the potential for the 'revitalization [sic] of buried possibilities for expression and communication'. Habermas speaks of the development of 'counterinstitutions' which generate:

> ....new forms of a 'politics in the first person', a politics that is expressive and at the same time has a democratic base....the counterinstitutions are intended to dedifferentiate some parts of the formally organized [sic] domains of action, remove them from the clutches of the steering media, and return these 'liberated areas' to the action co-ordinating mechanism of reaching understanding (Habermas, 1996e, p. 327).

For some theorists, the public discourse that is generated by civil society derives its value from the fact that it stands outside the institutions of the state. Habermas, for instance, asserts that autonomous public spheres are 'neither bred nor kept by a political system for purposes of creating legitimation' (Habermas, 1996f, p. 362).

One might infer from such comments that the development of discourse is dependent on the proliferation of diverse specialised publics throughout the terrain of civil society. However, this sharp conceptual division between the state and civil society has been questioned. For example, White (1995b, p. 11) suggests that this theoretical move points toward an image of instances of communicative action that 'can, in effect, only hurl themselves against an administrative Leviathan'. It has consequently been argued by some that Habermas has overstated the dichotomy between the state and civil society. Analogous to this is the importance of recognising skewed distributions of power between different structures of political action. Fraser (1992, p. 136) consequently argues that we need a conception of political space that would enable us to 'think about strong and weak publics, as well as about various hybrid forms....[this] would allow us to theorize [sic] the range of possible relations among such publics'. With this in mind, we need to be aware of the pivotal role of institutions of the state in shaping and influencing the contours of the spaces of civil society. As Walzer (1995b, p. 23) puts it, the state 'both frames civil society and occupies space within it'.

In recent years, Habermas' writings have become more reformist than was perhaps originally the case. As Outhewaite (1996b, p. 18) has remarked, the notion of socialism and the emancipatory intent of much of Habermas' earlier work has been largely displaced by the concept of 'radical democracy'. Habermas himself has argued that within complex and bureaucratic societies, instances of communicative action find themselves acting as steering mechanisms within arenas of complex social action that they cannot regulate. This scaling down of the specific direction of Habermas' project has implications for his understanding of what we might mean by processes of 'democratic will formation'. Drawing upon a broadly Parsonian notion of influence, Habermas (1992c, p. 453) now argues that '[D]iscourses....do not govern'. Rather, the public sphere, via sites of rationalised discourse, is seen to exert a 'pressure' (Habermas, 1992c, p. 452) upon established decision-making structures. The outcome of such processes is that communicative action is able to 'sensitize [sic] the self-steering mechanisms of the state and the economy to the goal-oriented mechanisms of radical democratic will formation' (Habermas, 1987a, p. 365). In this sense, instances of communicative action provide 'democratic countersteering' (Habermas, 1994b, p. 117) to the instrumental forces of the system. Habermas argues that some level of systemic steering is inevitable in complex societies. He therefore advocates a 'balance' between communicative action and steering media. This process leads to the 'expansion of democratic social control over markets and bureaucracies through extended public spheres combined with a critical attitude towards the normative basis of authority' (Ray, 1993, p. viii).

In his most recent writings, Habermas (1996b) has developed a more explicit picture of the complex interplay between civil society and the formal institutions of the state. This interaction is built around an increasingly politicised civil society that 'alters and fragments the boundaries of the state' (Warren, 1995, p. 170). With this in mind, Habermas has remarked that:

> ....the public sphere is a warning system with sensors that....are sensitive throughout society....the public sphere must in addition, amplify the pressure of problems, that is, not only detect and identify problems but also convincingly and influentially thematize [sic] them, furnish them with possible solutions, and dramatize [sic] them in such a way that they are taken up and dealt with by parliamentary complexes (Habermas, 1996b, p. 359).

The picture is thus one of a range of interconnected and overlapping political sites oriented toward discursively generated influence. With this in mind, Habermas has recently presented the practical development of discourse ethics in a more generic manner than might previously have been the case. The turn toward the underlying implicit nature of language has been criticised for representing a dilution of Habermas' early interest in concrete social institutions (Calhoun, 1992b, pp. 33-42). In consequence, it is suggested that Habermas is not particularly explicit about theorising the practical forms that such responses to colonisation might take. Ray (1993, p. 177) argues that, as a consequence, Habermas fails to adequately distinguish between the wide range of possible reactions to processes of colonisation, which might include apolitical withdrawal, defensive political participation and radical forms of rational-critical discourse.

Despite these criticisms, Habermas remains committed to the role of civil society and political participation within a rejuvenation of rational-critical debate. As Habermas himself puts it, 'the political public sphere is not conceived simply as the backroom of the parliamentary complex, but as the impulse generating periphery that surrounds the political center' (Habermas, 1996b, p. 442). As Warren (1995, p. 170) notes, Habermas feels that questions of democracy and rational discourse arrangements have become increasingly appropriate to civil society structures. It might be worth spending a few moments reflecting on how this relationship between the political practices of civil society and rationality can be conceptualised. Ray (1993, p. 63) argues that '[C]ollective action might occupy a broad continuum from defensive neo-conservative protests to campaigns that expand fluid, post-conventional identities'. This ties in neatly with the idea of political participation as a spectrum of activity. Offensive forms of political interaction represent those forms of activity that are potentially capable of developing discourse ethics. Conversely, defensive aspects of participation tend to be structured around more hierarchical and technocratic dimensions of activity, which foster the closure of critical-rational discourse. It must be noted that this offensive/defensive distinction 'connotes an organizational [sic] tendency' (Ray 1993, p. 63) rather than an all-encompassing form of participation.

Although there is increasing discussion about the potential role of civil society within wider processes of rationalisation, the concept of civil society should not be used lightly. The notion of civil society is often invoked as an ideal rather than as a viable political project. As Hall (1995, p. 2) notes, '[C]ivil society is complicated, most notably being at one and the same time a social value and a set of social institutions'. It is also important to avoid generalisations about the nature of civil society. The aims and internal structures of civil society organisations vary greatly. For example, the individual members of Greenpeace have no formal say in the internal policy process of the organisation. Amnesty International, on the other hand, provides opportunities for members to take part in its national and global policy structure. Writers such as Walzer (1995b, p. 23) have also suggested that 'civil society, left to itself, generates radically unequal power relationships'. Burns *et al* (1994, p. 250) refer to the outcome of power differences between factions within civil society as 'the way in which the amplification of some voices may lead to the muting of others'. It is important that we do not overstate the value of civil society without actually investigating the realm in some detail. As Staeheli (1996, p. 607) observes, '[T]he failure to recognize [sic] exclusion has idealized [sic] some spaces as public when they are, in fact, exclusionary, with the effect of continuing the marginalization [sic] and exclusion of some groups'. Burns *et al* (1994, p. 243) similarly observe that civil society needs to be conceived 'as a site for conflict, division and domination as well as conviviality, solidarity and mutuality'.

Given that civil society is increasingly identified as a major source of democratisation, it is important that dominant forms of political action and practice within this realm are subject to some scrutiny. This should not only occur at the theoretical level, but also through analysis of the 'real world' of citizen participation. Clearly, there is scope for analysing how different types of political structures within civil society foster different forms of political participation and discourse. This is especially crucial if we are to take up Habermas' notion of communicative action, and reflect upon its potential institutionalisation within the structures of citizen participation. In order to explore the extent to which the developmental tendencies of rationality are perhaps played out in the arenas of political participation, I now turn to a discussion of the practical uses of Habermas' overall project.

From Theory to Practice: Developing an Analytical Framework

Discussions around the themes of communicative action and rational discourse are often conducted in broad philosophical terms. Much of the debate that relates to the concepts developed by Habermas consequently takes place at a relatively abstract level. Recently however there has been an identifiable attempt to connect the theory more closely with practice. This move is not entirely unexpected. Although it has not always been obvious, Habermas has generally sought 'the possibility of a unity of theory and practice' (Calhoun, 1995, p. 28). In recent years a small body of work has emerged that deduces applied research questions from the theoretical directions taken by Habermas (Forester, 1985a; Kemp, 1985; Alvesson and Wilmott, 1992a; Dryzek, 1995; Blaug, 1997). Reflecting this growing 'applied turn', Dryzek (1995, p. 116) calls for critical theorists to 'come down from the metatheoretical heights to actually practice the critique they preach'. In this sense, if Habermasian analysis is to strengthen its dialectical relation to its object of inquiry then it is necessary to directly apply the theoretical imperatives identified by Habermas to real examples of political interaction and participation. As Blaug (1997, p. 116) notes, a Habermasian approach must therefore adopt research strategies that are closely allied to questions of practice and praxis:

> If critical theory is to do more than merely rock backwards and forwards whilst intoning the words 'public sphere'....it might do well to inspect the problems of democracy from the point of view of participants in a practical discourse. Such a use of theory might have implications for....recurrent problems that participants face in their efforts to be both fair and effective in their deliberation.

How can Habermas' work contribute to our investigation into the nature of political participation? I have already outlined a number of theoretical issues that can inform our understandings of the role of political participation. It should be clear from the preceding discussion that Habermas provides a backdrop against which we can begin to place an assessment of the current nature of political participation. According to Habermas the realm of citizen involvement both reflects broader processes of rationalisation and offers spaces for the reconstruction of public debate. The picture that is painted by Habermas' account of political participation is therefore of a sphere of often-conflicting tendencies. These inclinations are likely to be played out in the range of practices and activities that take place within the various realms of the political participation. In the remainder of this chapter, I draw together the threads of the preceding discussions by outlining the value of Habermas' theoretical insights as a source of applied analysis.

Virtually all acts of participation will have some significance as instances of political discourse, and are likely to reflect the scope of political rationality at work within the public sphere. By joining a pressure group or attending a protest rally or taking part in a Labour Party branch meeting, a citizen is not only making a statement on political issues but also, at a deeper level, acting in a discursive manner. The actual ways in which we participate in politics can tell us a lot about the wider nature of the political public sphere. The structures that constitute the actually functioning public sphere are therefore important as carriers of rationality and discursive activity. Participation in the bodies inhabiting the public sphere provides a point of interaction between everyday acts of political discourse and wider processes of rationalisation. As Forester (1985b, p. xiii) observes, Habermas' model raises the importance of 'the structural staging of intersubjectively meaningful action'. The 'quality' of political debate and the subsequent generation of political opinion and influence is central to Habermas' conception of democracy within advanced liberal democracies, and needs to be conceived as 'an empirical variable' (Habermas, 1996b, p. 362).

The task for the analyst is to examine the dynamics of these discursive acts and to uncover how and why certain forms of political practice become established. Hence, it is important to place an emphasis on the internal character of carriers of political communication and the types of activity that are fostered within them. In Chapter Two I introduced the concept of 'activism' and I highlighted the spectrum of activity that constitutes political participation. Drawing upon Habermas' thematic categories, I intend to consider how these aspects of political participation relate to discussions about the limits of communicative and instrumental rationality. The nature of actually existing forms of political participation can then be examined in relation to the possible distortion of political communication within the political public sphere. Assessment can be made of the extent to which the various forms of activism that take place across civil society embody the communicative rationality highlighted by Habermas.

The starting point for such analysis is the idea that the twin principles of communicative and instrumental rationality can serve as evaluatory pillars around which to assess political practices. The concept of communicative action provides a measure against which political relations in the real world can be compared. Habermas' work points us toward the importance of the identification of systematic distortions of communication that shape the contours of political discourse and participation. In the words of Meehan (1995b, p. 2), Habermas offers 'a model of subjectivity and an account of the pragmatic presuppositions of discursive validity, against which actual political and personal relations and discourses can be measured'. If one adopts such an approach then it might be assumed that the primary aim is to uncover the exercise of strategic action within sites of political participation. This would allow us to show how certain voices are excluded from proceedings whilst others are able to control the direction of interaction. As Dryzek (1995, p. 104) notes:

> ....all such practices are going to be in violation of precepts of communicative rationality to a greater or lesser degree. Conversely, glimmerings of communicative rationality should be apparent in almost all practices.

By starting from the point of the 'ideal speech situation' it can be shown how specific practices might contravene this procedural criteria. Dryzek (1995, p. 109) defines this type of analysis as 'pure' in the sense that it 'criticizes [sic] real-world practices to the extent they fall short of the ideal'. Closer inspection of this approach reveals a number of conceptual problems. When applying such criteria to the real world of political participation we need to be aware of the largely unattainable quality of 'discourse ethics'. Although Habermas points us toward the normative value of undistorted discourse, the principle of an open and free dialogue inevitably remains beyond our reach. The notion of allowing the force of the better argument to hold sway should therefore serve primarily as a critical principle, and not as a realistic practical aim (Scholsberg, 1995, p. 293; Dryzek, 1995, p. 104). The notion of discourse ethics can act as a critical device through which exiting arrangements can be scrutinised.

Habermas himself (1992d, pp. 467-468) has commented on the direction that such research might take:

> I think an empirically meaningful approach to our selective and even colonized [sic] forms of public communication is to see how they work within certain procedural dimensions of formal inclusion, of the degree of political participation, of the quality of discussion, of the range of issues, and, finally, and most important, of how the presuppositions of those public debates are really institutionalized [sic].

The question of the degree of participation has already been dealt with in Chapter Two. I have also suggested in Chapter One that a verdict on levels of political participation is something of a misnomer in the sense that there is limited historical data to ground such a judgement. The aim of the present study is therefore to explore the qualitative aspects of participation identified by Habermas. More specifically, I have taken up Habermas' concern with the ways in which systematically distorted forms of political communication become institutionalised. The question is then one of analysing how and why political participation becomes structured and shaped in particular ways, rather than merely attempting to describe the levels and composition of participation. This in turn requires us to ultimately consider the quality of these methods of public debate. As Dryzek (1995, p. 108) notes, the purpose of this type of research is 'not simply to offer arguments to support positions within policy debates, but, more importantly, to scrutinize [sic] the conditions under which debate proceeds'.

The aim here is to explore how seemingly 'neutral' processes of participation in fact mask an internal set of dynamics that may close off more communicative ways of conducting political discourse. As van Dijk (1993, p. 254) notes, 'dominance may be enacted and reproduced by subtle, routine, everyday forms of....talk that appear 'natural' and quite 'acceptable''. Alvesson and Wilmott (1992b, p. 13) suggest that critical analysis of this type should involve 'the questioning and opening up of what has become seen as given, unproblematic and natural'. With regard to political participation, these 'habits of argumentation' (Chambers 1995b, p. 177) clearly require further investigation. Underlying this point is the idea of 'informal impediments to participatory parity that can persist even after everyone is formally....licensed to participate' (Fraser, 1992, p. 119). As Fraser (1992, p. 118) further notes:

> The question of open access [to political discourse] cannot be reduced without remainder to the presence or absence of formal exclusions. It requires us to look also at the process of discursive interaction within formally inclusive public arenas.

This brings us back to the point raised in the preceding chapter about the importance of examining the inner dynamics of political participation. This theme urges us to ask why it is that certain participants tend to dominate discourse whilst other participants are often excluded from proceedings. It also points us back toward Habermas' more general point about the need to understand how disrupted forms of political communication continue to operate within formally inclusive vehicles of citizen participation. This, in turn, requires a clearer understanding of the nature of activism.

The aim here is to examine the relationship between participants in a discourse and the structures through which interaction takes place. This required applying the criteria outlined in this chapter toward an assessment of the 'systematic distortion' of communication and debate within political participation. As I have noted, this does not mean that instances of participation are held up to a series of critical principles for the purpose of unrealistic judgement. Rather, it entailed an attempt to acquire some hermeneutical understanding of the rationale and processes of political participation. Geuss (1981, p. 92) argues that working in the tradition of Habermas requires intensive methods of analysing particular groups in order to discover underlying, tacit norms:

> ....it....means that one knows something about their epistimic principles and their perception of their own situation, about what they take to be plausible motives for action, cogent arguments, good reasons for belief, relevant consideration etc.

I will discuss this theme in more detail in the next chapter where I consider the methodological direction of this study. The purpose of such primary research is to 'look carefully and closely at the complex and largely uninvestigated ways that normative claims are actually made in practice - to shape obligation, sense of membership and self, consent and deference, patterns of future action' (Forester 1992, p. 62). From this broad starting point, we can begin the process of 'deconstructing' the nature of political participation. It can be shown how unquestioned assumptions about the nature of political participation conceal a range of dynamics that contribute to the shaping of voluntary political activity and discourse.

The broad aim of posing these questions is to explore the various participatory cultures that can be found in the sphere of political activity. The relationship between acts of political participation and the structures within which they take place is therefore seen in a dialectical manner. I also intend to perhaps stretch existing understandings of the problems associated with attempting to draw concrete implications from Habermas' theoretical categories. What can analysis of the tangible world of participation tell us about the limits and possibilities of Habermas' notion of discourse and communicative action? Is there any evidence of genuine interest in discourse, or the 'anticipation of an ideal speech situation' amongst voluntary political actors?

These themes raise the question of the potential role that civil society and state structures can play in processes of democratisation. This, in turn, requires that we reflect upon the question of whether political structures must remain outside of the state if they are to develop the communicative tendencies identified by Habermas. A complimentary question concerns the extent to which state structures operating within capitalist liberal democracy have the capacity to develop structures of state-citizen dialogue in which communicative discourse can be sustained. One cannot also overlook the points at which political structures within civil society touch upon the established policy-making process and the potential effects of this upon the nature of the political discourse that occurs within such forums. These questions remain highly abstract unless we attempt to gain a closer insight into the forms of political activity and practice that actually take place within such structures. In the second half of the book I bring together an analysis that examines the range of political participation that can be located on the continuum that stretches across the state and civil society. Habermas has remarked on the different forms of participation that he feels may inhabit this political public sphere: 'Actors who know they are involved in the common enterprise of reconstituting and maintaining structures of the public sphere as they contest opinions and strive for influence differ from actors who merely use forums that already exist' (Habermas, 1996b, pp. 369-370). In other words, Habermas is arguing that the public sphere potentially contains a range of different categories of participation, each of which may have differing implications for the nature of the public sphere. However, the specific contribution of actually existing forms of political participation to the constitution of a functioning public sphere remains somewhat ambiguous.

In this chapter I have presented a theoretical argument that allows us to develop the empirical data outlined in Chapter Two. I have highlighted several interrelated categories that provide a set of criteria for interpreting the nature of political participation. I have argued that this theoretical framework provides a context within which discussion around political participation can be developed beyond statistical analysis of such activity. This requires greater attention to be given to the discursive character of different types of participation. In the remainder of this book I utilise the categories outlined by Habermas in order to assess the forms of participation I have studied in the course of my primary research. Having outlined the theoretical background of this inquiry I will now move on to a fuller discussion of the research itself. I begin with an outline of the methodological design of the primary research.

4 Methodology and Research Design

Any investigation that utilises primary research needs to give a substantial amount of attention to the design and implementation of an appropriate research strategy. In this chapter I outline the issues that have informed the methodological direction of this study. Attention is firstly given to a discussion of the broad philosophical questions I faced when choosing to adopt a predominantly qualitative methodological strategy. I then move on to outline the design of the research. The research process itself is then chronicled in detail, and I subsequently reflect upon some of the practical issues encountered during the fieldwork stage of the project. In conclusion, I reflect upon how I have been able to overcome resulting methodological dilemmas.

Qualitative Methodology and the Social Sciences

It was clear from the outset that the present study would be most closely identified with the field of 'political science'. This is an extremely varied area of study that contains a range of competing perspectives. There is as much disagreement about how to 'do' political science as there is about what constitutes political science. Nonetheless, Stoker (1995, p. 7) has defined political science as 'an academic discipline which seeks systematically to describe, analyse and explain collective decision-making and the values that underlie it'. Political science can therefore be seen as a discipline that studies the distribution of power within the machinery of political systems and institutions. It is also a form of analysis that falls within the broad category of investigation known as 'social science', in the sense that it is concerned with the study of society and human relations.

These are not arbitrary terms. Even a cursory glance at the literature on methodologies within the social sciences will show that it is not sufficient for a researcher to select methods purely on the basis of knowing how particular instruments of research might be put into practice. Restricting questions of method to issues of practical implementation overlooks a broader equation to which research needs to be sensitive. As Jones (1993, p. 114) puts it:

> ....what matters is not so much what a method is technically capable of doing, but what particular task it is asked to do....there is little inherent quality in a research tool; what matters is the uses to which a sociological researcher chooses to put it.

It is therefore important that the researcher does not become preoccupied with the means of research rather than the meaning of that research. With this in mind, Sayer (1992, p. 4) demonstrates that questions such as the object of study, the method of investigation and the purpose of research are closely interrelated and cannot be realistically separated out from one another. Put crudely, the question of how we should acquire knowledge of social life requires that attention be given to wider issues than simply the arbitrary choice of a particular method.

The social sciences have historically been contrasted most strongly with the natural sciences. The latter tends to draw heavily from the 'positivist' tradition. Although this is a highly ambiguous term, one can state with some certainty that this method of inquiry is primarily based on the idea that is possible to discover laws and regularities that operate within society through the application of natural scientific methods. Positivists assert that 'the truth or otherwise of a statement can be determined through systematic empirical observation' (Stoker 1995, p. 14). At the heart of the positivist tradition is the notion that generalisable predictions about human behaviour can be deduced from collected data. Positivism is most closely associated with behaviourist traditions, although the rational choice models to which I referred in Chapter Two also have a strong positivist undertone. Positivist philosophy has classically argued that knowledge of reality can only be generated in an 'objective' way, free of the subjectivism associated with more interpretative social sciences. However, phenomena such as cultural norms, interpretation and symbolic meaning are human attributes of social life that remain elusive to natural scientific approaches. This divergence has been reflected in the association between positivist traditions and quantitative methodology, and in the implicit link that is often made between the social sciences and qualitative methodology.

When approaching the field of political science one is initially struck by the prominence of quantitative or statistical forms of analysis (Miller, 1995). In part, this can be traced to the position within the field acquired by rational choice approaches. In the past two decades these approaches have been joined, and in many respects challenged, by new methods of 'doing' social science. During the 1970s, a wide ranging interest in phenomenology and sense making practices generated a scepticism over the relevance of the natural sciences as an appropriate basis for the types of analysis undertaken by the social sciences. The perceived limitations of quantitative approaches related to the tendency for such methods to generate a relatively static representation of phenomena which remains largely external to the experiences and interpretations of situated actors. In consequence, qualitative methods of data collection and analysis have been imported from anthropological and sociological traditions into the realm of political science.

Qualitative research differs substantially from its quantitative counterpart by exploring 'the meanings, variations and perceptual experiences of phenomena' (Crabtree and Miller, 1992b, p. 6). As I have shown in Chapter Two, quantitative data goes some way to indicating the extent of political phenomena such as involvement in political participation. However, it is an insufficient basis on which to formulate analysis of complex social and political processes or events. Qualitative methodology refers to forms of data collection and analysis that focus upon establishing an understanding of social processes and relations. The emphasis is upon gaining a close and intimate familiarity with meanings, as defined and experienced by agents. This type of approach requires making close and constant reference to the experiences of those who take a direct role in processes. As Devine (1995, p. 138) observes, qualitative methods are best employed 'where the aim of the research is to explore people's subjective experiences and the meanings they attach to those experiences'. Unlike positivist leanings toward measurement and prediction, qualitative methods are best employed when the purpose of research is to uncover causal dynamics. Devine (1995, p. 138) goes on to note that:

> The role of a rational objective science....is not to make predictions but to devise causal explanations about the world which involve describing both the observable and unobservable processes that link phenomena together. Explanation also involves describing and understanding people as conscious and social human beings, and their motives, experiences and subjective interpretations are an important component of causal processes.

Within qualitative methodology, respondents are given space to define and categorise the social sphere within which they function as agents. Qualitative methodology is therefore suited to analysis that is intended to be exploratory in character rather than being structured around the need to test a pre-defined and rigid hypothesis. With reference to the present research, a number of broad research themes were originally identified as central to the study. However, it was anticipated that the specific categories through which the data would be organised would, at least in part, emerge from the primary data itself. A strategy of this type is intended to enable respondents, rather than the researcher, to assign relevance and importance to particular subjects or categories.

Qualitative research is also notable for the ontological understanding of social reality which it expounds. A qualitative methodology is constructed primarily around questions of context and process. Context attains significance as 'a means of situating action' (Dey, 1993, p. 32). In this sense, qualitative research methods enable the researcher to locate activity within social 'mechanisms' (Keat and Urry, 1975, pp. 32-35) and to examine the causal relationships between each. The processual dimension of the qualitative methods 'seeks to illuminate the ways individuals interact to sustain or change social situations' (Dey, 1993, p. 37). The qualitative researcher must therefore be sensitive to the interplay between the capabilities of actors and the structures within which agents acquire status, role and agency (Dey, 1993, pp. 49-50). Given that I have attempted to shift away from a methodological individualism in my understanding of participation, this qualitative perspective seems well suited to the requirements of the research.

This does not imply that the present study should be considered as an ethnographic investigation in which the cultural values and meanings of respondents define the study. Within the field of social sciences, it is the development of interpretative or 'hermeneutic' approaches that have been most closely associated with the growth of qualitative methodology. This perspective has been concerned with the ways in which objects and experiences acquire meaning within social life. However, the hermeneutical approach has been criticised as being too subjective in its search for an interpretative sociology. Sayer (1992, p. 4), for instance, refers to a methodological imperialism 'which tries to reduce social science wholly to the interpretation of meaning'. The individual agent can easily become detached from the conditions of existence within which agency is able to function. By employing qualitative methodology it was therefore important that the fieldwork avoided simply providing a forum for subjective 'voice'. The hermeneutical approach can omit to explore the influence of structure upon action, and this is a move that would clearly undermine the approach adopted by the present research. However, as Outhewaite (1987, pp. 61-76) points out, there are aspects of the hermeneutic tradition that can usefully inform a more 'realist' approach. Outhewaite (1987, p. 72) observes that a hermeneutics based on interpretative epistemology has distinct problems in identifying distortions of communication, but this in turn points toward 'more structuralist and materialist conceptions of social theory - themselves of course hermeneutically grounded'. Therefore, although a 'pure' hermeneutics tends to isolate individuals from wider social relations, the methodological commitment to investigating the meanings attached to particular events or processes is relevant to the present study. In designing the fieldwork stage of the present study I was therefore seeking to draw upon qualitative methods in order to illustrate aspects of political participation that have previously remained largely overlooked.

The qualitative methods employed in this study enable the experiences and interpretations of political participants to be brought to the fore. Intensive, as opposed to extensive research, is fundamental to this form of analysis. The latter would usually involve the analysis of large-scale collections of data, perhaps in the form of surveys. Intensive research, on the other hand, adopts a more in-depth approach within a limited number of 'groups' or case studies. Attention is given to the workings of internal processes and how certain events are brought about and maintained within social and political life. As Sayer (1992, pp. 221-224) observes, the intensive approach seeks to identify causal explanations for the occurrence of particular events by attempting to 'identify structures into which individuals are locked and their mechanisms'. Intensive research strategies subsequently enable dynamic social relations to be studied whilst simultaneously tracing causal links with mechanisms and structures in some detail. As I observed in Chapter Two, the extensive research methodologies adopted by a large amount of political science in relation to levels of participation, provide only limited scope for analysis of this type. Qualitative methodology is premised upon a need to acquire a depth of knowledge rather than a breadth of data, and as such is ideally suited to the requirements of the present study.

Research Design

As I have demonstrated, the design of an optimal research strategy invariably entails a close convergence between practical questions of method, the themes informing a study and broader ontological and epistemological categories. Practical methodological considerations must therefore be closely attuned to the thematic and theoretical questions guiding a study. The field researcher needs to be aware that the choice of a particular methodological approach is undoubtedly related directly to the types of questions informing the research (Strauss and Corbin, 1990, p. 19; Robson, 1993, pp. 43-44). Certain methods of investigation will be more ideally suited to certain types of theoretical questions. As Sayer (1992, p. 85) puts it, 'little can be said about method without taking into account the nature of the things which the methods are to be used to study'.

Having established that the themes of this project required the adoption of a primarily qualitative methodological strategy, it then became necessary to design the specific programme that the researcher would operationalise. A primary methodological commitment related to the fusing of 'multiple methodologies' (Burgess, 1982, pp. 163-167) into a coherent research programme. In recent years, the attempt to circumvent excessive methodological and theoretical specialisation has become an increasingly common feature of social science research (Marsh and Stoker, 1995b, p. 289). One should of course be wary of adopting a 'scattergun' approach when utilising multiple methodologies. Nonetheless, it is increasingly common for social science research to simultaneously draw upon a range of methods when investigating a particular object of study. By utilising semi-structured interviews, non-participant observation and analysis of primary literature I was able to construct a methodological strategy that allowed the researcher to cross check findings from one data source against another. Hammersley and Atkinson (1983, p. 198) define such methods of 'triangulation' in the following manner:

> ....the comparison of data relating to the same phenomenon but deriving from different phases of the fieldwork, different points in the temporal cycles occurring in the setting, or....the accounts of different participants.

In this section, I seek to illustrate the various facets of a research design that adopted such an approach.

Interviews

A central feature of qualitative methodology is the use of interviews as a form of data collection. In the course of undertaking primary research, the present study made extensive use of interviews. Unlike quantitative survey-based forms of data collection, which tend to be based on highly structured and predetermined formats, qualitative interviews provide a more open and flexible space for the collection of data. This methodology has a number of advantages for the researcher attempting to examine aspects of a phenomena that have remained under explored, a feature reflective of qualitative methodology generally (Strauss and Corbin, 1990, p. 19). This is primarily due to the flexibility and adaptability of the interview format. It allows the interviewer to probe beyond initial answers in greater depth (Bell 1987, p. 91). The respondent is also able to elaborate and clarify responses in a detailed manner. As May (1993, p. 93) observes, these features facilitate a research environment in which the data collection process allows room for the respondent to define their experiences on their own terms, but still maintains a structural quality suitable for undertaking comparisons.

Inevitably, this aspect of the methodology prompts a specific hermeneutical relationship between the researcher and subject. Qualitative research requires an openness to the meanings and interpretations of the subject and his or her perception of their environment, or what May (1993, p. 14) loosely defines as a 'dialogical retrospection'. The interview process proceeds in a reciprocal manner, with the interviewee taking a more active role in defining the parameters of the interview content. This is a hermeneutical move that imports heavily from feminist and interpretative methodological principles and subsequently resists positivist traditions (Mies, 1993, pp. 68-73). However, one must be careful not to assume that the interviewer plays no significant role in defining the overall direction of the interview. A more productive route is to acknowledge that the field researcher will inevitably influence the responses of the respondent (Devine, 1995, p. 144).

Non-participant Observation

In order to supplement the interview component of the research, a sequence of non-participant observation of various forms of meetings was undertaken. The origins of participant observation lie in the field of anthropology and sociology. It involves the researcher immersing himself or herself in the social setting being studied. This mode of data collection reinforces the qualitative concern with acquiring improved understandings of established procedures, practices and relations within a particular context. By directly observing phenomena, the researcher is able to better understand the dynamics of routines, practices and relationships that might otherwise be overlooked. As May (1993, p. 115) puts it, 'to assist in understanding social reality, we must also directly experience that reality'. The researcher becomes more accustomed to the norms that define the context, and thus acquires a fuller understanding of the rationale that informs the context. However, I would again be wary of overstating the ethnographic credentials of the present study.

With this in mind, it may be relevant to distinguish this form of data collection from more participatory forms of observation. Although qualitative methodology often attempts to attain a fuller understanding of the meanings and understandings that operate within a particular research field, it is nonetheless valuable for the field researcher to maintain some formal distance, or 'analytical space', between himself and the object of analysis (Hammersley and Atkinson, 1983, p. 102). By observing rather than participating directly in meetings I have been able to fulfil this requirement. The ethnographic interest in asking questions that arise as a result of observation has been reserved for interviews, in order both to gain greater clarity and depth and to avoid interrupting 'naturally occurring' data (Hammersley and Atkinson, 1983, p. 2). Of course, it is important to note that all research in the social sciences is likely to be subject to some form of 'ecological validity' (Bryman, 1988a) in which the presence of the researcher influences the conduct of an event.

Documentary Analysis

An auxiliary component of the fieldwork has involved analysing various documents pertaining to the organisations being investigated. In the process of meeting with staff at the British Section of Amnesty International, I have acquired a number of internal documents. These have included unpublished membership surveys and profiles. With regard to the Labour Party, a broad body of documentation from within the public realm has been available to the researcher. This has included published interviews and official Party publications. Exodus has produced a number of short pamphlets and I was able to acquire copies of these. In the case of the Tenants' Associations, I was able to compile various documents including the minutes of meetings, constitutions, rules of association, leaflets distributed by members and relevant correspondence. With regard to the Residents' Association I acquired various documents pertaining to the history of the organisation. I was also able to gain access to the constitutional rules within which the Residents' Association operated.

Profiling Respondents

The material generated by interviews has been further complimented by the collection of information about each respondent. Although the project is primarily qualitative in character, I decided to compile a picture of each person that I interviewed by asking him or her for small pieces of statistical data. A range of information was collected, including socio-demographic details such as age, gender, ethnicity and employment. I also asked respondents to list their organisational affiliations outside of the group being studied. Finally, I enquired as to their past or present formal positions within the particular organisation being analysed. This information, although relatively limited in scope, was useful for a number of reasons. Firstly, it provided a resource for the cross tabulation of findings both within and between organisations. Secondly, the data enabled comparisons to be made with previous findings within the literature that have focused primarily upon the collection of data of this type. This acted as a form of 'check' to confirm that there were no glaring discrepancies between my samples and previous research. Thirdly, the information was useful in giving a more 'human' and fully rounded character to each respondent.

The Research Process

When undertaking research within a number of organisations and with a relatively large number of respondents, questions of practicality inevitably come to the fore. The observations of Buchanan et al (1988, p. 54) are particularly relevant when reflecting upon the likely successes and failures of fieldwork:

> In the conflict between the desirable and the possible the possible always wins. So whatever carefully constructed views the researcher has of the nature of social science research, of the process of theory development, of data collection methods, or the status of different types of data, those views are constantly compromised by the practical realities, opportunities and constraints presented by organisational research.

This advice is valuable in persuading the researcher to develop a pragmatic approach to research opportunities. Inevitably, the high expectations that are often developed during the planning stage are unlikely to remain intact during the fieldwork phase of an investigation. This was a factor that had to be borne in mind during the research process itself.

Securing and Negotiating Access

Given the varied nature of the research sites involved in this study, the process of establishing access required a great deal of attention. Each site had their own peculiarities when it came to the process of securing access, and I felt that I would also be well advised to be sensitive to the expectations, concerns and potential worries of the organisations being studied. It was anticipated from the outset that close collaboration with certain key officials would be an important aspect of the research programme. It was also expected that negotiating access to established institutions such as the Labour Party and Amnesty International would require extensive official organisational sanction, and this proved to be the case. It thus became necessary to establish successful and productive relationships with particular key actors through whom access could be secured. Hammersley and Atkinson (1983, p. 63) refer to such actors as 'gatekeepers' because it is these individuals who are likely to be capable of providing or denying the researcher certain levels of access within a particular organisation. Hammersley and Atkinson (1983, p. 60) also highlight the importance of such 'informal sponsorship' when conducting research within institutions. This was perhaps at its strongest in the Tenants' and Residents' Associations and in Exodus, partly as a result of these groups having less formal structure than the Labour Party or Amnesty International.

Having recognised that it was important to maintain a relatively close relationship with these agents, I nonetheless retained a commitment to protecting the integrity of the research programme. In particular, it was stressed during all stages of negotiation that all interviews with individual members of particular organisations were totally confidential, and therefore would not be available to these key actors. A small number of respondents in the Labour Party initially expressed concern over which members of the Constituency Party might have access to their interview. As a result of previous experience, one member was concerned that the national Labour Party might be able to gain access to his contribution. In these few instances, I was able to reassure the interviewee (both verbally and in one case through a written statement) that their confidentiality would be maintained. The interviews were then able to proceed.

In addition, it was made clear that the various organisations could not expect to have any influence over the design and structure of the research. As Hammersley and Atkinson (1983, p. 65) point out, these factors are of particular importance in view of the fact that gatekeepers will often attempt to 'exercise some degree of surveillance and control'. Fortunately, there were no substantial objections raised to my prerequisites. I made only one exception to this arrangement. During negotiations with the Communications Director at Amnesty International, it was agreed that Amnesty International would be able to include a small number of questions in the interview guide to be used with Amnesty International members. In view of the fact that these questions related closely to my own themes, and that I was able to continue using all of my own interview questions without disruption, this arrangement was not viewed as a methodological problem.

Interviews

The sampling process A criticism that is often directed at qualitative methodology concerns the validity and reliability of its sampling methods. It is suggested that those researchers drawing upon qualitative methodology overlook questions of bias and unrepresentativeness when designing a sample of interviewees. It is then possible that findings will be skewed. However, as Devine (1995, p. 142) points out, the ways in which a group of respondents is selected is as important to qualitative researchers as it is to their quantitative counterparts. It is therefore not surprising that a study which draws upon qualitative methods must be prepared to consider the question of how generalisable the testimonies of the respondents are. It was therefore necessary to be sensitive to the methods by which interviewees were chosen within organisations, for both thematic and practical reasons. Importantly, a fundamental intention of this research was to analyse existing forms of participation by extending data collection beyond the so-called 'activists' who have predominantly comprised the subject of existing analysis. In order to analyse the experience of participation it became necessary to interview a cross-section of respondents. Indeed it would be somewhat elitist to assume that those who are at the centre of political participation are the only suitable 'actors' for investigation. I felt that those who occupy the fringes of participatory sites could perhaps tell us as much about the nature of participation as those who are more heavily committed to political activity, particularly in relation to the question of why some participants are less engaged than others.

This implied that the research needed to avoid sampling methods that are likely to produce self-selecting samples. It was felt that this may be a particular issue for this study because those individuals most likely to put themselves forward for interview were also likely to be the most 'active' members of a particular organisation. Whilst it has undoubtedly been important to secure fieldwork opportunities with such respondents, it has been equally important to maintain the innovative nature of the study by incorporating the less engaged members. It was similarly important that the sample was not biased in favour of those respondents who had perhaps become disillusioned or alienated by the particular organisation of which they were a member. Where it was possible, these factors have entailed compiling a random sample of members in order to avoid a bias in the final sample. Each member of an organisation would therefore have an equal opportunity of being selected for interview.

However, circumstances dictated that a number of varied sampling strategies were employed across the range of organisations. Both Amnesty International and the Labour Party were able to provide highly structured methods of sampling. Despite agreeing to access, both of these organisations were understandably not prepared to provide unrestricted access to their membership lists in accordance with data protection issues. This issue was adequately solved following negotiation between myself and the Constituency Labour Party Secretary and the Communications Director at the British section of Amnesty International. It was decided that each organisation would compile a random sample of members from its membership lists within a particular locality and then enquire via a letter of introduction as to whether the member had any objection to being contacted by myself. The details of those who raised no objection were then passed on to the researcher. The logistics of retaining a random sample of members was thus retained, and the protection of membership data was not compromised.

The remaining research sites were much smaller in size, and were not mediated by a large-scale national structure. It was therefore less straightforward to employ a structured random sampling method. The Exodus collective has no formal 'membership' structure as such. Consequently, I utilised an informal 'snowball' approach (Devine, 1995, p. 142) in order to establish research opportunities within the collective. This entailed beginning from a core of respondents and gradually expanding the sample via recommendations and information procured from the original sources. I firstly established contact with the collective's most high profile spokesman via a mutual acquaintance. I was then able to discuss the project in detail with him and he subsequently introduced me to several members of the collective. He was also able to inform the collective that I was undertaking the research and would be interested in speaking to other members. A similar approach had to be adopted during the fieldwork with the Tenants' and Residents' Associations. According to the Housing Department regulations, the former should maintain up to date membership lists but this was not the case with either of the Tenants' groups in which I carried out research. The Residents' Association had a relatively small membership and it was not difficult to speak to all of the members once I had procured access to the organisation.

Contacting respondents From the outset of the fieldwork stage of this project it was felt that the initial contact between the researcher and respondents would be important to the outcome of interviews. I concurred strongly with the view of Hammersley and Atkinson (1983, p. 78) that those people being studied 'are often more concerned with what kind of person the researcher is than with the research itself'. This is not to deny that the respondents were often interested in the content and purpose of the research. However, I felt that interviews, and indeed field relations generally, were more likely to proceed in a productive manner if I was able to establish an open relationship with respondents from the moment of initial contact. I therefore attempted to establish a commonalty and rapport with respondents.

When first speaking to respondents I was also aware of the need to avoid biasing the interview. I felt that couching the description of the project in general terms would be less likely to steer the thoughts of the respondents in particular directions before the interview was conducted. For example, I tried wherever possible to avoid mentioning the term 'activism' in preliminary exchanges. The rationale for this approach was not in any sense based on concealing information form the respondents. Rather, the motivation for such an approach was twofold. Firstly, the format of the interviews was adopted as an exploratory framework within which respondents could raise issues that they felt were particularly relevant. I felt that supplying them with concepts and categories before the interview took place would be too restrictive and might inhibit the parameters of their discussion. By waiting for respondents to bring up concepts such as activism then the interview would be likely to proceed more on their terms than mine. I felt that such an outcome would also generate more spontaneous data. Secondly, contact with one Labour Party member during the very early stages of the fieldwork suggested that a small number of the respondents might be concerned that they did not 'measure up' to the label of activist. This was clearly an unsuitable scenario for securing research with the less engaged participants.

The interview process A total of sixty one interviews were conducted for this research. These included twenty one from the Labour Party, sixteen from Amnesty International UK, seven from Exodus, seven each from the Tenants' Associations and three from the Residents' Association. The interviews conducted as part of this research varied in length from twenty minutes to over two hours. This was entirely dependent on the level of response of the interviewee, and I made no attempt to cut interviews short. I felt that this open-ended aspect of the interviews was useful in giving respondents room to explore subjects at a depth they felt comfortable with. Whereas life history approaches often employ multiple interviews with individual respondents, I preferred to hold only one meeting with each interviewee. This was partly due to practical considerations. I had a large number of interviews to conduct and it appeared somewhat impractical to plan to return to individual respondents on a regular basis. In addition, I felt that there would be little to gain from undertaking multiple interviews with individual respondents. This is not to say that I was unavailable to respondents following interviews. I emphasised to all interviewees that they could contact me at any time after our interview. In addition, all respondents were supplied with a copy of the transcript of the interview after the event had taken place.

As I have previously observed, the relationship between the interviewer and the interviewee is important to successful qualitative research. The power dynamics of the interview situation is central to this consideration. Invariably, the format of an interview can generate some concern and hesitancy amongst respondents. It is often the case that the researcher exercises an informal position of power within the interview. The generation of an environment in which respondents feel relaxed and able to speak at length is therefore of fundamental importance to the qualitative interviewer. The power dynamics inherent in the interview situation require careful attention from the researcher.

The use of a semi-structured format is a first step in attempting to alleviate some of the potential problems resulting from the interviewer-interviewee relationship. By attempting to prompt and ask for explanation the researcher loosens the confines of a standard interview situation. A highly rigid or structured format provides little scope for the respondent to relax and overcome initial nerves or anxieties. I always emphasised to respondents that the interview was intended as an 'informal chat' rather than a rigorous question and answer session. This provides the respondent with the space within which to respond on his or her own terms, rather than in a manner that I had deemed appropriate. As Devine (1995, p. 138) notes, interviews 'allow people to tell their own story in language with which they are familiar'.

The exploratory nature of the interviews was reflected in the structure and format that I established for the exchanges. It was felt that the research required that the interviewees be given sufficient room to prioritise those issues that they felt related most significantly to the areas they were being asked to reflect upon. I started the interviews with a set of loose themes or categories within which respondents were able to articulate definitions and experiences as they saw fit. I also encouraged respondents to introduce themes and issues that they felt were of relevance to the discussion. It has thus been consistently made clear to respondents that they should feel encouraged to introduce opinions, perspectives, experiences and subjects into the interviews that they felt were of specific relevance to their individual relationship with the organisation in question. At the end of all interviews I offered respondents the chance to talk about any points that they perhaps had not had a chance to raise in the interview proper. This part of the interview process often produced particularly rich data. This was perhaps as a result of a feeling on behalf of the respondent that the pressures of the interview situation were now over, and they were consequently able to relax.

Following each interview I spent a short time recording my own thoughts and reflections upon the interview. I included points on my impressions of each respondent, how successful I felt the interview had been and any other relevant observations. These brief notes were not intended to contribute directly to the final data but they proved useful in organising my own thoughts and reminding myself of each interviewee. Hammersley and Atkinson (1983, p. 164) highlight the importance of such an approach by emphasising the value of 'regular reflection and review'.

All interviews were taped and transcribed by myself. Although this proved to be a particularly time consuming process, I was keen to retain control over all aspects of the research programme. By spending time transcribing a recently conducted interview I was able to remind myself of the particular character of each respondent. The process was also useful for reminding myself of the main points that I had often made a mental note of during the interview. The transcription process also forces the researcher to pay close attention to the entirety of an interview, and to listen intensely to what is being said by the respondent. This in turn facilitates the emergence of findings that may have initially been overlooked during the interview itself. These factors were also generally useful in retaining and reinforcing my closeness to the raw data generated during the fieldwork process. The transcriptions were as near replication as was deemed necessary. It was felt that omitting certain sections in a discriminatory fashion during transcription may undermine the data analysis stage of the programme, when existing bits of data can sometimes appear in a new light. There were a few exceptions to this principle, particularly when respondents wandered quite substantially from the subject onto an unconnected area. However, this was the case on only a small number of occasions.

Non-Participant Observation

The aim of utilising this method was to enable the researcher to observe at first hand the deliberative forums in which the various modes of political participation being studied actually operate. In the course of the primary research, I was able to study meetings and interaction within the Tenants' Associations, the Residents' Associations and Exodus. However, I felt that this was justified by virtue of the fact that interviews with the remaining organisations were able to focus explicitly on the ways in which respondents experienced meetings. With regard to the Tenants' and Residents' Associations, I was able to observe the conduct and structure of meetings. This was supplemented by observation of the interaction and relationship between various attendees. Where possible, I attended meetings and took field notes whilst the meetings proceeded.

Data Analysis

An issue of particular concern to qualitative researchers is the process of analysing data. As Devine (1995, pp. 144-145) points out, the analysis of qualitative data proceeds quite differently from the systematic statistical analysis that is applied to quantitative data. All qualitative data is likely to be capable of generating different interpretations. It is therefore important that the researcher is sensitive to methods of organising and classifying data in order to establish a systematic process for the generation of findings. Although qualitative research is such that there is no 'correct' manner of organising and analysing data, I attempted to develop a specific method for analysing the data. Integral to the process of data analysis is the construction of some form of classification system into which data can be arranged. Adopting a flexible format for the interviews meant that a number of these categories would emerge from the data itself. I had developed a set of broad themes around which interviews were loosely structured, and this provided an initial framework for structuring categories.

In order to organise the data in a thematic fashion, it was necessary to undertake the systematic shifting of data in order to identify and classify key thematic categories. It has been suggested that the initial development of such categories should proceed on a 'middle order basis' (Dey, 1993, pp. 104-105). This avoids pre-empting the entire direction of the research, but simultaneously enables the researcher to develop some preliminary distinctions within the data (Dey, 1993; Becker and Geer, 1982). Thus, once a transcript was fully completed I was able to read through the interview and annotate the text in order to highlight what I felt were the main points of importance. I then made a summary of these points for each interview. Each respondent was thus equated with a synopsis of the major thematic categories that could be drawn form their particular interview. As the number of interviews summarised in this way grew, it then became possible in some cases to identify new issues that had perhaps been overlooked or not considered on initial readings of early interviews. This process was useful not only for continued data analysis but also for feeding back into interview guides as the fieldwork developed. Once the fieldwork stage of the project was drawing to a close it became possible to collate the findings in a more systematic and wide-ranging fashion. A number of large diagrams were produced that mapped out the findings and included reference to the location (i.e. interview name and page number) of relevant data. This format enabled me to trace the connections between the findings more clearly and to make comparisons between organisations. This enabled similarities and differences to emerge from within the data itself.

Ethical Issues

An important consideration for the social science researcher is the question of ethics. In particular, the adoption of a qualitative methodology invariably raises a number of specific ethical concerns over the practice and conduct of both data collection and data dissemination. In particular, feminist methodology has raised the profile of the relationship between the researcher and respondent. The use of interviews as the primary source of data collection has required that the researcher be aware of ethical issues such as confidentiality and informed consent (Berg, 1989, pp. 137-138; Seidman, 1991, pp. 48-55). It has been made clear to all interview respondents that their responses will be presented in a completely anonymous manner during the write-up and dissemination of the data. The use of individual pseudonyms is a common technique (Berg, 1989, pp. 138-139), but I have instead adopted a more general reference to respondents in term of their organisational affiliations. This issue of anonymity was raised whilst negotiating with a Tenants Participation Officer within the Council Housing Department, a Constituency Secretary of Labour Party and the Communications Director at Amnesty International UK. All expressed a preference for the anonymity of locale and members. Although the majority of individual respondents have expressed to the researcher that they have no objection to their names being included in the presentation of findings, it was felt that the anonymity of respondents should be protected.

Another area where the researcher must be sensitive to ethical issues relates to leaving the field. This can raise tensions within the researcher-respondent relationship (Taylor, 1991, pp. 244-245), particularly if the subject feels exploited. In order to address this issue, all respondents have been offered a complete transcript of the interview. It is felt that this contributed to the development of what Seidman (1991, pp. 83-84) refers to as 'equity' in the qualitative research relationship. Providing the respondents with a transcript of their interview was intended to counter the sense of exclusion that respondents may feel from the research process. This type of approach could perhaps be criticised as being tokenistic and failing to develop a fully dialectical relationship between the researcher and respondents. However, I was aware of these points and felt that this project could not realistically sustain a more developed series of links between the respondents and myself.

It should also be noted that the use of non-participant observation raises fundamental concerns over the nature of field relations, and in particular the securing of consent from participants during observation. Throughout the project, observation has only taken place following the securing of sanctions from holders of formal organisational authority, such as Chairs, and following an introduction by myself before meetings. No participants have raised objections to my presence at meetings.

Having examined the methodological approach employed in the course of data collection and analysis, I will now move on to providing an overview of the organisations studied in the course of the research.

5 Case Studies

In Chapter Two, I outlined the range of structures within which political participation takes place. In order to provide an adequate survey of the different facets of political participation it was necessary for intensive research to take place within a range of organisations. This required the use of what has been widely defined as 'case studies'. Yin (1984, p. 23) defines the concept in the following manner:

> ....an empirical study that....investigates a contemporary phenomenon within its real life context when the boundaries between phenomenon and context are not clearly evident....and in which multiple sources of evidence are used.

A number of diverse organisations were studied in the course of the research. These included the British Labour Party, the British section of Amnesty International, an alternative lifestyle collective known as Exodus, two Tenants' Associations and one Residents' Association. This selection is not intended to be exhaustive. Rather, each body was chosen in order to provide a representative range of participatory organisations. Clearly, each of these case studies is illustrative in it's own right, but I was particularly interested in examining the similarities and differences that existed between the nature of participation within the research sites. Taken together, the organisations I have studied therefore provide a spectrum of political structures within which citizens participate. This stretches from traditional state initiated structures through to a major political party, a single-issue pressure group and a radical political experiment.

Given that I have stressed the importance of examining the dialectical relationship between organisations and members, it is necessary to spend some time examining the organisational and structural characteristics of each group in turn. This aspect of the study provides some understanding of the context in which the 'inner workings' of each of these groups takes place. Below, I intend to provide a brief outline each of these bodies. Limitations of space inevitably limit the scope of this analysis, but it is hoped that an adequate picture of each body is provided. This will also serve to illustrate the rationale for including each group.

Tenants' and Residents' Associations

In the course of the fieldwork I have undertaken research with two Tenants' Associations and one Residents' Association. All three bodies were based in the South East of England. The Tenants' Associations were both established by the local council as a mechanism through which council tenants could consult with their respective Housing Departments. One of the Tenants' Associations had only been established for less than six months, whereas the other had been in existence for several years. Local residents originally set up the Residents' Association in the mid-1950s with no formal support from local authorities. It is still run on an independent basis although it regularly consults with the local council via committees such as Home Safety Meetings and the Home Safety Advisory Committee.

The development of effective strategies for extending public involvement in the delivery of public services represents one of the most prominent policy trends of the past decade. The management of public housing has been at the forefront of attempts to extend channels of accountability beyond the confines of established electoral processes. Between 1975 and 1986 the proportion of local authorities in England and Wales with arrangements for tenant participation almost doubled from forty-four to eighty per cent (Joseph Rowntree Foundation, 1990). There has also been a long history of pressure from the community level for increased consultation over housing matters (Grayson, 1996). Recent years have witnessed the development of a number of innovations in the council-tenant relationship. Principles of joint management and control have been implemented in those local authorities adopting some form of 'decentralisation' of public services (Burns et al, 1994). However, the implementation of devolved power to tenants via direct input into decision-making structures remains rare. For many local councils, the development of a working relationship between a Housing Department and local tenants is likely to function within the parameters of what Arnstein (1971) has referred to as 'consultation'.

The Tenants' Association remains a fundamental component of the relationship between local council tenants and Housing Departments. A number of specific functions of Tenants' Associations have been identified (Chartered Institute of Housing, 1994). These include: raising issues of local concern; representing the views and interests of tenants; providing expert local knowledge; providing information for the wider body of tenants; acting as agents for Housing Management within the local community; and acting as a focus for local campaigning. In addition to these pragmatic roles, it has been suggested that Tenants' Associations are able to fulfil what might be referred to as a more 'developmental' role within the local community. Goodland (1994) defines this concept as relating to the potential social or educational effects of tenant participation. Previous findings have indeed suggested that tenants often view associations as providing a place to meet and socialise, and as a forum for the creation of some form of 'community spirit' (Joseph Rowntree Foundation, 1990).

There is only limited agreement about what tenant participation means in practice. Nonetheless, there are a variety of established mechanisms that local councils have used to connect with tenants. These range from methods that focus upon the individual tenant (including letters to tenants) through to collective forms of involvement (primarily via the formation of Tenants' and Residents' Associations). Increasingly common is the use of face-to-face contact between tenants and council officers in the form of meetings and discussions (Chartered Institute of Housing, 1994, pp. 40-46; Goodland, 1994, p. 119), although in 1990 less than half of local authorities employed such methods (Joseph Rowntree Foundation, 1990). This method of tenant participation can take the form of tenant representation on relevant housing committees and advisory bodies, but perhaps the most basic unit of face-to-face activity is the use of regular meetings between an established Tenants' Association and Housing Department Officers.

As a unit of citizen participation, the Tenants' Association has a number of common features. A number of organisational positions are usually created for local tenants to fill, including Chairperson, Secretary, Treasurer and so on. It is common for a Committee to undertake administration duties within the association, and an Annual General Meeting is held to nominate and elect members to office holding positions. A series of general meetings are held throughout the year in which members are usually able to converse with Housing Department representatives. It is common for Tenants' Associations to adopt a standard constitution covering rules of association. The bodies studied in this research conformed to all of these norms. Despite the fact that it is not formally linked to the local council, the Residents' Association had adopted a constitution very similar to the council sponsored associations. I will discuss these issues in more depth in the next chapter.

Amnesty International UK

During the course of the primary research, I also undertook data collection within the British section of Amnesty International. Interviews with members took place within three local groups, all of which were based in the South East of England. This fieldwork was complimented by interviews with several key staff members within the Campaigns Department of the British section. These included the Campaigns Coordinator, the Outreach Team Leader, the Individual Action team and the Groups Coordinator. In terms of the research agenda developed within this book, Amnesty International represents a prime example of the large-scale campaigning groups associated with the 'protest businesses' identified by Jordan and Maloney (1997).

Since its inception in 1961, Amnesty International has established itself as one of the largest and most high profile international human rights campaigning organisations in the world. The mandate adopted by Amnesty International focuses upon global violations of human rights, and seeks the release of those prisoners of conscience imprisoned solely for their beliefs, ethnicity, religion, gender or language. Central to the activities of Amnesty International is the contribution made by members. There are more than 1.1 million members worldwide, and according to it's own publicity material Amnesty International prides itself on remaining a participatory, democratic organisation. There are more than fifty international sections, and each of these sections contains internal structures developed specifically for involving, mobilising and communicating with members. The British section of Amnesty International is a long established part of the organisation's global structure. Drawing upon a body of sixty-five paid staff (NCVO, 1997) and many full and part time volunteers, the British office oversees a wide range of activities and campaigns within the United Kingdom. The British section is divided into five main departments including Campaigns, Fund-raising, Communications, Administration and Finance, and the Directorate. Each of these departments is further subdivided into Offices. In this sense, the central structure of the British section of Amnesty International is built around a 'compartmental structure' (Christiansen and Dowding, 1994). This structure facilitates the lobbying of external agencies such as British and foreign governments.

The internal policy making structure of the British section of Amnesty International is designed along formal democratic lines. Individual members, local groups and affiliated organisations are all entitled to submit resolutions and take part in voting at the Annual General Meeting, the highest policy making body within the British section. Each individual member of Amnesty International is entitled to a single vote at the national Annual General Meeting. Individual members can also submit policy motions for discussion at the Annual General Meeting. The Council is responsible for implementing policy and deciding on policy matters.

Perhaps the most important aspect of the British section's mandate within the global structure of Amnesty International is the coordination and development of the activities of the membership. There are a number of ways in which members can become involved in the activities of the organisation. At one end of this spectrum we find the most basic unit of Amnesty International participation: minimal subscription or financial donation. Secondly, the recently introduced Individual Action Network utilises basic methods of membership participation including signing postcards or displaying posters. This scheme is intended to enable members to take part in campaigns without becoming directly involved in the local group structure. The most common form of membership involvement in the campaign activity of Amnesty International is letter writing. This involves individual members acting upon appeals and campaigns by sending formal letters of protest to relevant government ministers. The Urgent Action Network entails members sending messages on behalf of prisoners who are felt to be in imminent danger of execution, torture or neglect. The Occupational Outreach Networks are structured around particular occupations and interest groups. Members from these groups form networks in order to share information and take joint action. Examples include Amnesty networks amongst journalists, academics, and students. Networks have also been developed within religious bodies, ethnic minority organisations, gay and lesbian groups and trade unions. Within this overall framework, Specialist Groups in the UK include Children's, Medical, Lawyers and Military, Security and Police groups. Finally, over three hundred and thirty groups represent the British section of Amnesty International at the local level. These bodies provide the largest scope for active membership involvement. The groups are run by volunteer members and actively campaign, fund-raise and generate publicity for Amnesty within particular localities. Groups undertake regular meetings in order to discuss administrative and campaign issues.

The Labour Party

The primary research conducted within the British Labour Party took place within a Constituency based in the South East of England. Much has been written about the internal structure of the Labour Party, and I do not intend to reiterate these points by providing a complete overview of the internal structure of the Party (Garner and Kelly, 1994, pp. 160-194; Fisher, 1996, pp. 64-93). Suffice to say that the Labour Party has been the site of many conflicting tensions in the past three decades. Although the Labour Party's internal constitution has traditionally been seen as 'self-consciously democratic' (Webb, 1994, p. 109), the past thirty years have witnessed periodic debates about the way in which the Party governs itself. During the early 1970s, for instance, there was much discussion about the perceived need for increased involvement of rank-and-file members in internal policy-making processes. By the late 1970s, the Party was experiencing an influx of radical members who adopted a critical approach to the Party leadership (McLaverty, 1996, pp. 16-17). This would eventually lead to the internal turmoil of the 1980s. Yet, Garner and Kelly (1994, p. 180) make the observation that the Party leadership has often been able to 'manage' the internal politics of the Party in accordance with their own ideological principles.

Perhaps the main point that needs to be considered in relation to the recent history of the Labour Party is the continuing influence of internal reform. As Garner and Kelly (1994, p. 160) point out, organisational change has been a major theme of internal Labour Party politics since the late 1970s. This has become especially acute since the election of Tony Blair as Party leader. According to Perryman (1996b, p. 1), the Blair leadership has been the 'ultimate inheritor of the portents of change'. A number of major changes have been made to the internal policy process of the Party, and the nature of Party membership has consequently undergone substantial revision in the past decade. For instance, the expansion of the National Policy Forum to 175 members and the creation of a Joint Policy Committee which has taken on the major role of initiating policy, have contributed strongly to the reconstruction of the internal structures of the Party. In Chapter Five I will explore in more detail the nature of the institutional changes that have been implemented within the Labour Party. In particular, I will consider the implications of internal reforms for the nature of Party activism.

The Exodus Collective

The final case study investigated in the course of this research was the Exodus collective. Based in Luton, this alternative lifestyle group emerged in the summer of 1992 when a group of young people began to stage a series of free outdoor 'raves' and parties for local people. These open-air dances were set up in response to the perceived commercialisation and expense of the dance scene in local nightclubs, and were originally organised without a Public Entertainment Licence. Attendance at the early informal and spontaneous raves was mainly comprised of unemployed or low-income youths from Luton and surrounding areas. The audience of these events grew rapidly over a relatively short period of time, and by 1994 weekly parties were regularly attracting up to 6,000 attendees from around the country (Exodus Collective, 1994). In 1993, a New Year rave attracted an audience of over 10,000 people (*The Guardian* 12th November 1993).

During this early period, the organisers of these raves developed a broad ideological agenda that quickly became closely associated with their activities. Those who were involved with the organisation of the raves began to describe these events as 'community dance parties'. The raves soon became seen as more than simply a regular outlet for the local youth population:

> ....by staging the events we were making a statement. We believe in the freedom of self-expression rather than the road that the dance scene had seemed to be taking - one of exploitation and intimidation of the youth. We staged free parties so that the people did not feel exploited, allowing them the freedom to express themselves in a beautiful atmosphere of peace, love and unity, our motto (Exodus Collective, 1996).

Many of those who were involved with Exodus during this period also soon became involved in 'community squatting'. The aim of this was to directly address local issues such as homelessness, unemployment and youth crime. A derelict hospice on the outskirts of the town was occupied and is currently being converted by members of the collective into accommodation for the homeless. This location is known as the Manor. By pooling the housing benefit of inhabitants, the Manor currently provides refurbished housing for thirty to forty people (Exodus Collective, undated). This scheme is known as the Housing Action Zone, and is 'supposed to be there to pick up the bottom end of society, to give them support. It is also supposed to a forum, an opportunity to do things' (Exodus Collective, undated). The inhabitants of the Manor make use of waste materials to regenerate the derelict rooms, a process known as 'wombling'. Other recycling strategies have included 'paletology' which involves constructing furniture from discarded wooden pallets. The collective has also converted an abandoned farm site originally used for raves into Long Meadow Community Farm, known simply as the Farm. The collective has also put forward proposals to the local council for a community centre to be known as the Ark. This would offer a permanent indoor venue for dances and raves. The proceeds from these events would be reinvested into the Ark and would support local cultural activities and self-learning schemes. Exodus has also outlined a range of facilities that would be available within the Ark including an arts and crafts market, a music studio, training opportunities and counselling services. Since it first emerged in Luton, Exodus has had a troubled relationship with the local authorities. Several large-scale police raids have taken place on locations occupied by Exodus and a number of members have been arrested and charged with various drugs related offences.

It is difficult to investigate Exodus without giving some attention to the collective's identity. There are a number of interrelated dimensions to the agenda that Exodus has developed. Firstly, the collective describes itself as part of the 'movement of Jah people', and claims to be motivated primarily by an attempt to create an alternative to the competitive environment of what is referred to as 'Babylon'. There is a strong sense of spiritual awareness amongst those most heavily involved, and Rastafarianism is a major influence on the collective. According to one of the collective's most prominent members, the collective 'respects all routes to God'. He further describes those involved as 'spiritual strugglers'. A former member to whom I spoke observed that 'their faith, or spirituality as they call it, rules their do's and don'ts and rights and wrongs'. Secondly, Exodus is vehemently anti-capitalist and anti-profit. The raves themselves are intended as 'profit free zones'. A rave organiser to whom I spoke stressed that 'I don't do it for profit. I do it for love'. Linked to this stance is a strong counter cultural and almost anarchistic dimension to the collective. Thirdly, Exodus reflects an openness to cultural diversity, and is clearly committed to crossing racial, sexual and gender boundaries. As one member has observed in a recent television documentary, 'We came together and we had to thrash out our differences. Sexual, spiritual. All these barriers that society has inbred in us. We had to come to a oneness' (Channel Four, 1995). Underlying the general philosophy of the group is a commitment to a community based ideal of collectivism. The collective is seen to provide the source of an individual's capabilities and resources, and this is evident in the ways in which Exodus organises itself.

In this chapter I have provided an outline of the organisations studied in the course of the research. In the remainder of this book I will draw upon the theoretical framework outlined in Chapter Three in order to consider the various forms of participation that take place within these forums. I will begin this process by analysing the expectations and policies of the organisations towards their members.

6 Structures of Political Participation

According to the perspective developed by Habermas, the internal structure of participatory forums is crucial to the potential development of a discursively structured public sphere. Clearly, political participation does not take place in an institutional vacuum. It is therefore important to begin our analysis of the nature of political participation by examining the expectations and attitudes of civil society organisations toward their members. The roles ascribed to members by institutions of political participation should not be overlooked if we are to critically assess the nature and scope of contemporary political activity.

In this chapter I intend to analyse the policies of the various organisations toward their members. This chapter asks to what extent the different organisations actually want some form of communicative rationality to develop within their internal structures. Habermas identifies the generation of discourse within civil society structures as an integral component of the emergence of communicative tendencies, but one must firstly pose the question of how contemporary political structures actually perceive such a development. And if deliberation is sidelined then what do the organisations actually want from their members? I will raise two main areas that have arisen from discussions with staff members, or equivalent, within the various organisations.

Firstly, the analysis will examine the policy or decision-making role that the organisations offer to their participants. Secondly, I will consider the attitude of the various bodies toward the question of 'activism'. It will be argued that the openness of organisations to discursive tendencies is not a clear-cut question. I will demonstrate that there are a series of internal tensions that can be located within each of the bodies. Moreover, it is clear that, to a certain degree, these conflicting tendencies transcend the spectrum of organisations under examination. The analysis that I present in this chapter will, in turn, provide the groundwork for moving on to examine the actual types of participation that develop within these various contexts.

Policy and Decision-Making Roles

Within Amnesty International UK, several members of the Campaigns Department staff felt that Amnesty International needs to provide a policy role for members. For instance, the Outreach Team Leader observed that 'In terms of Amnesty's structure....the AGM is weighted in favour of ensuring that the local group membership have a very significant role in deciding what Amnesty's strategies and priorities should be'. He went on to note that 'The membership lead Amnesty, unlike other organisations such as Greenpeace....we are lay led'. Taken in conjunction with the details presented in Chapter Four, we can see that it is only a partial representation of Amnesty International UK to suggest that it does not provide opportunities for members to take part in internal decision-making processes. As the Campaigns Co-ordinator puts it: 'the parameters of the organisation are in some shape or form decided by our members'. However, it is important to note that there are discernible limits to the perceived role that members should play in such a process. On the one hand, the Campaigns Co-ordinator went on to outline the practical difficulties associated with an inclusive policy making process:

> Sometimes it is just a complete mess to go through all this consultation and dialogue all the time, but it is quite important for bringing people along with the thrust and direction of different policy directions. And a lot of the biggest policy changes that have happened in Amnesty have come from bits of our membership. So, for example, deciding whether Amnesty should adopt people as prisoners of conscience on the grounds of sexuality was something that came out of the membership....but that probably took about ten years to actually get changed. And even then it was a bit of a fudge. But it got there...in terms of big changes to areas that Amnesty works on it requires a level of global consensus. And that can be a process that takes a long time. And sometimes it can be laughed out of court for being slightly barmy. But there is a dynamic that goes on between the centre and the membership.

At the same time, I detected a more negative interpretation of the value of the involvement of members in policy formation. The emphasis on internal democracy was not necessarily perceived in a purely normative manner. For example, a member of the Individual Action Team warned that:

> If any idea was mooted and we had to consult before making any decisions with some kind of representative body, or to whom we were responsible, it

would be an anathema to us. It would really hold up our work. It wouldn't contribute anything useful. It might make us more democratic and we might be more accountable but there are plenty of other mechanisms for holding us accountable.

There is clearly a tension between the concern with ensuring a policy role for members and achieving the specific aims of Amnesty International. The Urgent Action Co-ordinator was critical of the idea that Amnesty International UK needs to pay extensive attention to the concept of internal democracy. He stressed that Amnesty International is ultimately interested in addressing human rights problems, and this is the primary factor guiding the design of the organisation. He did not feel that improved democracy within the organisation would have any direct effect on patterns of participation. As he put it:

I don't know to what extent the democracy of the organisation actually affects levels of activism. I don't know whether it is an incentive at all for it to be a democratic organisation. I think the vast majority of members couldn't care less. They don't join because it is a membership based organisation and they will have a democratic right to change the structure or the mandate of the organisation. They join because they want something to be done about human rights.

The notion that members do not necessarily view Amnesty International as an opportunity to take part in the organisation's internal affairs were echoed by the Campaigns Co-ordinator. He noted that 'the things that will piss off our membership are basic things about our services and their expectations of what they expect us to be able to deliver....things like delivery standards, training for the phones and those kinds of service standards. Those are the things that will produce the most complaints'. We can thus identify a tension between the perceived necessity of maintaining a policy role for members and the institutional criticism of the extent to which such a process is even possible or desirable. This is important because it also raises the question of whether members actually want such a role within a large-scale organisation such as Amnesty International. This is a theme that I will explore in more detail in the next chapter when I consider the perceptions and expectations of individual members.

One can detect similar tensions within the Labour Party. Habermas has commented on a number of occasions about the continuing assimilation of political parties into the apparatus of the state. He argues that within the liberal democracies of advanced capitalist societies, political parties are increasingly compromised by their position within the political public sphere. Political parties 'treat the political public sphere as the system's environment, from which they extract mass loyalty' (Habermas, 1996c, p. 218). Keane (1988, p. 142) similarly refers to 'the wholly conventional trend, commonly observed of the compromise party in recent years, of choking off inner-party discussions and controversies'. As I have noted in the previous chapter, the period during which the research was conducted was an era of intense change for the Labour Party, and the role of the individual member within the Party was subject to upheaval.

In the past few years, the Labour Party has undergone a 'genuine transformation' (Marquand and Wright, 1996, p. 287) of its internal structures and decision-making processes. The *Labour Into Power* reform package has ushered in a range of substantive changes to Labour's traditional internal decision-making structure, based on the submitting of resolutions to an annual conference. In the past few years, the methods by which the Party develops policy have been restructured away from traditional debate at annual conference toward the creation of a series of local, regional and national Policy Forums. In many respects, the introduction of structures such as Policy Forums can be interpreted as a deliberate attempt to move away from the perceived shortcomings of traditional membership mechanisms in order to develop a more rational and open policy process. I will return to this theme shortly.

Turning to the Exodus collective, one encounters a radically different approach to the management of internal affairs. In view of the description given of Exodus in the previous chapter, it comes as no surprise that the collective has no formal membership 'policy' to speak of. This does not however mean that the collective is opposed to all forms of structure and organisation. As one founding member put it 'we're not anti-organisation'. However, he distinguishes between an organisational structure that serves the interests and needs of the collective and a 'control' structure that restricts and limits the actions of members. As a political organisation, Exodus has a number of distinctive features that mark it out as an innovative form of contemporary political activity. Conventional modes of political involvement have been picked up by the collective as a starting point, or foil, against which Exodus can be defined as an organisation. One of the founding members of Exodus had previously been involved with the Socialist Workers Party, and he remarked that he had become disillusioned with the 'double talk' of such organisations. Another member commented that 'I've been along to a couple of [Socialist Workers Party] meetings. They bear little or no resemblance to the real world. They just jabber on at great length'.

By reducing the status and importance of a hierarchical structure it is felt that members are able to participate and contribute in a more meaningful and substantive manner. In this sense, the actual structure of the collective is seen to emerge directly from the combined contributions of participants, and to be susceptible to change over time. As one founding member of Exodus put it, 'Exodus has an evolving structure'. In line with this, the format of the collective is seen by a number of members as having evolved and developed in a range of largely unpredictable ways. As one Exodus rave organiser put it: 'it has unfolded in certain directions that nobody could have predicted.....you could never have planned it...the whole thing is organic, it's like a seed that has spread'. There is a deliberate attempt within the structures of the collective to avoid hierarchies and leadership structures. One member referred to the attraction of being able to show that 'we can do things and we can do them differently, and there is no need for all that shit, all the bureaucracy and red tape....let's get away from all that'. Underlying the general philosophy of the group is a commitment to a 'community' based ideal of collectivism. The collective is seen to provide the source of an individual's capabilities and resources: 'we all realise that as individuals we can't get anything done, but as a group we can'. Another member has observed that 'communal and community are the key words around here...we live together, we love together, we work together and we play together' (Channel Four, 1995). These factors were also evident as a member spelt out his motivations for joining the collective:

> As a community you can produce things more easily. If you want to build a house and there are ten of you to build it, it's a lot cheaper. If you want to work the land. If you want to be successful and go further and be a craftsman and learn and develop yourself and become a better person. Learn more, be more constructive. But with the help of other people. The idea that the group is larger than the sum of its parts. If I wanted to start up a little course teaching people, other people could teach me things.

There is certainly a sense of mutual self-help and co-operation within the loose structure of Exodus. In many respects, this is seen to facilitate the non-hierarchical and organic nature of the collective. There is a direct opposition to the hierarchical distribution of responsibility. One member observed that 'nothing works here through giving orders'. Rather, Exodus is premised upon the development of particular 'niches' in which individual members can become specialists. The ongoing synthesis of these skills is seen to provide the collective with a mutually reinforcing base from which everyday activity can take place. Comments from the member responsible for information technology within the collective illustrate this: 'I'm not manual in any way....those guys that know how to do that, full respect to them from me. And it works the other way. They respect all the effort that goes into this kind of thing. It all gels together as one big help for each other'. In many respects, these factors encourage the adoption of a more open and deliberative style of discourse within the collective. I will take up this point in more detail in Chapter Seven when I discuss the actual process of taking part in different types of political participation.

However, comments from other respondents suggest that one should be wary of assuming that an internal culture of this type is necessarily conducive to some form of political radicalisation. One former member remarked that 'most people who go to Exodus parties couldn't give a toss about their politics or their ideas. They're just interested in well, it's free, it's a sound system, and then they go home afterwards'. One former member also highlighted the sense in which a radical group such as Exodus might generate exclusionary tendencies, particularly for those who do not feel able to commit to such a form of political action. As he put it:

.....it's cool to be part of Exodus. It's cool if you're a macho single male or a single female. Or if you are prepared to go with that youth culture. You just see so many other people in society who are actually scared by this. I've been on convoys through villages, and you see these people....it's two o'clock in the morning and there is this truck with a red flashing light going through their village. They all stand outside and look at it. They have this forlorn look....what is going on? Are we going to be safe? These people look frightening.

He went on to suggest that 'part of the appeal is probably being able to do that. Being part of that. We are the bigger group and we are more frightening than the next lot. You're not going to mess with us because we're a unified group and there is a lot of us'.

As I have observed, the Exodus collective initially sprung up within a space that is far removed from local state structures. However, in recent times this relationship has been subject to revision. The collective has become increasingly involved in negotiation with the local council, particularly in relation to the development of the Ark project. This shift has implications for the internal structure of the collective. The collective has gradually broadened its agenda and has taken on a number of new features since its inception. As one member put it:

> We didn't set out to be a political organisation, but what we now do is political. Take the Manor and what we have done there....that is political. It's a political statement. ...and we are the ones they said were drop outs. That's a big political statement. But people look at politics and think it is all about higher level stuff but it's not. It all starts from the ground. That is what politics is for, that is who its is supposed to affect. And really we didn't like the way politics was treating us so we kind of went our own way.

He went on to state that 'we now realise that we have got to work with the authorities in order to get anywhere....you can't get away from it all in one fell swoop....you have to mould you future....and talk to these people'. Clearly, there is a tension between these comments and the following sentiment: 'Really, what we want is total autonomy. We are gradually getting away from it all and we want to be self-sufficient and totally autonomous'. This conundrum is crucial to uncovering the extent to which Exodus is susceptible to the instrumental tendencies of established participatory cultures. One former member even remarked that 'the idea that they are an alternative....all of a sudden, they become the same....and all of a sudden those dividing lines are crossed'. I will take up this theme in the next two chapters when I consider the nature of the activism that emerges within Exodus.

Questioning Activism?

In Chapter One, I referred to a growing critique of 'activism' to be found amongst policy practitioners and existing political bodies. During the interviews I found strong evidence of this trend, particularly within the Labour Party, Amnesty International UK and Exodus. One cannot however assume that all of these organisations were critical of activism for the same reasons. One must also be willing to query exactly what it is that these organisations are questioning in their membership policies. Within Amnesty International one can identify a skepticism over the capacities of local groups to sustain open and inclusive forms of membership participation. With regard to the Labour Party, the critique of traditional forms of Party activism has taken a similar path, but has also formed a major component of the wider internal reforms associated with the leadership of Tony Blair. The Exodus collective has been founded on an assumption that the shortcomings of existing forms of activism require the development of seemingly alternative forms of political culture.

Discussions between myself and staff within the Campaigns Department show that Amnesty International UK is keen to stress its credentials as a membership driven organisation. Amnesty International UK is also reliant upon those members who are willing to take a more substantial role in the campaigning activity of the organisation. A promotional leaflet stresses the value of becoming involved in a local group: 'Working together can have a far greater impact and be much more enjoyable than working alone'. This can be clearly detected in the comments of the Campaigns Co-ordinator who felt that:

> ....a key strength of Amnesty is that it really is an organisation about ordinary people doing ordinary things, and getting ordinary members of the public to do stuff and say that they are concerned about human rights violations.

Members are consequently viewed as a major resource of campaigning activity that the British section of Amnesty International is able to undertake. The Local Groups Coordinator commented: 'local activism is the root of Amnesty really'. Similarly, the Outreach Team Leader noted that:

> What would distinguish us from some other organisations is that we put a premium on membership activism because our campaigning depends on it...the staff exists to support our volunteer activists....our strength is our numbers of active members and our volunteers.

However, it was also clear to me that the Campaigns Department is currently engaged in a questioning of the role of this structure. In part, this stems from a concern over the numbers of members who are prepared to become involved in Amnesty International activity. This was expressed by a number of Campaigns staff members, and the Urgent Action Co-ordinator noted that 'even in the most optimistic sums....you are still talking about one fifth of our membership actually doing anything to do with campaigning'. He went on to note that 'you are talking about 80 to 90,000 people who just do nothing'. The Local Groups Co-ordinator similarly observed that 'there is a bit of a concern about whether the network of local groups is going to increase in the future, and if not how we are going to maintain the pressure of activism'.

In the late 1980s, Amnesty International UK set up an Active Membership Working Group in order to examine recruitment methods and investigate new ways of persuading members to take on posts within local groups. At the time of conducting the present research, the Campaigns Department had recently revived these themes and set up an Individual Action Team. The Individual Action Co-ordinator, who was responsible for the Team, summarised the aims of the initiative: 'Our brief now is to get more members active....the aim is to activate more of the membership, and to activate in terms of campaigning so that more of them will send appeals or will do something within any campaign we are running'. At the same time, it is too simplistic to assume that Amnesty International UK necessarily wants increased levels of membership participation. As the Campaigns Co-ordinator observed: 'There is a kind of organisational disincentive to make it increase as well...the more successful your campaigns are, the harder the work is'. He went on to observe that 'if there was a sudden dramatic increase in levels of participation it would be a bloody nightmare. The capacity of the support structures here would be really pushed'. This comment is interesting for demonstrating that there is a perceived maximum level at which membership participation becomes unmanageable. In this sense, Amnesty International UK appears to be dependent on only a limited amount of its members actually taking part in campaign activities.

The interest in developing new methods of membership participation within Amnesty International UK is not only restricted to questions of the quantity of membership involvement. Interestingly, the Individual Action Co-ordinator stated that the concern with these areas came primarily from 'a recognition that the group structures aren't growing....the traditional Amnesty group structure doesn't work'. He went on to highlight a number of problems associated with the local group as a mechanism of membership activity. He commented that 'groups are not the way forward. They aren't growing, they are overwhelmed, they don't get new members'. This was echoed by the Local Groups Co-ordinator who observed that 'the core of our membership that are involved in groups tends to be fairly stable at best'. The Individual Action Co-ordinator also spoke of his own experience of local groups by observing that 'we go to quite a few meetings and you can have a group meeting that only has three people at it. And they are receiving campaign materials and you just know that most of it has never been read and never been acted upon'. He argued that at the root of these dilemmas was the tendency for groups to rely too heavily on small numbers of highly active members. As he commented:

> More and more is being asked of groups when there is less and less capacity within the groups to deal with it. Groups tend to be very small and they have a core of between five or ten people who do everything. And they burn out

after a few years and the group falls apart. Those that are active do a lot of work but I think we have to rely on them too much. And we have to take it for granted that when we send something to them that there will be a response.

The Campaigns Co-ordinator made very similar comments when he noted that 'Quite a few of the local groups struggle along and rely on a handful of individuals who are committed and do things. And to a certain extent it is a bit like say the Labour Party. Individual wards frequently rely upon a secretary and a Chair and a Treasurer, and if key people pull out then they are stuffed'. The Individual Action Co-ordinator went on to argue that 'there needs to be a sea change. Let's forget about group structures and think about the individual member and how we can involve them in a campaign'.

There has also been substantial effort to remould the local culture of Constituency Parties within the Labour Party over the past five years. According to Mandelson and Liddle (1997) recent reforms have generated a new culture within the Party, both at a national and local level. They speak of the development of a more campaigning and open face of the Labour Party. Tom Sawyer has similarly spoken of a modern mass membership Labour Party that is more willing than ever before to represent and reflect the complexities of communities in the Britain of the 1990s. Since Tony Blair's election as Party leader, the Party leadership has criticised the traditional role played by the most active party members. Mandelson and Liddle (1996, p. 213) claim that local constituencies 'became easily dominated by individuals who were unrepresentative of the wider membership' and claim that 'an unrepresentative, activist-driven structure....generated politics and attitudes at odds with what Labour has traditionally stood for' (Mandelson and Liddle, 1996, p. 212). According to Taylor and Bentley (1997) the Party leadership has attempted to develop 'good communitarian activists'. Mo Mowlam (1996) has stated that 'we are changing from a party that is small and inward-looking to one that is more campaigning and open'. In a similar vein, Tony Blair (1996) has commented:

> We have altered our structures and organisation to remove the damaging domination of small groups of activists that almost wrecked the party. The activists are now far more in touch with the broader party; and the broader party, thanks to an expanding membership, in touch with the people.

It has been argued that the traditional resolution based politics of the Party needed to be replaced by more open and outward oriented constituencies. Mandelson and Liddle (1996, p. 215) suggest that 'instead of activity dominated by meetings, minutes and agendas, constituencies [must] undertake campaigning, education and socialising, which are more interesting and stimulating for old and new members alike'.

The Labour Party has also been eager to develop more direct methods of consultation between the leadership and individual members through the introduction of mechanisms such as One Member, One Vote and postal ballots. Recent consultative surveys such as *Shaping Our Future* (Labour Party, 1997) are structured around a postal system which contains no direct face-to-face contact between individual members and an internal policy process. The views and opinions of members are increasingly solicited through questionnaires. A Constituency Party Secretary to whom I spoke was concerned about the changing nature of Party membership. He noted that:

> People say that democracy has been widened, and you have got direct involvement. But you could almost do that by post...and then there is no interaction with the political process. You get a statement from the aspiring candidates and you choose between five or six people. Well, that's not democracy. Democracy does depend on debate and you get that when you get into the face-to-face level.

Advertising and publicity material produced by Amnesty International UK clearly highlights the potential contribution that individual members can make to human rights issues by becoming a member of the organisation. For example, one leaflet states: 'You will make a difference simply by joining and giving a donation'. Comments from the Campaigns Co-ordinator demonstrate how the Campaigns Department views financial subscription as an important basis of membership activity:

> ....we use the terminology of active and non-active but I suppose the fact that people are members is one level of activism. Just signing a cheque, and being bothered enough to say yes I am motivated enough, or I have been pestered enough to want to get you off my back. But they have made a commitment. It is not nothing.

As the Local Groups Co-ordinator observed, this type of membership is important for lobbying purposes:

It is always useful for us to say that we have got 120,000 members when it comes to lobbying, to show that we have got quite broad support. I think it is also useful for local groups when they go to lobby their MPs to be able to say in this constituency we have X hundred or thousand members.

She went on to note that the relatively high membership of Amnesty International often acts as an index of the wider status of the organisation: 'We are the largest human rights organisation and because of our membership base I think we are seen as a bit more legitimate'. The notion that the overall size of membership provides some form of validation for a campaigning group such as Amnesty International is indicative of the previously discussed 'protest businesses' identified by Jordan and Maloney (1997). The Local Groups Co-ordinator observed that:

Sometimes we have to be careful that we don't always think about quantity and not quality. But we know that with certain techniques that we use it is the quantity that matters and certainly not the quality....high quantity and low quality appeals are something that people can engage with.

One can also detect a critique of certain aspects of established forms of activism within the Exodus collective. There is a clear attempt in the collective to move away from established norms of practice, and to operate according to alternative models of deliberation, decision-making and organisation. Specifically, rigid structures are rejected in favour of mechanisms that are seen as more likely to foster relations of equality and mutuality. Interestingly, the main organisers within the collective have attempted to introduce these strongly egalitarian structures and mechanisms in a self-conscious fashion. Again, one can detect a questioning of traditional aspects of participation that have become largely discredited in the eyes of the original members of the collective. This is a point I will discuss in more detail in Chapter Seven when I examine the tendency for long-term participants in established forums of political activity to question the usefulness and validity of existing modes of discourse. The collective is keen to bypass the perceived inadequacies of these forums such as political parties. These are perceived as largely discredited by many members of the collective. As one member put it:

....the Labour Party could be seen as part of that system again. It has got that same hierarchical base....it's ideas have been tried and tested and become immersed in society as it stands....it is just another part of that system. Equally as rejected as the Conservative Party....they are all part of the same thing....they are part of the problem itself. They are the problem, we are the solution.

The collective purports to operate within a loose and organic structure with no formal rules or norms of membership. One prominent member observed that Exodus is 'the most unorganised organisation I've ever known'. Another observed that 'it is different here because there is no set structure'. This is seen to contrast directly with the more rigid organisational structures widely encountered in established political groups. It is primarily these various organisational factors that one founding member believed distinguishes Exodus from other established political groupings. He referred to the 'design and fault' character of existing political organisations such as the Labour Party, but reverses this to define Exodus as 'fault and design'. Whereas groups such as political parties are premised upon an established design or structure against which any discrepancy is defined as a fault, Exodus prefers to try out an idea first and then develop a design or way of doing things from problems that are encountered. In many respects, this appears to reverse more traditional assumptions about the nature of participatory membership. Rather than new members being advised on how to successfully adopt existing procedures, Exodus appears to be more interested in enabling members to influence the design and nature of the system through which the collective operates and governs itself. Another member observed that the innovative structure of Exodus means that 'you don't necessarily need the authority and the organisation that a normal group would have. You don't have that structural need....we don't have to be told'.

Reinforcing Activism?

Attempts to critique existing forms of activism were not so evident in discussions with the Housing Department responsible for the Tenants' Associations. The Tenants Participation Officer noted how Tenants' Associations have to be prepared to rely upon the contributions of small numbers of key individuals. When discussing the role of the Chair in local Tenants' Associations, he noted that the Chair 'tends to be the most important person in our groups....we would see the Chair as being the person who gives direction to the group, a focal point'. He also noted that these key individuals are seen as 'a person we would maybe approach to start with on any issues that we have got on consultation'. Reflecting the data presented in Chapter Two, the Tenants' Participation Officer also went on to comment on the tendency for Chairs to play a central role within the group over long periods of time:

> They are very much the, if you like, linchpin of how the groups operate. They are usually the person who is either the one who help set it up or was most involved when the groups got underway. And it tends to be a role that continues for them. I can't remember the last time we had a Chair actually voted out. So they are a link with some sort of continuity. They were on the old committee and they are on the new committee.

Interestingly, he was aware that the prominent position often held by the most heavily involved tenants was something that could not be easily denounced. He felt that a minority form of participation was an inevitable aspect of the council's relationship with local tenants. When discussing the low levels of participation, he observed that 'I don't know whether it is good or bad. I think it is inevitable'. He went on to state that 'local democracy, just like any form of democracy, involves some people actually becoming activists. But the number of people who will become activists is limited....literally handfuls. So, good, bad or indifferent, I think it's inevitable'. He noted that 'we are realistic and realise you're not going to pack halls out....to get them to elect tenants' committees or even come and listen to things which may be important to them. Because it is very difficult to get people into public meetings'. Elsewhere, he observed that 'you are never going to get more than a small group that actually want to become involved....so I think that provided they make every effort to just keep people informed, then that is about the best we can hope for'.

These sentiments place a strong emphasis on those individuals who become involved in such groups. This, in turn, raises the question of what types of members such organisations might need in order to continue to function in their current format. The Residents' Association Committee members to whom I spoke provided some insight into this theme. One member of almost forty years standing observed that:

> I think the main skill which people have to apply in local organisations such as ours is the writing of reports, the writing of minutes, the formulation of your ideas or your complaint so that you can get a proper drafted letter and get everything done correctly. Because there is nothing worse than having an association which looks foolish in the eyes of the bureaucrats......if you can keep your association to a high level of sophistication and efficiency then it commands more respect.

This ability to work within certain formal administrative parameters will be taken up in the next chapter when I explore the prevalence of forms of participation built around management and organisational factors. These comments are also instructive in illustrating the level of formality that becomes necessary when civil society structures enter into communication with institutions of the state.

A further dimension of the forms of participation sought by local authorities was highlighted by the Tenants Participation Officer when he noted that 'I think we would expect the Chair to make sure that the various members of the committee were actually fulfilling the roles they need to do'. In this sense, the most centrally involved participants are encouraged to play a key role of personnel management. A similar sentiment was evident in discussions with the Campaigns Department of Amnesty International UK. The Local Groups Co-ordinator highlighted the perceived value of local group members who are able to manage the internal life of local groups. She noted that:

> A local group can still be effective when it has got a dictator in charge. Because either everyone thinks that person is wonderful or because everyone has known each other for a long time....dictator groups can work and they can be very, very effective because they are very purposeful and they pull people along.

In conclusion, one could initially suggest that the location of a structure on the spectrum that stretches between the state and civil society exerts a strong influence on its internal membership policy. For instance, Tenants' Associations have been shown to have a highly rigid and long established policy toward the nature of membership. Exodus, on the other hand, has a more open and flexible model of membership.

However, one should not assume that this endorses clear-cut conclusions about the approach of such bodies to the role of their members. The findings discussed in this chapter have also illustrated the range of conflicting tensions that currently inform the structures operating within the political public sphere. For example, the question of active involvement of members has been shown to be a source of some contention. Amnesty International and the Labour Party are both currently engaged in developing critiques of traditional forms of membership activism. Opportunities for internal deliberation and input into policy processes have been shown to be a problematic issue for these organisations. Whereas the management and administration of organisational tasks has been highlighted as a key form of membership participation, opportunities for input to policy processes has been shown to be currently subject to substantial revision. With this in mind, there is a sense in which the organisations in question tend to instrumentalise the political process by limiting the role of members within the organisation. This is perhaps not entirely surprising, but the fact that a group such as Amnesty International displays instrumental tendencies at the expense of a more open form of deliberation may force us to question the position of such groups within the schema developed by Habermas. One can also see from the findings that although Exodus defines itself by its rejection of more traditional political cultures, this does not necessarily preclude the development of exclusionary tendencies.

The data outlined in the present chapter has also raised questions about the attitude of the members of the organisations. For example, how does the drive for large membership levels adopted by Amnesty International and, increasingly, by the Labour Party impact upon the perceptions and assumptions of members? Indeed, one might also pose the question of the extent to which members of such organisations actually want a deliberative input into such groups. If the motivation of members is shown to be largely instrumental in character, then fundamental questions can be raised about the relationship between such forms of participation and the Habermasian model. It is also apparent that there is currently a widespread critique of activism within large-scale political organisations. But what is it exactly about existing forms of participation that inspires such skepticism? In some sense, this question feeds into the broader lack of understanding about what might actually constitute activism to which I have already referred. In the next chapter, I will take up these points by discussing in more detail the various types of participation that actually function within the different organisations. This will enable me to develop a typology of the forms of participation that exist within the political public sphere. This overview of voluntary political participation is intended to lay the foundations for a more detailed analysis of the process of taking part in various forms of political participation. This, in turn, will shed more light on the question of exactly how particular forms of political participation become embedded in the various structures of the political public sphere.

7 Mapping a Typology of Political Participation and Activism

The attitude of political structures toward their members provides only a partial picture of the nature of the political public sphere. Having examined the perspective of the various organisations toward their members, it is now necessary to focus more closely on the nature of participation itself. In this chapter I begin this task by presenting a typology of political participation and activism. This is intended to illustrate the range of activity that occurs within the various organisations studied in the course of this research. Having investigated a relatively wide range of organisations, one might have initially expected to encounter radically different forms of participation. Somewhat surprisingly, the findings indicate that there are a number of strong similarities that bridge the activism that occurs within the various organisations. Of course, important differences remain but the findings suggest that it is productive to view political activity as variations located along a continuum rather than assuming that there are strictly compartmentalised forms of activism. However, I begin my analysis with an aspect of the participatory schema that is specific to large-scale organisations.

Minimalist Participation

The first dimension of political activity that I intend to outline is what I have labelled as 'minimalist participation'. In Chapter Two I highlighted the continuing growth of what Jordan and Maloney (1997) refer to as 'protest businesses'. Richardson (1995) argues that in contemporary liberal democracies, the political role of citizens is increasingly akin to that of a consumer. He asserts that a market of political participation and activism has developed to meet the changing political needs of citizens. In the context of the growth of increasingly specialised single-issues and high membership turnovers within campaigning groups, it is argued that 'participation today seems to be characterised by the equivalent of impulse buying in a supermarket' (Richardson, 1995, p. 129). Jordan and Maloney (1997, p. 70) similarly refer to the support of Friends of the Earth as 'couch participation'.

During the course of the interviews, I came across strong evidence to suggest that this image of an increasingly commodified sphere of political activity has some validity. Not surprisingly, this was especially true of Amnesty International, but it was also clearly apparent in my discussions with Labour Party members, particularly those who had joined recently. The emergence of such forms of participation has ramifications for the types of expectations that citizens have about becoming a member of such groups. Increasingly, they tend to anticipate an extremely restricted role within these bodies.

For a large number of the Amnesty International members to whom I spoke, the value of being a member of the organisation stems primarily from the ability to make some kind of 'personal statement'. Perhaps because of its high public profile and large size, Amnesty International is widely perceived as the main forum for expressing such a statement about human rights. For these respondents, membership is seen primarily as a chance to express a commitment to the theme of human rights but not as an opportunity to directly take part in the campaigning activity of Amnesty International:

> Amnesty is very much a one way organisation in that it is about giving. I'm not going to get a knighthood or MBE for being in Amnesty. It is an organisation through which you can demonstrate your opinion and what you stand for.
>
> I am pretty certain that I joined because I wanted to make some kind of a statement. I wanted to do something.
>
> I suppose it was a way of registering a statement saying I am bothered, I care.
>
> I think it was probably more of a case of wanting to be a number and make a statement and be counted rather than just talk about it with my friends.

The decision to join Amnesty International is consequently perceived by some members as a preferable alternative to merely supporting Amnesty International and making no effort to contribute. Joining is therefore seen as the bare minimum that can be done by concerned individuals. These comments illustrate this more clearly:

> I see what I do within Amnesty, even if it a little bit, as useful to the organisation.
>
> I think it is better than nothing. Better I am a member than doing nothing at all.

Closely related to this is the suggestion that by becoming a member, the profile of Amnesty International and human rights is being increased. As one member observed:

> If there aren't people committed to being part of it, being part of the organisation, to increasing its size and numbers then it isn't likely to succeed....I think it is so that they can actually show the size of the organisation. A card-carrying membership is an indication of the strength of an organisation like Amnesty.

The idea that joining a large-scale organisation is an opportunity to express some form of political statement is not only restricted to Amnesty International. During the interviews with some Labour Party members, I detected similar sentiments to those expressed by members of Amnesty International. I have shown in the previous chapter that the membership policy of the Labour Party has undergone significant change in recent times. It has been shown that changes to the internal structure of the Labour Party have perhaps cultivated a membership that is structured around less active contributions from individual members. There was evidence from some respondents that these changes have had implications for the nature of Party membership. It interesting to note that comments to this effect came primarily from Party members who had joined in the past few years. One such Labour Party member commented on how he perceived his decision to join the Party as a way of expressing a statement:

> I don't have a lot of expectations. I mean, basically a lot of it is actually about making a statement against the state of things at the moment....but I don't expect a great deal from within the Party.....I don't expect to suddenly become a major activist within it or to get into politics and all the rest of it on a major level. It is just a little bit here and there to help out. A token gesture.

Another Party member described in similar terms how he perceived his involvement in the Party:

> I want to be a member and leave it at that.....I'm a sleeping partner really....there is the National Executive Committee that we elect, and that's one job you could say I do. And there are questionnaires. I've had two of them and I fill them in. So that is something isn't it? So I participate to a degree.

A key aspect of the rationale for joining Amnesty International is the idea that it provides some financial support for the campaigning work of the organisation. For those members who do very little within the organisation, this was seen as a particularly useful contribution. This was evident in the comments of two members:

> There is an element of, to be honest, just putting a tiny bit of money where my mouth was. I think it was also a feeling that if organisations like Amnesty aren't properly supported in that sense then they won't have the voice that they need.

> ....even if I'm not actually doing anything I am at least contributing one membership fee to the funds.

Once again, a Labour Party member who had recently joined the Party expressed similar statements to his Amnesty International counterparts. He observed that 'It is basically about just being a member....financial contributions....not particularly to get major involvement.....I want to keep it fairly low key'. With the expansion of this form of participation, one can see that the definition of what comes under the auspice of 'activism' is expanding. A Constituency Party Secretary to whom I spoke observed that:

> I think you find that people's definition of activism is now different. Wherever they are on the spectrum of activity they will now see themselves as being active. So, paying a subscription and offering a minimal commitment is now seen as active....so I think the definitions of activism have changed because the nature of the membership has changed.

Another long-term Party member felt that the underlying nature of Party membership was undergoing substantial change. He argued that the growth of the Party membership was tied to the growing effort of the Party leadership to mobilise people on a minimalist basis:

> I would feel they [newer members] are different. They are partly different in profile, they are different in the sort of people they are. And I think they are different in terms of what they expect the Party to do....they expect the Party to do the more modern things like putting them on mailing lists and trying to sell them a T-shirt and merchandise, and selling them credit cards and so on. I'm not sure they want or expect to go to meetings....I think they are quite different from myself and maybe more long standing members who see the membership of the Party as very much a way to influence existing democratic processes....it is a whole new way of looking at Party life.

The growth of this minimal form of participation throughout large-scale political structures has significant effects on the perceptions and expectations of members about the organisation in question. With regard to Amnesty International, a large number of the respondents reported notably low expectations about their relationship with the organisation. Others made very similar comments:

> I don't feel they [Amnesty International UK] need an awful lot from us apart from the money to continue.

> I pay the sub and I try to read the literature. I take that much interest. I don't think they expect a lot more from me.

> I don't know if they expect anything from me. I think they would hope that we would get involved with what they are trying to do but that is all.

These comments were made despite the fact that there appeared to be something of a consensus amongst the members interviewed in the course of this research that the membership is fundamental to the work of Amnesty International. A few members contrasted Amnesty International with organisations such as Greenpeace that offer very little space for members to participate. According to the interviews with members, a distinctive feature of Amnesty International was the role and position afforded to members. Comments from several members illustrate this clearly:

> Amnesty is structured in a way that the membership is absolutely crucial. It survives or falls totally on that. Not just in terms of having members but on those members actually doing what needs to be done. Amnesty could not survive just at head office....so Amnesty is totally dependent on its grass roots. And to me there is something very healthy about that.

> I think the membership is fundamentally important. It seems to me that without a body of opinion that is capable of being mobilised then Amnesty would have much less credibility.

However, it was also clear that for a large number of members this 'ideal' often fails to translate into reality. Rather than experiencing a close relationship with the British section of Amnesty International some members feel that there is a distance between themselves and the organisation itself. One consequence of this is that Amnesty International is often perceived as somewhat remote by members. For example, one member remarked:

> I'm close to the issues. But close to Amnesty? Probably not very close...it is very easy for me to give forty pounds a year and get the magazine. But other than that, I don't feel very close.

Other members similarly commented on the distant relationship that they experience with Amnesty International:

> It is all just a little opaque to me. I thought a moment ago you were going to ask me what do you see when you think of Amnesty and I don't. I have no real picture of it. It is not particularly visible to me as an organisation.

> I used to feel involved on the fringes, but now it would be difficult to know who to write to at Amnesty. I just feel remote from it all.

> I have experienced an increase in interest in the issues over the years, but only at a conceptual level.

Some members clearly experience a gap between themselves and the structures of Amnesty International. It was also apparent that a number of members perceived Amnesty International as a highly instrumental organisation. Several respondents felt that Amnesty International was primarily motivated by the need for funds, and they suggested that this defined their relationship with the organisation. One such member remarked that:

> My impression is that they just expect me to pay my subscriptions and write a few letters. I feel that maybe they respond differently to members who don't do a lot. They don't seem to contact me much anymore and I'm not really sure why that is. Maybe they have just given up on me because I haven't been actively involved.

Comments from two other members illustrate this theme more clearly:

> I do object to feeling that the only time they are really interested in us is when they want our money. They already have my money.

> They only ever phone if they want us to go and collect money for them. They don't phone to say have you written your letter yet or would you like to write another letter....they only ever contact us if they want us to go out and collect money for them.

A number of members were somewhat disillusioned with Amnesty International, primarily because of the perceived view of members as a source of funds. Perhaps somewhat surprisingly, a number of the respondents were concerned about this situation. Several members felt that Amnesty International has become too cumbersome and is rapidly becoming detached from its membership base. According to these members, the emphasis within the organisation has gradually switched to principles of the business world. As one member put it:

> ....it almost becomes like a business but it isn't meant to be a service industry.

> It is almost as if it has got too big and too successful. It has got to the point now where Amnesty relies on its members for money and more money.

> Perhaps you expect a certain amount of efficiency but you also expect to feel valued in some way....I haven't felt valued at all as a member.

The question of internal democracy within Amnesty International is consequently rather remote for many members. As one respondent commented:

> I would assume that it [Amnesty International UK] is democratically organised, but to be honest I don't really know.....I have this image of a group of people waving a magic wand somewhere. I don't even know if they have paid employees....I suppose there is a core group of people who administer the whole shebang. I suppose I see them as the ones who do it all...

Closely related to this is the sense in which some Amnesty International members felt that membership of the organisation entailed 'buying into' a pre-defined policy agenda. As one member put it:

I always feel that one of the strengths of Amnesty is its clarity. Whilst I totally accept that there are grey areas, one of the options for Amnesty is to stay as they are and say we don't deal with these other areas. We deal with this and that is what we base it all on....the other option is to go into the grey areas but then you are going to have debate. What will happen is that some people will come down on one side and some on the other. And then you are into some problem areas....there is a bit of me that would be very reluctant to go into those areas. I think there is a whole area that could be a minefield of confusion when you start to go outside of your remit....in practical terms my heart would say let's stay dead clear on this and stay exactly on those lines.

The findings presented above suggest that this minimalist form of political engagement exerts a strong influence within the realm of political participation. However, it would be naïve to assume that a more traditional form of active involvement in political life no longer plays a key role in the political public sphere. In fact, the interview data indicates that minimalist participation is only one of a number of influential facets of particiaption.

Administrative Participation

During the course of my interviews with those respondents who displayed high levels of involvement in political life, I became aware of a strong tendency toward forms of activity that were built around administrative concerns. By this, I mean that many of the more active respondents to whom I spoke appeared to be directing their energies not toward the discussion of what might be classed as 'political' issues, but toward questions of internal management and organisation. The political activity of these participants consequently becomes inward looking and concerned with the handling of short-term tasks that maintain the organisational structure of the participatory structure in question. Indeed, for some respondents there was almost a celebration of this administrative side of their participation. It should be noted that this 'backroom' dimension of participation could be detected in all of the organisations to varying degrees. The members of Exodus to whom I spoke were keen to move away from what they see as a traditional political concern with administrative issues, but this appears to be increasingly compromised as the collective has become embroiled in the local policy process. I will discuss this in more detail shortly.

Initially, the focus on 'backroom' participation was most evident during my interviews with active Labour Party members. A number of these respondents defined their involvement as a form of activity that takes place 'behind the scenes'. Some members to whom I spoke had become heavily involved in administrative tasks, and stressed the importance and value to the Party of such work. One branch election organiser to whom I spoke made reference to what he perceived as his administrative skills when he first joined the Party:

> On my letter of application to the branch I actually said I wanted to use my organisational and administrative skills to the benefit of the Party. So I did join in order to bring what I classed as my own personal skills in organisation....I'm in an administration type job so we thought why don't you use your talents in doing something like organising.

A Constituency Secretary remarked that 'I think it does reflect politically on our level of activity if things like the admin side are kept under control'. Similarly, another member noted that 'in terms of political benefit it might be very back room stuff but my view is that....it is unsung stuff'. But this was not only restricted to those members who had taken on a formal role within the Party structures. One member defined a Party activist as 'somebody who is willing to do the donkey work to be perfectly honest'. He felt that this entailed a variety of tasks including canvassing, delivering leaflets and attempting to recruit new members. Another member made a very similar point when she observed that:

> You are the person who takes on the donkey work aren't you? The Party bosses might get off their backside and sign a bit of paper, but you are the actual man in the field that is doing the work....you are the person who is doing the actual work or the manual part of it.

She went on to identify fund raising as a major part of Party involvement: 'the main thing is to raise money to keep the Party going....that is an important part of it all'. For some members remaining behind the scenes in this way is an important aspect of how they interpret their own participation. A few active Labour Party members indicated the perceived importance of this type of participation by describing in detail to me their efforts to work in the 'backroom'. For example, a branch election organiser gave an account of his attempts to redesign the workings of the local branch at election times:

> We wanted things done right....it was very old-fashioned. We basically had to drag some of the procedures with the elections into the present time. It's no good saying they had never heard of computers because that's not true

but they weren't interested at all in doing any kind of computerisation. The newsletters and such were still being done on a typewriter and all of those things were being done the slow way....so from the first off we produced a very highly stylised type of newsletter.

He went on to describe how he had first become involved in the organisational side of a local election:

I remember going to one election....I wasn't in charge of it, and I was told that whoever was running the committee wasn't up to it. And I was told never mind about upsetting anybody, go in there and take over. I wasn't quite happy about that, but then again I knew what they were saying because the person was a very nice person but they didn't think they were a strong enough person to run the election committee....the first thing we found when we got there was we found out they had done all the cards and they had written them in felt tip pen and it hadn't gone through....that is the sort of thing that was hours of wasted effort. And so I did go in and take over. And I enjoyed it. But even in those early days I think they recognised that I am an organiser.

This pride in working within the administrative aspect of participation was also evident in interviews with some Amnesty International members. One respondent who had been involved in his local group described in detail a similar process of restructuring the group's newsletter:

....and for a couple of years I did the newsletter. Quite a task really. Getting things in, getting the information there, getting it photocopied, collated and sent out to these people...that was a good contribution and it was appreciated....I had great fun with the newsletter because it had been done the same way for so long. And I just started playing around with that....it was all about rearranging it and making it different.

Very similar sentiments can also be detected in the comments of a Labour Party member who had been involved in redesigning the management structure of the local Constituency Labour Party Headquarters. He rated this as the most important aspect of his involvement in the Party and noted that 'I have actually been instrumental in changing the whole structure there....so getting the structure right has been part of the fun'. He went on to observe that 'this is my job now and I have the power to say we are going to do this on finance, and we have actually got a sensible thing working'. A Constituency Party Secretary to whom I spoke outlined the nature of his participation in the Party in a similar vein:

> I think it is the business of maintaining a Party....you need to keep the thing spinning along. It is like plates on sticks. One plate at the end of the row is starting to fall off again and you have to run to the end of the row and start the plate spinning again. Parties are a bit like that, so they need help as well....it needs constant maintenance and attention. You just can't let it go.

Interestingly, this concept of backroom involvement was alluded to not only on numerous occasions, but was also contrasted quite sharply with what was seen as more overtly 'political' activity. Indeed, the label of 'political activist' was largely shunned by many of the more heavily involved respondents. With regard to the interviews with Labour Party members, I was struck by the lack of enthusiasm for what might be defined as the political or policy side of the Party. For example, an experienced branch secretary confided to me that 'I never wanted to be, and never shall be, in the limelight...I feel much more confident and I work better behind the scenes rather than in the front'.

This distinction between the administrative and political realm of participation is interesting for the way that it subtly pushes away certain aspects of discourse, most particularly the discussion of policy issues. For these Party members there was a positive affirmation of the administrative aspects of their involvement but an evident caution about wanting to become involved in political issues. For instance, the member who had been instrumental in redesigning the Constituency Labour Party Headquarters management structure was keen to describe himself as a 'party worker' rather than a political activist. He stressed that his involvement in the restructuring of the Headquarters was providing important support for the wider political aspects of the Labour Party. He stated that

> I would use the phrase active in the Labour Party, but I don't think I would describe myself as a political activist....I suppose I would like in quotes to be a bit more involved in the political side of the Party but I suspect that I won't readily do so.

Similarly, the aforementioned branch secretary stated that 'I look upon myself as an active member of the Party, but not a Party activist'. Another Labour Party member observed that 'I don't have vast political ambitions, so I feel I can actually do my bit in other ways'. The distinction between political and administrative domains of Party involvement was also detectable in the comments of one member who posed the question:

Are you just going to be active and help them do what they [the Labour Party] want or are you going to go the other way and go over the top? I'm thinking of this bloke they call Swampy. I think he takes what he is doing too far. The same as some Party activists go too far. They go over the top. Instead of working for the Party they work so hard the other way that they defeat it. They get too bigoted....I suppose I have been more of a doer than a talker.

This distinction between a 'doer' and a 'talker' contains an implicit distinction between those members who are willing to undertake administrative tasks to support the Party and those who are more inclined toward ideological or policy debate. I also spoke to one experienced Party member who noted how he was well aware of the tension between this backroom form of participation and the political dimension of the Party. He observed that:

You are there as a foot soldier. This was a problem for me almost as soon as I joined. I'm not a natural fundraiser. I'm not somebody who is very good at going out and rattling the tin....one of the main things that you feel you are a member for is to go out there and make money. You know, jumble sales, raffles, fairs, stalls, wonderful new ways of making money. That was the whole thing I realised about the Party after about two years....I felt very much that was what they wanted us to be....to get new members, but above all to make money. To make it all tick....you quickly realised you are there basically as a vote gaining machine. This is how it felt as a member. I was either there to make money for the Party or to get votes for the Party. What I wasn't there for was to make significant social and political change. That was loud and clear.

Others were familiar with the conflict between these two aspects of Party involvement, but were more willing to see a connection between the two. One member shrewdly observed that:

I guess what tends to predominant is organisation. I would say organisation is important. Fund raising. Leaflets. Elections. Campaigns. I think you would find that the predominant view is that that tends to dominate in meetings for instance. But I also think that historically the Party has always tried to introduce discussion as well. How do we develop ideas? How do we develop individual members? Thinking on things. And that is difficult to do those two things.

The Constituency Party Secretary to whom I spoke interpreted his involvement as primarily administrative in character, but he was quick to highlight the importance of such activity to the political side of the Party. As he put it:

> I try to ensure that there is a local Party organisation, which is possibly more administration than activity. Well, administration is activity....there does need to be a local Party base and I see my primary role as ensuring that I help that to continue. Making sure you have got the local structure to support the national Party. Because I think those things are actually quite important in political terms. I don't differentiate between the administration and the political side. One needs the other. They are mutually inclusive I suppose.

This Constituency Labour Party Secretary was aware of problems associated with focusing too heavily on this 'backroom' activity. But he also acknowledged that the pressures of ensuring that Labour candidates were elected locally and nationally often made this difficult:

> Our priorities are making sure we have got an organisation for campaigning for general elections....and then you have got the regular local elections and the European elections as well. So there is that cycle of business that we have to got through...the process of selecting candidates, then you have the campaign, the election. You have to be carefully it doesn't become the means to an end, in that all you are doing is going out there and trying to get councillors elected.

It is clear however that it is not only the vagaries of the election process that cause the prominence of this administrative aspect of participation. This aversion to activity that might be defined as 'political' was also evident amongst many of the active Tenants and Residents' Association members that I spoke to. One long-term committee member of the Association remarked that 'there is one thing that we don't end up in, and that is politics'. Another Committee member who had been involved for a number of years observed that:

> I've no time for people who are anti this or anti that. I don't believe in it. There's too much of that....I'm not going to strut around with banners and God knows what else saying we don't want this or we don't want that.

It is important to highlight the informal way in which this exclusion of political issues often occurs. Detectable in the comments of the Residents' Association members is an unspoken assumption that Committee members would resist efforts to include more overtly political discussion. For instance, one Residents' Association member recounted how the Committee had subtly blocked efforts to raise such political issues:

> We have had one or two people who have come in and tried to be political....there was a chap and he was a strong union activist. And he tried to ease politics into it, but he got very quietly eased out. So one or two people have tried to bring little minor political matters in but we always turn it round so that it becomes non-political.

It was clear to me that for a sizable portion of the active respondents to whom I spoke the administrative character of their involvement was quite appealing. One Labour Party member even went so far as to suggest that 'I guess there are certain people....who quite like to get bored by that nitty gritty stuff'. An Amnesty International member who had been involved in various environmental and campaigning groups made a very similar point about the people who are attracted to participatory bodies. He felt that those people who become actively involved within groups are often motivated by a desire to administer and manage these groups:

> These things tend to attract people who are like that....the people who want to run an organisation. The ones who want to formalise everything. Maybe they are frustrated officials or something....I want to get away from all that now while still being as democratic as possible.

This point will be expanded in the next chapter when I discuss the relationship between activism and the tendency toward controlling participatory mechanisms.

But what about those members who were not particularly involved in the groups I studied -were they aware of the influence of this backroom activity and those who practice it? And did this have any effect on their involvement? One Amnesty International member felt that local groups tend to become concerned with issues of administration at the expense of more pertinent issues:

> It seems to me that some local groups deteriorate to such a point where they become a money raising machine and nothing else. So all they are doing is becoming the Amnesty jumble sale group....I think that is why I don't want to get involved. I've done jumble sales. I did that at playgroup. To me, that is not what Amnesty's about.

Other Amnesty International members similarly felt that the purpose of the organisation becomes subverted by the influence of this administrative participation. This is clearly shown in the following comments:

> The actual point of an organisation like Amnesty is then perhaps lost in the fund raising and the quizzes and so on. But we certainly didn't join it for any sort of social input. We don't want that social life and we don't want the jumble sales.

> For me, there has to be some kind of trade off. If I am going to do it I want to have some tangible result. I don't want to say aren't we good, we raised £100 this Saturday. I want some poor bugger to be released out of some horrible jail in Columbia or somewhere. If we are just talking about making money then we are not doing the business locally....raising money is not much of a challenge.

This concern about the dominance of administrative activity is also felt within the Campaigns Department of the British section of Amnesty International. As the Local Groups Co-ordinator observed:

> The business of a group is quite tedious, and groups need to organise things so that meetings are not all nitty gritty planning things that can take forever....people don't go to a group meeting to find out who is running a stall. They want to know how they can help somebody directly who is a prisoner of conscience. So I think the groups need to focus on what Amnesty is really about because groups perhaps get lost in that organisational aspect.

The influence of this aspect of participation is also recognised by members of the Exodus collective. Reflecting the general interest in constructing an alternative to dominant modes of participation, the collective has made a conscious effort to move away from this administrative type of activity. One member referred to the attraction of being able to participate in a group that tries to avoid excessive administration:

> That was a big attraction for me. To be able to be a part of that. To show that we can do things and we can do them differently, and there is no need for all that shit. All that bureaucracy and red tape....let's get away from all that.

However, it must be noted that the administrative dimension of political participation has become more prominent as Exodus has become more directly involved with the local policy process. The description that one member gave of his role in the collective is strongly reminiscent of the comments from active Labour Party and Amnesty International members:

> There can be days when not a lot happens. Maybe just one fax will come over and I will just ring up whoever it is for and let them know it is here. Other days we can be working until five or six in the morning. That's the way it goes sometimes. If something needs to be done quickly....it is like this has happened, let's have an idea, how can we use the computer to make things easier for ourselves. It pretty much revolves around it now.....letters, faxes, can we email them? Or we might do a letter for one person and we end up faxing it to half a dozen different people.....forwarding letters and copying them to people. It is all quite involved really. All those bits and pieces....that is what I have sat doing basically, just training myself.

The question of why this aspect of political participation is so prominent within the structures of voluntary political activity is crucial to understanding the disruption of political communication. The fieldwork shows that in order to become successfully active within participatory structures it is often necessary for participants to gradually scale down their original aims and intentions once they have entered the organisation in question. A narrowing of political discourse occurs in which questions of a moral-practical nature are sidelined by more pragmatic and administrative issues. This often leads to an instrumentalisation of their participation, and the sphere of administrative activity provides an available forum within which some forms of limited political identity can be developed. I will take up this point in more detail in the next chapter when I discuss the question of what participants learn from their involvement in political life about the reality of political activity. It is also evident that organisations such as the Labour Party, Amnesty International and Tenants' or Residents' Associations need members who are willing to take on administrative tasks on a regular basis. This type of activity is consequently sanctioned and encouraged at an organisational level, as we have seen in the previous chapter.

Social Participation

A further aspect of political activity that bridges the various organisations relates to the 'social' dimension of political life. For some of the respondents, active involvement in political life offers the facility for establishing social links. One Labour Party member observed that '...in a sense the Labour Party offered me the opportunity to get to know a lot of people....people who will have things in common with me'. Another member observed that 'it does almost become like a mini social circle'. He went on to say that 'we have found everything from baby-sitters to other people we have got to know through it'. He also added that 'it fulfills that function as a bit of a social organisation....in a funny way it is a part of our life, so to speak'. Another member similarly referred to 'people that just like to be there. It's a good way of meeting like-minded people and organising dos and things'. These sentiments were echoed in the comments of two more Labour Party members:

> I felt I wanted to be part of something....so in a sense the Labour Party offered me that opportunity to get to know a lot of people. People who will have things in common with me.....at the end of the day, it does have a social dimension. I went to lots of dos at High Street [local Labour Party Headquarters]. We went to people's house. We went to community centres. All sort of things like that.

The good thing is that a lot of the time, after the meetings it becomes a bit of a social event. That is the time to stay and join in if you can. There are no formalities then. You are not working to an agenda or going over x, y, z that has been written down. And that is when it will come out that I only live up the road form you. Knowing that if you meet them in the street and you have got a problem you can say that is the bloke, give him a ring and he can sort it out.

For some members, this social aspect of Party involvement may even displace the 'political' dimension of activism:

> ....plenty of people I know are quite active at the level of seeing it particularly for the social side of it. They go to branch meetings, they like going to the pub afterwards, they will have a commitment to go down the Socialist Club, they will organise social functions. And for them it is a key bit of their social life. But the last thing on earth they would want to do would be to be on any of the committees and to start getting terribly involved in the political activities.

An Amnesty International member made a similar judgement about some of those who were active in local groups:

> I bet that if you went to any of the local groups you would find people who were there because they want to be there because they feel it is the right and moral thing to do. But there are other people there who need the group. They need that kind of thing because they don't have anything else in their

life....they are looking for some kind of social life. They see a regular thing happening with a group of pleasant people and there is the occasional coffee morning....and that is quite a nice thing to do.

She went on to suggest that these people are likely to take part because of their own personal needs for social contact:

You meet people who are like-minded and you all get together. You end up going along because you know you are going to meet people who you are going to get along with. It is a conduit. It is something that they can relate to and enjoy doing. But the secondary knock on effect is that they meet a group of people. And it is a nice thing to do and then they get involved. And they feel good about themselves.

One Amnesty International member who had been quite involved in a local group observed that 'we had the odd social sort of thing....you chatted to people and we also had a break in the middle, so there was a social level to it all'. He went on to highlight the attraction of the social dimension of participation: 'Well, there is a group of people there. And I suppose in a sense I don't have very many social groups....and I just enjoyed the mixing with people'. A Labour Party member made a similar point about the social attraction of involvement in the local branch:

It was a question of dashing up the road because we wanted to socialise afterwards. We wanted to have a drink afterwards....we felt that once the meeting was finished we wanted to stay together and socialise. Probably still discuss politics if you like, but in a more relaxed way. In fact, round the table with a glass of beer in your hand.

One Amnesty member noted that this aspect of activism is important in maintaining individual participation in the face of waning interest: 'if you begin to get fed up and you have got those people there who you see as friends as opposed to acquaintances then you would continue to go'.

Careerism

A further dimension of political participation that the findings revealed relates to the tendency for some people to adopt a careerist approach to political activity. These respondents had adopted a highly instrumental approach to their involvement in political life. This was most evident during my discussions with members of the Labour Party. One member defined the 'careerists' in the following manner:

> And there are undoubtedly the careerists....people that clearly want to involve themselves because they have got an ambition to be a councillor or whatever....they clearly see themselves as wanting to have a major impact on things within the Party. And to involve themselves in absolutely everything so that they are at the forefront of what is going on. So that clearly they are in there when you're looking for people to nominate at council level.

Another Party member remarked on how this form of careerism is often more influential within the Party than ideologically motivated forms of participation:

> I suppose a definition of activism is that it is something to do with the degree of commitment....these things are important and by doing a set of actions loosely associated with the Party I can make a contribution to achieving these ideological ends. Or alternatively, and perhaps more powerfully, careerism, to use a pejorative word. So by attending these meetings and by making the correct interventions in the variety of forums I can then become a councillor, chairman of such and such a committee or an MP and so on.

One Labour Party member recalled how he had rejoined the Party in order to possibly become a councillor:

> I've got friends who are Party agents who said why don't you become a councillor? I said I don't know I've never really though about it....So I said I would think about it....that is still ongoing. I'm considering it. That is what I'm hoping to be able to do within the Labour Party and get more involved that way.

Another Party member similarly remarked on how he had become involved in his local branch in order to be nominated as a school governor:

> I guess that the main active involvement that I have had was that by becoming a member of a political party I could then automatically be put forward as a local education nominated governor. And that happened and so I am now chair of governors at our local school. So it gave me that opportunity which was good.

Clearly, the sphere of voluntary political activity is susceptible to highly instrumental motives. This appears to be particularly true when one forum of participation is seen to represent a route to another form of political engagement, and thus acts as a basis for some form of participatory careerism. However, it would be overly simplistic to assume that the existence of this aspect of the participatory repertoire implies that all participants approach the political sphere with a highly developed and cohesive scheme for developing a political 'career'. In the next section, I explore the dimension of political participation that leads to many participants being informally coerced into taking a more active role in certain organisations.

Informal Coercion and Political Participation

The popular image of a political 'activist' is one of a highly politicised individual who has developed a habit of responding to political issues. The findings indicate that this is, at most, only a partial version of the reality of political participation. One area where this is most pronounced is in the informal coercion that is often imposed on participants to become more involved. Rather than assuming that all 'active' citizens decide to take up participation on a purely voluntary basis, the findings indicate that some participants find themselves pressurised informally to take on greater responsibilities and duties. Somewhat surprisingly, this informal coercion was firstly detectable amongst those respondents who had little involvement in their respective organisation. Many of the respondents who were less involved in their respective organisations were aware of the likelihood of being pressured into taking on tasks once they took the step of becoming more involved. This often created a tangible wariness about taking further steps into the world of participation. These worries were not unfounded. For example, a number of active Labour Party respondents spoke of being pressured into taking on office holding responsibilities within their local branch. Others referred to experiencing an informal obligation to remain within formal positions once a post had been taken up. There was an obvious concern amongst many of the less active respondents that once they entered the realm of more intense participation it would be difficult to protect themselves from informal pressure to become increasingly involved. Many feared being forced into taking on excessive workloads as part of their commitment to the group. A number of the respondents felt that once they had started attending meetings then they would have entered this higher level of involvement. Several Amnesty International members raised this point:

> There is a worry or feeling of being pressurised if you go along. I think there would be an expectation that one would have to become committed.

> I wouldn't want to go along and think that I would have to bring a pile of tasks away with me.

> I don't want to get drawn into the local organisation of Amnesty because at the moment I just can't cope with all that. It is too much.

> I think if I got involved locally with Amnesty it might be too much.

A number of the respondents consequently placed a restriction on the parameters of their own participation. These concerns about becoming more involved also appear to stem in part from a worry that there is little flexibility about the level of participation that one can take up. For these respondents, taking part in a more active manner necessarily implies a static and heavy commitment. This was summed up neatly by two Amnesty International members:

> I would be worried about not being able to determine to what extent you are going to be involved.

> I want to be able to make my time commitment and not feel obliged to make any more.

Clearly these respondents had made important assumptions about what would happen once they entered a local Amnesty International group. There is a feeling that one would be expected to take on a more active and elaborate role within the organisation. We can detect this in the testimony of this Amnesty International member when he outlined what he felt it would mean to start attending his local group and playing a role in local campaigning:

> If I were involved at the local level then I would expect that my role would change. I would then be becoming an agent of Amnesty. And I would be mediating with other individuals. In that case, I would want to be a lot more sure of my grounds. If only because if they ask me a question it would be insufficient to say I have got as much information as you have. That wouldn't seem to me to be adequate. So almost by definition, if my role changed in that way I would have to be much better informed.

He went on:

> It means to me that I don't just become a conduit. I become more of a mouthpiece. I'm capable of defending a position or proposing a position from a more solid basis of personal understanding.

The reluctance of a sizable portion of the Amnesty International respondents to become involved in a local group stems from this worry over commitment and informal pressure. However, this is not purely due to a distaste for such active involvement. A number of members also noted that they would feel some level of guilt over not being inclined to participate to the extent that other group members were able to. For example:

> What I don't want is to go along there and feel bad because everybody else is doing a lot while I have set my boundaries to do less...I would feel bad that I wasn't doing more. It is irrational of course because it is actually okay to do less. But I still feel bad if I am not doing more.
>
> I would hate to turn up and let people down.

A Labour Party member described similar feelings of guilt at not being more involved in his local branch:

> I do feel guilty on occasions but the guilt...is more because I can remember how much I used to do...I still dutifully trot out and deliver my leaflets, without feeling that it is a particular chore. When I'm doing that I usually think my God, is that what it has come to? Is this the full extent of my contribution this month? You know, deliver a pile of leaflets and go to the odd meeting.

Several Party members referred to the amount of 'guilt tripping' that goes on within local branches. One respondent described the pressure that members are under if they go on to become a councillor:

> It seems to me that the level of commitment of, for example, a councillor is absolutely grinding. I toyed with the idea of putting my name for council. I thought I just fancy maybe giving it a go. But I withdrew it actually before the end and I'm not sorry. The....machine grinds people into the ground in the end. The range of bloody meetings they go to. If you are a councillor you have the council meetings and the group meetings and so on. On top of these they really are expected to go to General Committees and Executive

Committees and be on this and be on that. I mean it really is a seven day a week meeting. It is like a guilt trip. You have to be there.

One Labour Party member referred to the 'little group that don't want to become councillors or can't....it is being looked upon for them to be Chairs and Secretaries and things like that. But they don't always want to do it'. This was evident in my discussion with a branch secretary who recounted how he had been asked to become a councillor on numerous occasions:

> ....some people, some councillors, they know me through one way or another. And they would like me to be with them in there. And some people have asked me because they think I would make a good councillor. And some people just ask because they think I ought to do it. And in fact one very good councillor was very insistent.

Another member observed that 'I'm fairly tough minded about not being guilt tripped into doing a whole load of things. There are a whole load of jobs and bits and pieces that could have been pushed on to me during my time'. It would therefore appear that the fears of the less active respondents have some basis. This is further supported by those respondents who confided that active participants will often seize upon any new member who shows an inclination toward some involvement. As one Amnesty International member observed:

> I do find that if you show an interest, however genuine, to an organisation like Amnesty then you are there. You are grabbed. They are desperate for people who are interested. They are desperate for people who want to be involved and want to do things....they want people to put displays up in libraries and go to meetings, but I don't need that.

A Labour Party branch election organiser similarly observed that:

> As soon as you get any kind of new blood you're pounced on really....they want you to join this and do you want to go on the GC and do you want to go on this committee....it is piled on to you very quickly.

He went on:

> With myself, one minute I joined....and within a matter of weeks I was taken up to see what the count was....and that was within weeks....almost straight away from the moment I joined I was out door knocking.

Another Labour Party member described how her active involvement had quickly developed in such a manner:

> Once you have got into one of these organisations you tend to then get sucked in deeper. I'm not saying that in a bad way but once you get interested and you start going deeper you do then start going in other things. So from then being at one meeting it becomes two meetings a week, or three meetings a fortnight and so on.

A Labour Party branch secretary to whom I spoke had decided to take a year off from his position, but his comments suggest that there is still a palpable pressure for him to continue in his role within the Party:

> I have already been warned that this time there is no way out. I must not look for an excuse because if I do then I will not be able to walk home. In other words, I will be kept in the branch office and that is where I will stay. The branch members will not let me come home.

In this context of informal coercion, routes into active involvement within the Exodus collective are relatively unusual. There is a clear opposition to the recruitment of new members. Rather, there is an interest in providing a space for those individuals who choose to approach the collective with a particular skill, ability or need. As one member observed: 'For those initial moments when they are coming into the collective it's never we go and ask them. It's always they come and approach us'. It is felt that by allowing new participants to offer their involvement then that individual's participation becomes, in the words of one member, a 'wanted input'. It is suggested that members then develop their own niches in a more 'natural' and organic fashion. It was noted that this was a suitable process for discovering whether 'people are on it, rather than trying to recruit people and then giving them assignments and little jobs....it just doesn't work like that'.

Yet at the same time, involvement in Exodus does tend to demand a great deal in terms of individual commitment. As one founding member put it 'all aspects of my life, including my children's future is tied up with Exodus now. It is a real way of life'. Another Exodus member similarly remarked that 'you can't be in Exodus and not be active. They go hand in hand with each other. If you expect to be part of it all then you can expect to be active'. This is of course not surprising in view of Exodus' efforts to develop and construct a community or collective structure. It does however suggest that the intense involvement with Exodus can appear especially demanding, particularly to those who remain on the fringes of the collective.

I have shown that the discourse of a sizable portion of political participation is predominantly administrative in character, but the picture of political participation still remains somewhat static. We therefore need to know something about how and why participants adopt the types of activity that I have outlined in this chapter. This question leads neatly into the theme of what actually takes place within the process of political participation, and how participants interpret the process of taking part in political life. This and a number of other related themes will be discussed in the next chapter.

8 Analysing the Process of Political Participation

In Chapter Two I sought to argue that analysis of political participation needs to be extended to include greater emphasis being placed on the actual process of involvement in political life. It was suggested that understandings of political participation should be rooted in the machinations of political life as it is experienced by those who actually take part, albeit in the context of a broader awareness of the forces shaping the political public sphere. In the past two chapters I have developed a picture of the dialectical relationship that exists between various political structures and different forms of participation that emerge within these contexts. Thus far, I have presented a picture of different forms of participation that develop across various political structures. I now move on to consider in more detail the ways in which these forms of political participation proceed. What exactly does it mean to take part in political participation? And how is this perceived by those who enter the political public sphere?

Arising out of the discussion presented in the previous chapter is the conundrum of how these different forms of participation actually develop within the structures of the political public sphere. In Chapter Three I have already identified the question of how skewed forms of political communication develop within the structures of the political public sphere as a key component of a Habermasian approach. The present chapter attempts to address this theme by analysing the types of political culture to be found in the 'real world' of citizen political participation. Drawing upon the testimonies of respondents and my own observation of group activities, this chapter seeks to focus on the experiences of the respondents within the various organisations and to draw some conclusions about what it actually means to be involved in these different arenas of the political public sphere.

There are two main stages to this investigation. Firstly, I consider the nature of the face-to-face discourse that takes place within the organisations I have studied. The interviews show clearly that at the heart of citizen involvement in political life is the interaction that takes place within the organisations. It is therefore particularly important to scrutinise those occasions in which internal group relations are mediated by membership meetings or similar discursive structures. I include comments from those who have been involved to some degree, but I also examine the assumptions of those who have not taken part in meetings. Rather than simply provide details of the mechanisms that sustain membership interaction, I intend to examine what goes on within these structures and how the respondents actually feel about these discursive processes. This dimension of political participation feeds directly into Habermas' concern over the ways in which discourse proceeds within the structures of the political public sphere. The impressions and meanings that participants take from their participation are central to this issue.

This leads neatly into the second major theme of this chapter. When referring to the political cultures that inhabit the structures of voluntary political participation it is important to pay some attention to the socialising processes that take place. From a Habermasian perspective, this issue is of particular significance. The ways in which certain forms of action acquire a status of normality can provide a useful index of the directions in which the political public sphere is developing. It will be shown that informal learning processes are a crucial component of the development of different dimensions of political participation. The main aim of this section is to consider the ways in which participants come to adopt certain norms within political participation, and to then analyse the nature of those assumptions. I will also consider the long-term effects of involvement in the different organisations, and reflect upon the extent to which the most politically experienced respondents have come to question various aspects of political participation.

Face-to-face Meetings: Analysing the Discourse of Political Participation

It has already been suggested in Chapter Two that the conduct of political participation often contains persistent inequalities. It was shown in Chapter Three that these findings are particularly important in the context of Habermas' concern with the ways in which formally inclusive political structures potentially sustain distorted forms of political communication. The data generated in the course of this research shows that the question of face-to-face interaction is a central component of this debate.

The interviews show that rather than acting as passive recipients of discursive mechanisms, the respondents invariably make active judgements about the value of turning up for an Amnesty International local group meeting, for example. Importantly, this applies not only to those who are actively involved in these bodies but also to those who are less embroiled. The interviews clearly show that the discursive character of various forms of participation plays a significant role in contributing to the decision to take part in a group. A number of respondents reported negative feelings toward meetings, and were wary of becoming involved in such discourse. Those participants who are regularly involved within group meetings also play an important role in encouraging or discouraging wider participation. With these preliminary comments in mind, let us now turn to a fuller discussion of what actually happens within meetings and how the respondents perceived such discourse.

Central to Habermas' idea of discourse ethics is the notion that communicative exchanges can potentially act as a channel through which participants develop and challenge their own subjective assumptions. Rather than simply reinforcing existing perspectives, discourse of an intersubjective character leads to participants internalising the attitudes of others and consequently developing reciprocal relations. As Calhoun (1992b, p. 29) puts it, communication then 'means not merely sharing what people already think or know but also a process of potential transformation in which reason is advanced by debate itself'. This notion appears to have little place in the participatory environments in which many of the Labour Party respondents found themselves. It was reported by a number of Party members with experience of meetings that these forums sustained little in the way of the developmental tendencies identified by Habermas. In particular, I was often told that meetings involved certain attendees merely going through the same discussions they have had with one another on numerous occasions before. Consider the comments of these four experienced Labour Party members:

> You feel as though you have been here before. And within that, at most meetings that you go to the same people are there. At a branch meeting I know pretty well who is going to be there. And to be honest with you, you could almost write the script. It's like watching Eastenders. You know who is going to say what. I know who has got which scenes and they are going to plot them out without ever really breaking free of that cycle.

> And they [regular attendees at branch meetings] are all people whose entrenched positions I know well. So you can actually predict who is going to say what.

> What we don't like so much these days is the GCs. Because they are merely boring talking shops where the same people have to get up and speak. And

you can almost know what they're going to say. And you could basically push a button on them and they would say the same things and they would have the same views. And to my mind although its supposed to be the committee because it is the members, a lot of it is just a complete and utter waste of time because it is just people saying the same things over and over again........it's very much a question of people who just like the sound of their own voices perhaps very often, or feel its expected of them to talk. There are people when they look round the room and they say who's next and they say so and so and you will here an audible groan because they know who is getting up and that's that for the next five minutes, if you're lucky.

....there are people, like any group, any committee, any organisation that feel they have to speak on everything and anything....very often their input is a complete and utter waste of time because they've only repeated what someone else has probably said two or three times before, even at that meeting.

The effects of this tendency are evident in the comments of one Amnesty International member. She was wary of becoming involved because she felt that 'would all be the same with the same agendas that you have to work through. All of that puts me off'. The suggestion that the format of traditional meetings fosters repetitive exchanges suggests that discourse of this type fails to sustain the communicative potential highlighted by Habermas. Perhaps not surprisingly, a number of respondents felt that this aspect of meetings often leads to an active minority dominating meetings. Several Labour Party members made similar observations:

The trouble is....at all meetings you have got the people who will sit there quietly. And you have got two or three who try to dominate the meeting. And you will find that it is the same two or three every time.

I think that what tends to happen at meetings is that certain people tend to talk whatever.

There probably needs to be more exploring and discussing policy. And actually discussing instead of everyone just standing on their soap boxes with their own agenda. That is what tends to happen.

The data also showed clearly that underpinning this is the attitude of the key participants toward meetings. When asked how they perceived the aims and purpose of internal meetings, many of the most heavily involved respondents highlighted the importance of a predetermined agenda. Many of the most involved respondents to whom I spoke saw such interaction in very narrow strategic terms. For example, a Labour Party Branch Election Officer made the following comment:

> You can try to be friendly and get them [new attendees] involved but a branch meeting is a business meeting when all is said and done. You have got business and so on to get through. It is not a cosy chat round the table.

A Residents' Association committee member to whom I spoke made a very similar point about committee meetings. He noted that 'we have to have some sort of formality....it is run in a very light hearted sort of way but we do mean business. We're not just there to play dominoes. We do mean business.' This attitude was central to ensuring that debate was conducted within a highly rigid discursive framework. The meetings of Tenants' and Residents' Associations consequently tended to cultivate what might be referred to as rule-governed cultures. This was evident in the comments of one Residents' Association committee member:

> We do try to stick by the rulebook. We don't bring it out at every meeting and start reading from it but anybody who knows anything about democracy knows what democratic procedures are.

Others respondents felt that there was a connection between this culture and a strong sense of routine within meetings. As one experienced Labour Party member put it:

> What happens at a typical branch meeting is this....people assemble and then they say right, we had better start....this is probably quarter of an hour after we were due to start....you then sit and work through the agenda and minutes of the last meeting. And then we will have a big discussion because somebody is unhappy about the nature of some wording, And then we will move on to the next item on the agenda which is usually correspondence. So the secretary will shuffle a load of papers out of his briefcase and then read them verbatim. And then that is about an hour into the meeting....so what happens is that all these socialist and environmental associations have written to us....blah, blah, blah.

This format was often replicated in the Tenants' and Residents' Associations meetings that I attended. I witnessed several instances where Chairs or Secretaries reading out correspondence in full length. A number of respondents also referred to difficulties associated with reaching beyond 'activist' members. At the heart of the reality of political participation is the trend for a small core of members to regularly turn up and take part in a large number of meetings. One long term Labour Party member wryly observed that 'I could go down High Street [local Labour Party Headquarters] and the same people would be down there that were there thirty years ago. Nothing changes there'. Further remarks from this Labour Party member highlight this phenomenon more clearly:

> Some people only ever see almost the same people....it's like when you have functions you can sit down and say so and so will come, and so and so will come......you still get a lot of people who will turn up at anything and everything. So consequently you still get a lot of people that will turn up at anything and everything and consequently you're dealing with the same people. You're not really dealing with outsiders.

As one Labour Party member put it: 'There have always been the same three or four people who are extremely active [in the local branch]'. One member bemoaned the persistence of this trend: 'it is also a matter of regret that you go to a branch meeting....and there are half a dozen of the same people every month'. Another member referred to 'people who are really active who seem to feel they have to be in meetings all the time'. A member of Amnesty International identified a similar trend in the local group that he had taken part in:

> There were some people who just turned up sometimes, there were some people who turned up all the time, there were some people who are on the local group list and pay their subs but never come to anything. And then there was a small group of people who actually do.

Another Amnesty International UK member similarly described a situation of a small core of active members surrounded by a largely passive local membership:

> Well, they pay their subs, they get their newsletter, they turn up at a meeting every so often. They are a face you sort of know. But they don't do anything for the organisation....as far as Amnesty was concerned there were just a few people who were active. And I have seen that in other organisations. I don't think that is something that is specific to Amnesty.

My discussions with those respondents who had less experience of such an environment highlight the strong alienating effects that this type of culture has on attendees. The effects of meetings are fundamental to developing an understanding of the internal dynamics of participation. Crucial to understanding the effects of both small bands of active attendees and established procedure is the reaction of new or inexperienced participants. One Labour Party member observed that the effects of a small core of active participants can be off-putting, particularly for new members:

> Very often you get new members and you can get them to come to GC meetings and they are so pleased at being chosen to represent the branch at GC. And they will come to one, they will come to two and they just disappear.

The outcome of this trend is for new members to be unlikely to become heavily involved in the local branch:

> It is so difficult to get people even at the branch level ....a new one starts, comes along, and it is so difficult your first time to understand what a meeting is all about anyway.

> New members appear and come on to the fringes...but in my three years of involvement in this branch I can't think of anybody who has really got very involved.

It is also sometimes difficult for members to enter this 'inner circle' of active participants. One Labour Party member admitted that 'Everybody is a bit cliquey really, like most organisations where people have known each other for too long'. He went on to observe that 'It is hard work to fight your way in to become an insider of any sort'. The Urgent Action Co-ordinator at Amnesty International UK was aware of such problems:

> I have been to meetings where a new person will sit at the back of the room and no one will say hello to them. And that person just gets up and leaves and will never come back to that group....some of them are just atrocious. They do reinforce that thing of this clique who come along to this drafty church hall, and then you are just sat along on the edge of it. I have had that as the guest at a group meeting where no one talks to you....so there probably is a large group of members for whom it is just a time thing. But I am sure there are just as many who have been to one group meeting and then never gone to any other after that.

Another Labour Party member highlighted the problems associated with encouraging participation from inexperienced members:

The odd new member will occasionally appear and may just persevere like I did because they know their way round the system. But new members, who are really new to the Party, it is difficult for them to get involved.

Particularly interesting in this comment is the idea that new members need to have some experience or knowledge of procedure in order to be able to effectively contribute to meetings. Comments from these members echoed the importance of this:

Personally, if I walked into a meeting that was cliquish I would make a point of talking to everybody. But I'm used to it all. I can imagine it would be very off putting for somebody if you go along to a meeting and nobody talks to you.

I think if somebody was coming into a Labour Party meeting for the first time it would be quite daunting. It would be very confusing. And I don't think that unless they attended quite a few meetings on a regular basis they would get the gist of how things are done.

Somebody going along for the first time, it's gone. You might follow it for a few minutes and you are then just sitting there and you want to sleep. You just want to go.

One Labour Party member highlighted that the effects of procedure and a small clique of members are closely related:

Another thing about the tendency for certain people to get involved in everything is the way in which, if a new member sticks his head around the door at a meeting, what does he hear? Just jargon that he doesn't understand. He says right, that's it. And he's gone.

In a similar vein, a Labour Party member observed that:

....what also happens, which doesn't have to happen, but does happen, is committee procedure. You find you spend your whole time sodding around with procedure....instead of actually doing anything. The procedure is necessary up to a point but it gets full of people who love procedure and forget that there is anything to do....most activists seem to me to do nothing but play at procedure....they are so wrapped up doing that that they forget to make anything happen.

The interviews suggest that meetings often serve to alienate those who do not take part on a regular basis. This is not only a result of procedure and formality. Several respondents raised the issue of the influence of the more 'active' participants. One Amnesty International UK member who had attended a handful of meetings of his local group felt that 'it appeared to be almost like a little cult group. It was very small. You are talking about ten or twelve people'. Another Amnesty International member felt that the active group members created an atmosphere that he found quite off putting:

> It was just people sounding off about how important they were. They were very patronising. Be quiet, we're talking. That sort of thing. So that put me off the local part of things. There were probably good people in that area who were put off by all that. So where did they go?

Another observed that the negative effect of attending a local group were reinforced by a feeling of social and political remoteness within the group:

> It smacked almost of a small handful of do-gooders wanting to get together and talk about some issues or maybe write one or two letters. The people didn't really seem to be that much in touch with everyday life. Quite far removed in fact. It wasn't like here is 10 or 12 ordinary, mainstream people. It was almost like a cosy, eccentric little band of people fighting for a completely and utterly lost cause.

He went on to describe the alienating effects of this experience:

> It was a bit depressing and demoralising....you come away thinking oh dear, this is a really, really remote group who really believe they are making an important contribution but they don't appear to be. Let's say I was trying to recruit someone to the importance of Amnesty and I took them to a meeting like that, I think it would just switch them off.

Another member spoke of attending a meeting at one local group where 'they had one of those very bustling groups where everyone ran around organising everybody'. He felt that this 'would drive me loopy'. Furthermore, he suggested that 'it was all based on being bossed about by fussy people. It all felt very fussy and almost like a stereotype of the Women's Institute. It was that sort of group. That put me off completely'. Another Amnesty International member reported similarly negative feelings about his dealings with a local Amnesty group:

The guy on the list put 'doctor' next to his name. I thought oh dear. I don't particularly want to meet this guy. It just puts up a whole barrier...I thought it is just going to be a bit of an ego thing. You think to yourself, can I hack that? You could just imagine what the guy was going to be like. So I spoke to him on the phone and he just talked down to me. He was not on this planet. A real academic type, completely on a different plane.

I was also able to explore the expectations and assumptions of those respondents who had no direct experience of meetings within their respective organisation. Although the attitudes to meetings were mixed, there was a strong wariness about becoming involved in local groups or branches. Some Amnesty International members, for instance, were worried that meetings might simply be 'talking shops' where little was actually achieved. As one member commented:

It would be OK if it is sitting down and knocking out some letters. But some groups would tend to spend the whole evening talking. What have you achieved? I like to actually achieve something or do something.

One can see from this comment that there are problems in assuming that those citizens who engage with civil society will necessarily be seeking some form of deliberation. Whereas previously I have pointed out the relationship between highly instrumental attitudes toward meetings and an exclusionary tendency, we can see from the comments of this respondent that she would actually prefer a more tightly defined focus for her participation.

Another Amnesty International UK member stated that she tried to 'avoid belonging to groups where I go to meetings...I would rather belong in the background because otherwise I have to get too involved and I end up taking on more than I can cope with'. Another Amnesty International UK member to whom I spoke felt that 'I wouldn't be the sort of person to go along to meetings. One has stereotypes of these things, but I imagine that everyone would be very zealous and the meetings would just be people sitting and talking'. She went on to note that 'I think that even if I had the time I wouldn't find it very attractive'. Yet another member encapsulated these concerns by noting that:

I don't trust organisations. So I need to satisfy myself with a local organisation about where they are putting their focus and emphasis, and why. What is the dynamic of the group who are most active? How prejudiced are they? How open and clear are they? These things count for me.

When asked to elaborate further, he identified existing participants as potentially off putting:

So what do you mean by problems with group dynamics in these organisations?

The way people behave together in a local group. It is not unknown in campaigning organisations, political and voluntary, for people at the local level who are active to be pretty single minded....I just don't get on very well with people who are single minded because it extends into prejudice. They may be good people, but it is a case of this is the party line and that is what you have to do....that is the watchfulness that is there for me. I am cautious about these things at the back of my mind...my experience with campaigning organisations at the local level does tend to put me off rather than convince me....you can't thoroughly discuss issues. A few people make up their minds what the group is going to do and that is what then happens.

Thus far, I have examined the perceptions and attitudes of a range of respondents to traditional forms of face-to-face discourse. However, if we are to gain a closer understanding of how these discursive mechanisms function within the structures of political participation then we need to examine in closer detail how meetings proceed. All of the Tenants' and Residents' Association meetings I attended were extremely formal events. Below, I present findings that emerged from my attendance at one particular Committee meeting. My first observation was that the agenda of the meeting was notable for the amount of acronyms and specialist jargon that was used. The following excerpt demonstrates this more clearly:

4. T.M.O.
5. TSC/submission to ombudsman
6. Housing Manger LBC
.....
10. C.C.T.

During the meeting, the Chair took the central role in initiating action within the Tenants' Association. Examples included the Chair proclaiming that 'this is something I want sorted out'. The Chair also displayed far more confidence in asserting what she saw as 'facts' about the Associations' relationship with the council. For instance, she stated on one occasion that 'that is the way it should work, and that is democratic'. She also remarked on another occasion that 'I might be wrong but I am pretty sure I am right'. Integral to this capability to act in an assured manner was an extensive knowledge of established procedures within the Housing Department. The Chair was able to impart this knowledge in a manner that provided her with informal rights of expertise within the meeting. Examples include her statements such as 'I have dome some work on policy and legislative issues' in order to support what she saw as appropriate courses of action. On another occasion she stated that 'I feel they have broken this rule under legislation, and I would like it taken up'.

I also observed that on several occasions the Chair and the Secretary made reference to meetings that they had attended within the Housing Department. These were often made in a veiled manner, and my impression was that the Chair was keen to retain her role as a mediator of specialist knowledge. For example, she began her comments at one point by stating 'what I have been hearing is this....' I felt there was a strong sense in which the meeting provided an opportunity for the Chair and the Secretary to stress their own political identity as meaningful actors. A prime example of this was provided when the Secretary made reference to a recent council meeting on Compulsory Competitive Tendering:

> Only five tenants turned up. It is pitiful. It's no good these tenants shouting at us if they can't be bothered to get off their backside....it shows you that it needs people like us to fight the tenants' case because they just won't do it themselves.

The Chair was consequently able to provide approval for certain acts of the local council whilst others were questioned. I consequently found very little evidence of disagreement or deliberation within the meeting. The other attendees made very few contributions, and when they did so it was largely to make short factual reports that the Chair and the Secretary then commented on. When a point was opened to the floor for discussion there was often no response, and the Chair then had little option but to prompt the Secretary to make a comment. In consequence the exchanges tended to be dominated by either of these two participants. It was also clear that the Chair and Secretary had informally discussed the agenda beforehand because at one point the Secretary introduced Any Other Business in the following manner: 'Right, as part of this AOB I think Lorraine wants to talk about this point'. The Chair was also able to control the agenda and the discussion of items in a number of ways. For example, an issue was raised but the Chair stated that 'we have got to talk to the committee about this, but not at this meeting'.

The mediatory role of the Chair was further emphasised during the final stages of the meeting. The Tenants' Associations had received details of courses from the Tenants' Participatory Advisory Service and the Chair spent a few minutes deciding which course would be appropriate for the Tenants' Association to consider. She did not open this up for discussion. She made comments such as 'personally I think this is something you should go on' and 'no, we don't want that'. She also displayed a reluctance to allow other members to become involved in the administration of meetings. As she put it during the meeting: 'running committees....that is an important one, but if you don't know how to do it then Rob and I can do it'.

Of course, this meeting could be seen as unrepresentative. Nonetheless, it is clear that many of the comments presented earlier in this chapter indicate the alienating effects of such deliberative processes. Turning to the Exodus collective, one initially finds a radically different approach to the conduct of meetings. Meetings are generally viewed as crucial to the running of the collective. On the one hand, meetings are seen to represent a fair and inclusive mechanism for decision-making. They are also intended to function as a forum for the development of communication skills. It has been suggested that these factors have established the meetings as events that members actually enjoy attending. One member observed that 'we come out of them saying that was a good meeting wasn't it?' Indeed, the meetings have become the focal point for collective decision-making such that 'the general consensus is that if you are not at a meeting then you can't moan about anything because that is your chance to hear what other people are saying'.

The meetings are designed to address the inequalities that may arise within group discussion. By adopting a loose and open format, meetings are intended to avoid domination by those with an established faculty of public argumentation. Everyone is given an opportunity to participate and contribute to the meeting. The collective aims to achieve this in a number of ways. Firstly, rather than hold regular formal meetings of a pre-defined length, the Exodus meetings appear to be organised in direct relation to need and requirement. One founding member stated that 'if we have got nothing to say then our meetings will only last twenty minutes'. In addition, meetings are often cancelled if a large number of attendees are unavailable. It is hoped that this general approach creates a deliberative environment that is able to develop a widespread attitude of wanting to attend meetings, as opposed to members feeling obligated to do so or being coerced into taking part.

Secondly, the meetings themselves are very informal affairs. Attendees relax on beanbags and several smoke marijuana. There are relatively few procedural rules. As one member puts it, the meetings are intended to be 'very human rather than mechanical'. It is intended that this fosters a different type of atmosphere to traditional meetings, such that 'we are all there and it is kind of like there are no inhibitions in the meeting'. A third aspect of the meetings is a rejection of what is referred to as 'ego tripping' or 'power tripping', whereby 'people get told to shut up or someone takes over'. No individual is seen to be capable of a superior or more worthy contribution than any other attendee, or as one member put it 'no one man takes the lead'. This strategy echoes aspects of the women's movement during the 1970s, in which it was assumed that 'equal respect is hard to sustain where there are clearly leaders and led' (Phillips, 1991, p. 122). As such, it is intended that meetings are not controlled and dominated by particular individuals or groups. Rather, meetings are run upon the premise that 'if the meeting isn't boss then bosses would develop'. Members are thus encouraged not to speak over each other. If there is a problem then it is common for attendees to shout 'one meeting', and the privileged position of the meeting itself is restored. As a result of this approach, the importance of establishing some level of consensus has become paramount. This is generally viewed as the fairest way of coming to decisions. One can detect elements of embryonic discourse ethics in this approach, and it clearly represents a strong contrast with the features of more traditional meetings that I have previously outlined.

Finally, there is also a strong enabling and inclusive dimension to the conduct of meetings. There is a professed interest in encouraging input and contributions from those attendees that may not otherwise take part. For instance, meetings at the Manor are sometimes attended by local youths that are not living on the premises. One member noted that there is an active attempt to involve these youths:

> We say this is for you, ski hat crew. You should get involved in this. And maybe one of them will speak for their little group. It's nice for these kids who would never normally have access to that kind of thing, or be involved in that kind of thing.

According to one member to whom I spoke, the meetings are thus able to act as 'a training ground for improving communication'. This is seen to be particularly important in view of the fact that a large number of Exodus participants 'come from cultures of not communicating'. This developmental dimension of the meetings is also seen as a valuable source of increasing the range of contributions and input. It may be the case that 'one of these young lads might turn around and say I've had this idea, and then suddenly he has become involved in it all'.

However, other members perceive the meetings differently. One observed that 'you could say that anyone at those meetings could stand up and say what they want to say', but he also noted that 'what actually seems to happen....is that there are people who are able to stand up and speak. These are the active participants'. He went on:

> What you get is it all in microcosm. So say there is forty people sitting in this room that they have done out....what you will get is that out of those forty people, I would suggest that there is six who are able to stand up.....

Another former member observed that 'there are only a few people who actually make the decisions'. He referred to one active member of the collective who 'policed' meetings:

> ....he doesn't actually say anything of worth. He just reflects whatever the popular ideology is. He doesn't say anything of his own. He does speak, but it tends to just be to re-affirm something that somebody has already said. Or if someone has disagreed with something that the collective has said, he will normally jump in there and say no, he was right. But to say he speaks is just to say he is a heavy.

In addition, it is not necessarily clear that the collective opens itself up to discussion of its own agenda. As one former member observed: 'When you cross-question it then you are told that you are not on the coup. You do not understand....and when questioned about it they always say, oh no, but we are righteous. This is a stock reply'. He further argued that the meetings masked informal barriers to participation by excluding comment on the collective's ideological agenda. He even went so far as to claim that the formal structure of a Labour Party branch meeting would provide a more communicative environment than an Exodus meeting:

> When you come to a Labour Party meeting it is structured for one thing. There is still a hierarchical air about it but if you have got a legitimate complaint or a legitimate argument against what is being done in the Labour Party, then I would suggest that you would stand more chance of having it voiced and having it discussed properly. In Exodus, what you get is rhetoric. You will get straight forward you are not on the coup, you're not spiritually enlightened, go away. You're not one of us. So it is a bit more totalitarian when it comes to that area.

He went on to suggest that the informal nature of the Exodus collective can actually create impediments to participation:

> The Labour Party will perhaps uphold democracy if you like, even if it is big and unwieldy and awkward and you still have to be pretty sure of yourself to stand up contrary to a prospective candidate or whatever. I feel it would be possible. I feel it would be possible to go to a meeting in which [local MP] was the head, and to stand up at the meeting and argue against her and be heard. Although it would have to be tabled or whatever and you would have to go through that formality, there is a structure there where you could perhaps be able to put forward your views. It is possible....if you had the same scenario except you replaced the Labour Party with the Exodus collective and you have got somebody who wants to speak contrary to the collective, I would feel very much that there would be that one individual who would be almost totally jeered off stage. Booed. He wouldn't stand a chance. Even making the speech would be an impossibility.

Political Participation and the Control of Mechanisms

Following the analysis of meetings, a point that requires further exploration relates to the tendency for certain participants to seek to control participatory mechanisms. One Amnesty International member who had been involved in his local group felt that these groups are liable to become an opportunity for the most active members to pursue some form of personal project. He commented:

> I think the groups become the baby of certain people....and for them it is very important....the people I am talking about were all very committed about actively taking part in the Amnesty campaigns. But it was also something more....it is their baby, and they have been in it since it was formed and they will be having their ninetieth birthday there.

This process often requires some form of informal control of participatory mechanisms by active participants. It was evident from my interviews that there is often an implicit desire to retain a power and authority over tasks and mechanisms within the organisation in question. The aforementioned Amnesty International member candidly described in detail how he had found himself developing an interest in maintaining control over the local group newsletter:

> People tend to think if I am the newsletter editor for instance, then that is my contribution. What will happen if I don't do it? What if they can't find

anyone else to do it? And if I don't do it what else am I going to do that is a positive contribution? I think there is also a bit of a feeling that will anyone do it as well as I do? So there is some stuff in there about territory and possession in that. Even when you are feeling overloaded by it....not wanting to let it go despite the fact that you know that it is all too much and you can't actually hack it anymore.

A similar concern with ensuring that only 'approved' participants are able to take part was also detectable in the comments of an experienced Residents' Association committee member. He stated:

....sometimes they [local residents] write in and ask us....if they can come to a committee meeting and put their problem personally....we do allow members of the association who are not members of the committee to....we do allow these people to come along and sit in on our committee meetings, particularly if they have a problem or a very strong suggestion to make. But they don't have any voting rights obviously. So they simply come and sit in and we talk about the matter and decide what we will do about it.

A branch election organiser in the Labour Party to whom I spoke was keen to identify the group of participants who he felt did not measure up to the requirements of 'genuine' activism. Clearly detectable in his testimony is the construction of an informal barrier between what he sees as real activists and pseudo activists. This is not simply a conceptual boundary – his distinction has practical consequences for the relations that develop between established active members and those who occupy the peripheries of these participatory structures:

You've got somebody like Janet and myself who are there when the polls open at eight o'clock and we invariably open up the polling stations and we start them off. So you're there before it opens up. You're actually there setting up the polling station very often. You're there to check that the boxes are empty and all the rest of it. Now, during the day you will get some members, notoriously of the Asian variety, who will come and say I've come to help. And you'll say right well, here's a card and go and knock those doors. And you could give them perhaps fifteen or twenty or perhaps a few leaflets. Something that would spend quarter of an hour, twenty minutes, half hour at the most. And they will go and do that. One, you might never ever see them again. Or they might come back and you say do you want to do some more? Oh no, I've got to go somewhere. And they really believe....although obviously that piece of help does contribute....they really believe that they have done the day's work. They have been an activist.

He continued:

> When the actual results come out you have a party down High Street [local Constituency Labour Party Headquarters] for the local members, and these people turn up. And they're there as if to say where's my medal? And yet Janet and myself and some of the others have turned out every single night door knocking. And these people really, really believe that if they spent quarter of an hour, twenty minutes that they've won the election. Now I know that they contributed but they're two inches taller because they've done that. And it's frightfully annoying because we say well you ain't off now are you? We need you to do this. Oh no, sorry, I've done my piece for the thing. And that can get awfully frustrating.

Putting aside for the moment the overt racism on display here, it is interesting to note how this active Party member is reluctant to allow certain members to become involved in the running of elections. He appears to see himself very much as a gatekeeper for deciding who should be allowed to enter the domain of the active participants. An experienced Party member highlighted the persistency of this dynamic within the Party. He felt that there is an informal assumption that active members need to 'earn' their rights of membership before they can be accepted into the realm of the active members:

> I suspect that there are some people who are quote activists unquote for whom it is almost like being part of the select few. One thing that I have always had difficulty with....and it has certainly been prevalent amongst quite a lot of Labour Party people I have known....it is almost as if, if you don't go to a whole load of meetings or whatever you are not really committed and you shouldn't have the same rights as other members.

One Labour Party member spoke about how he saw reliance on procedure as a tool for filtering members who might want to become more active:

> I believe that some procedures are made so complicated, deliberately so....they make everything complicated so that they can, if you like, suss you out before you get a chance to be involved to a full extent...so that they know what sort of person they have got before they allow you to become an activist.

Underlying many of these comments is the idea that certain forms of activism are connected to exclusionary tendencies. This has also been clearly detectable in the analysis of meetings. A major implication of this tendency is the development of cultures of expertise within structures of political participation.

Expert Cultures and Political Participation

During the course of my interviews with the respondents I was struck by the presence of what might be productively defined as 'expert cultures'. There is clearly a tendency for certain respondents to acquire the role of a 'professional' participant within their respective organisation. This is particularly interesting in view of the Habermasian notion that 'professional mystique is itself a source of hierarchy and distortion in policy debate' (Dryzek, 1995, p. 108). The development of expertise within political activity is unlikely to foster conditions in which communicative action might be able to flourish. As Ray (1993, p. 50) puts it, this 'insulation of expertise has a deforming effect on everyday life since the possibilities for democratic participation in decision-making is restricted'.

A number of the more experienced Tenants' and Residents' Association members tended to see themselves as 'experts' within the local policy process. For example, one Residents' Association committee member described how local residents could bring issues to his attention:

> If you thought it was a rather delicate subject and you wanted a bit more expertise on it....instead of going straight into action as you might do in some matters writing to your borough council....I mean, there's no reason why you shouldn't write to your borough council and try and get an answer from them. And that is sometimes the best way to do it, is to go to them and get some feedback from them as to what the council's attitude would be, or the water company or anyone else. And then if you don't like the answer you get back then you come to us and we will try and sort matters out for you. We don't guarantee to sort matters out. We can't do that. But we do try to sort matters out because as an association we are a little bit bigger body and we're recognised at the Town Hall, rather than a single individual. We have had people come to us with problems where they didn't go to the council.

Another Committee member similarly recounted the lengthy procedure that any issue raised by a local resident has to go through. Again, the key mediatory role occupied by active Tenants' Association members was apparent:

....the problem would be discussed with a committee member. The committee member would then take the problem to the next committee meeting and the committee would then decide just which particular department of local government the problem was directed to. We would then write to that department of the Town Hall to try to get that problem resolved.

A Constituency Party Secretary and a Branch Election Organiser to whom I spoke similarly described their respective roles within the local Party as a mediatory position:

....you have got to ensure that branch activists know what they are doing, so I try to keep them involved. I think I'm usually the first port of call for any members if they have got something they want to raise....I try to give them advice and help.

I think organising is the main role of it all. You have got people who can be active but they want to be told what to do. They need to be given the job to do rather than them assume that that is what they should be doing....so yeah, basically to organise them.

One can clearly see the instrumental relations that might underpin such a role. The Branch Election Organiser went on to describe in rather disparaging terms how he put these principles into action:

We have got a member who would be....better be careful how I say this....but he would probably be useless at almost everything and anything, but he is a wonderful leafleter. And you can give him a great pile of the things and send him out and you might not see him for hours but you know they are going to go through the doors....they are all individually labelled. This road, that road. So he has got a bundle so he knows I have got to go and do that road now or that road today....he really works bloody hard. He just shoves the things through the doors. And he works a lot harder than some people who just come for the half-hour and think oh I've done well.

Socialising Influences: Learning to Participate

It is evident from the interviews that in order to become heavily involved within specific organisations it is often the case that participants go through an informal learning process. The findings show that if we measure participation purely by the number of meetings or functions attended, then we overlook a whole stratum of activity that is integral to the development of the previously described forms of expertise. In order to operate successfully within their respective organisation, it was clear to me that participants often need to conform to particular ways of working.

This is particularly relevant in the context of identifying those informal socialising influences that shape participants' assumptions and patterns of belief about legitimate, and indeed illegitimate, forms of activity. Dryzek (1995, p. 108) states that those analysts investigating political interaction from a Habermasian perspective need to 'elucidate socializing [sic] forces that distort participants' assumptions and perceptions'. In other words, it is important to know something about how agents learn to act in particular ways. For our purposes this means uncovering details of how respondents might come to pick up norms of participation that contribute to the shaping of the political activity of participants, and then examining the nature of these assumptions and beliefs. It is crucial that this process of learning to participate is not regarded as a neutral process. The definitions of 'normal' ways of working that the respondents may have developed are inevitably patterned in certain directions. Conversely, alternative modes of action are likely to be sidelined or closed off. It is this process that contributes to the construction of what Forester (1992, p. 61) refers to as 'bounded rationality'. Our broad task is to begin to assess the extent to which these learned participatory techniques and forms of rationality deviate from Habermas' notion of communicative action.

Furthermore, the question of how participants experience these socialising influences is particularly important if we are to explore the scope of 'communicative competence'. This is important because, as Chambers (1995b, p. 167) observes, when Habermas outlines the conditions of discourse ethics he often talks 'in terms of non-interference as opposed to positive requirements'. In other words, Habermas spends a great deal of time outlining the procedural requirements for ensuring that participants are able to contribute to a discourse in an open manner. However, he tends to overlook the question of whether participants are likely to feel inclined to actually take part in a discursive manner:

> Successful discourse involves more than ensuring that people who want to engage in discourse may engage in discourse. Successful discourse involves fostering the desire to participate; it involves....a positive responsibility to engage in the process (Chambers, 1995b, p. 167).

A number of respondents highlighted the need to become familiar with the inner workings of the relevant method of participation before one can become 'active'. For example, one Labour Party member observed that 'You can't really become active until you have worked out how the system works and got involved in the system and been in the system'. He went on to observe that by learning to take part in this way, the process of participation becomes more familiar:

> I feel once you can understand the system fully and completely....really understand it....it all becomes like having a cup of tea. It is then second nature. And once it becomes second nature you can get really involved.

Other respondents referred to the need for persistence in order to become heavily involved in participation. A central aspect of learning to become active is a willingness to commit to attending meetings and picking up the 'rules of the game'. Consequently, the process of learning to participate in particular ways is, in many respects, rooted in the face-to-face discourse I have already discussed. This was evident in the comments of the following Labour Party member:

> Well, you need people who are prepared to put time into the Party. Time not only just to attend committee meetings but can spend time, particularly at election times, canvassing and being involved in elections. Delivering newsletters, that kind of thing. Someone who is prepared to give of their time....you could be an activist and never leave your home to a certain degree, but I think it is more a case of you going out and being involved. And not necessarily just with the Labour Party stuff, because remember the school governors are political appointments. And as such that is a whole new series of additional meetings, on top of Party meetings. So, I think you need to be prepared to give of your time most weeks throughout the year.

One Labour Party member who had taken a conscious decision to commit to such a learning process consequently noted that:

> I will still stick with it if I possibly can. Because if you do that for the first time, then the second time you will understand it better and better.....once you see it and you suss it out for a few weeks....then you can get to the real bones if what is happening....and then it starts to make a bit of sense and it becomes really interesting.

Another member observed that 'I am quite willing to give it a couple of years to watch and learn'. She went on describe in more detail how she had begun to experience this process:

You have really got to give three or four meetings before you dare open your mouth. I went along just to look, so there was no point in opening my mouth because I didn't know anything about what was happening. But I think that is what people should do....after a couple of months you start to recognise the faces as well. You might then ask a couple of questions and get into it like that.

In order to become involved to any great degree it is clearly necessary to be willing to apply oneself to a process of learning. It was clear from my discussions with those who had taken an active role in various organisations that it was often necessary to submit oneself to formal procedures of learning participation. For example, a former member of a local Amnesty group similarly noted that:

There was a lot to learn about Amnesty itself, about the way it works. When you see the mandate you think oh God how can you possibly do that? How can you achieve aims like that? And then almost by contrast letter writing is such a dominant part of it....there was a bit of me that just went you must be joking. The two things seem discordant. So there was a lot of information to get to grips with.

Interestingly, the learning processes also take place on an informal level. One Labour Party member spoke of the learning process as an informal 'apprenticeship':

I suppose it's sort of like an apprenticeship which you can't define. Some people when they pay their subscription and they get their right to attend branch meetings might not have experienced anything else like it before.

A number of Labour Party members pointed to the importance of interacting with other members in an informal manner. One member observed that they had learnt a lot about being involved 'by going to the meetings and listening to other people. And having a chat afterwards'. One of the Tenants' Association Chairs to whom I spoke referred to having to pick up a lot about the nature of tenants' participation. She had only been involved in the Tenants' Association for a few months and she highlighted the importance of informal interaction with experienced Tenants' Association activists. She noted that:

It's just that I have never done this sort of thing, so.... I'm still learning. I have to learn off other Tenants' and Residents' Associations. So you're supposed to be very formal, which I'm not. But you are supposed to be. Like they're supposed to say you know, Chairperson and agendas and so on.

I spoke to one of the Residents' Association members who had advised her and he described how he had been able to help her with the new Tenants' Association:

> So when I first got introduced to Josie she said I could use you. I need you. I said well I'm quite willing to help you. I said if you have just started up I know quite a bit about it with 31 years experience. I said I will help you. So that is how I came to be at their meetings. And I have also been over to her flat and given her quite a lot of information….so what she has done is co-opt me onto it…I don't have any voting powers but I'm there to give advice and information. I think she's picking it up well.

Learning from Political Participation

What exactly did these respondents report learning in the course of their participation? Is it possible to detect certain types of rationality that consequently come to be paramount within the sphere of political participation? Firstly, The Residents' Association members that I spoke to were keen to stress the importance of becoming familiar with the formal rules under which their Residents' Association operated. One area of these rules that was stressed to me was the formal procedure necessary to run meetings. One member felt that 'you have got to have a reasonable amount of formality to control the meeting. You have got to make progress through your minutes and through the work.' Another Committee member similarly stressed the importance of formal rules as fundamental to participation:

> ….every committee meeting if it is properly administered has to follow a set of rules which we commonly regard as being the right set of rules right across the country. Every group, every club, every society should follow a set of rules and procedure of committee meetings.

Comments from two Labour Party members similarly noted how they had come to see these procedures as an integral part of involvement in the local branch:

> ….almost accepting that that [the procedure associated with meetings] was part and parcel of the baggage that went with being a Labour Party member. You sat through all of this because the branch was an important part of

proceedings. You believed it was appropriate for the branch to discuss issues and pass resolutions and look after the particular interest of its bit of the town, but it doesn't actually do that with any kind of effectiveness at all.

I take all of that structure of meetings as part and parcel of not just the Labour Party but any group....I just try to treat it as one of those humdrum things that has to be done.

These comments can be related directly to the previous discussion about the importance of meetings within political participation. I spoke to one Labour Party member who provided detail of how he had come to learn to operate within the parameters of formal meetings. This involved him acquiring knowledge of the technicalities of meeting procedure:

I've been to meetings that are quite involved and I've said something and they've gone round the thing and I've had my hand up and the Chairman has deliberately bypassed me because I'm not speaking the way they want. I say mister Chairman I had my hand up three-quarters of an hour, I'm getting tired. I want to speak. Sorry, no more time. That has happened....it's very annoying. So, next meeting put it in writing so it is on the minutes. Then there's no way of bypassing it. But I've learnt that over the years. If you can't get it in any other business because they want to get the meeting finished and they know you are going to say perhaps not what they want to hear, then put it in writing.

He went on:

But new members would take a while to suss that out. They would take a while to see that....but the trouble is then they will have a meeting about that letter beforehand and suss out how they are going to deal with it. That gives them an opportunity then to work out how to deal with it. Bring it up in any other business you can catch them unawares. You have to know how to deal with this, either if you want to take pot luck and put it in any other business and catch them unawares....I'm getting a gist of the Labour party now...sometimes you have got to raise things in such a place and at such a time to get the shock factor. And then it tends to get through. Whereas if you put it in writing you might not get what you wanted from it.

The aforementioned Tenants' Association Chair noted that assistance from existing tenant representatives advised on the appropriate way of working within established procedures:

I'm on the Steering Committee in the Town Hall now....and because I'm new there, they carry me along. They say....before I go, well look this is what we're going to do and this is the way it will go. But if I want to say something and if I don't say it right, they'll say this is the way you should do it.

Secondly, it became clear that these learning processes often encourage participants to develop low expectations about the likelihood of their involvement having an identifiable policy impact. As one Labour Party member put it:

There is no point going in and thinking right that's it, I'm in now. Because it ain't going to change. Nothing will change tomorrow or the next day.

For a number of the Labour Party respondents there appeared to be little direct connection between their active participation and discernable outcomes. Many of the most heavily involved Labour Party members to whom I spoke appeared to have accepted that their involvement is unlikely to lead to any substantial policy change. As a Constituency Party Secretary put it:

When they join the Labour party they want to change the world....so you go along to your first branch meeting and you think this is taking a long time to change the world here, I think I will go and do something else. But that is how it all works....if they can assimilate their political aims into how it becomes practice and comes into the policy process then that is a success. But it is not easy to be able to articulate things and be successful in that way.

He went on to describe how the expectations of new participants can often be frustrated when they come up against the reality of involvement in the Party:

I mean, the whole way meetings are run, not just in the Labour party but in any organisation....they [new participants] might not be familiar with it all. You know, you speak through a chair, you have an agenda, matters arising, any other business, all that procedure. Motions, people speaking in debates, seconders....we don't have any formal way of explaining that to people.....I mean, there is the whole use of acronyms and things like that. The jargon. You can try to keep that to a minimum so that the people don't feel....not disorientated....disenfranchised really from the political process. They may also find the process of meetings is boring. It's not something they looked for.

One can detect in these comments the sense in which there is a barrier that participants encounter. This was further emphasised by another member who had recently become involved in her local branch described her initial reaction to attending the branch meetings:

> You don't know what they are talking about and you don't know who they are talking about. And half the time you don't give a damn. Let's face it, you don't. They are all talking about the drains up the hill or a football field down the road or somebody's dog. And you think what the hell has this got to do with what I'm here for? I want to talk about politics. You just can't see the connection....I didn't really know them as well as I do now. And you just sort of sit there and it seemed as if there was about one hundred people there, but it only about thirty. And they all seemed to be talking about local houses and fields or something. And I was sitting there thinking what the bloody hell are these people on about?

She then went on to describe how she had gradually become accustomed to the focus of deliberations within the Party. It was clear that she had accepted that her participation would be focused on narrow issues and would not be likely to bring about any substantial policy change.

Thirdly, several Labour Party respondents also spoke of developing an 'intuition' for participating in an appropriate fashion. A Constituency Party Secretary referred to a 'political calculus' that he uses in his own mind to make decisions. One respondent stated that 'I'm not sure how you would put it really....you can call it a sense if you like....it is being able to tell whether something is unsolvable or not'. Evidence of such an 'intuition' was presented by comments from a branch election organiser. He referred to the technicalities of canvassing at election times in a manner that emphasised the assumptions made during such activity:

> So what we do is, Janet picks and chooses who goes to what doors. And it's sensible to say that if you have got a little old lady about seventy or eighty then with all due respect you don't send an extremely large black man to that door because she won't open the door. So obviously if you have got a female on the thing, or if you have got a white man....so you have to pick and choose who you are sending....you have to basically know, when you are running the card, who you are sending to which door to get over that business of having a certain response....when you're canvassing, strange as it may seem, we treat people differently and we dress differently. I wouldn't go around these houses wearing jeans and a T-shirt. I would go perhaps like this to some of the places. But I would wear a tie and trousers simply because, I wouldn't say part of the image, but it's the way I think it should be. A lot of people don't like jeans and scruffy dressing as I would call it,

whereas for other people it doesn't matter...I think we're a little more careful in some of those areas that are not our strongest areas. We try to put across a good impression.

The findings outlined above suggest that there is often a barrier which new participants come up against when they enter established arenas of political participation. However, such responses to the process of political involvement are not restricted to new or inexperienced participants.

Questioning Traditional Structures of Political Participation

During the course of the interviews I spoke to several respondents who had been involved in either one group or a number of different bodies for a long period of time. This provided an opportunity to consider the long-term effects of the forms of political participation in which they had engaged. Interestingly, a number of these respondents reported experiencing a sense of having reached a 'glass ceiling' with their own involvement in political life. For some respondents this was a case of realising that their heavy involvement might take over their personal life. As one Labour Party member put it:

> We said hang on, count me out. There is life outside of High Street [local Constituency Labour Party Headquarters]. I think that it is one thing to be interested....it is good to be enthusiastic and it is good to be involved, but it soon gets boring for the simple reason that you can be too involved. And I think you need to look at other aspects of your life rather than perhaps take on a tunnel vision in which the only people you see and speak to are the same old people.

Perhaps more significant were those respondents who reported that they had found themselves questioning the legitimacy of established forms of discursive activity, and indeed the actual purpose of their involvement. For instance, one Labour Party member observed that:

> There have very much been times when I have actually taken on responsibility and gone and done something, but a lot of me just doesn't want to do that anymore. Maybe I have gone through that part of my life, which lasted quite a long time.

He went on to observe that he was currently 'unlearning' procedural norms associated with active involvement in the Party. An Amnesty International member similarly observed that this tendency can often lead to withdrawal from active participation:

> People do run out of steam. That is a reality of it all. So then maybe they will just sit back on the committee or sometimes they will walk away from it. That is what happened to me with Amnesty in the end. I ran out of steam. I had been doing the newsletter and then it was getting out late and then one of them was missed....and I think part of fading away form the local group was linked to all that.

Underlying these comments one can detect a questioning of the norms of participation that may have been acquired during a process of socialisation. This process often leads to a gradual decline of enthusiasm for traditional methods of participation. In particular, a number of respondents highlighted a growing disillusionment with meetings and associated procedure. For example, one Labour Party member of thirteen years standing stated that:

> When I was younger I used to think it was quite good fun going to meetings, but now I just can't really be bothered with meetings anymore unless it is really worth going to. I find them pretty tedious really, the meetings.

Another respondent who had been a Party member for over thirty years similarly stated that 'it is horrendous when you look at another agenda and see canvassing, door knocking and those kinds of things. How can you get excited about that?' He had previously been a Labour Club secretary, so was familiar with such activities. Yet another revealed how he had begun to question the legitimacy of meetings and associated procedures:

> The procedures....maybe once I accepted that one had to work in this way. Maybe I just didn't question it. Maybe I just thought this is how it is done. But increasingly I wonder about how we do things.

Comments from an Amnesty International member provide a telling example of this tendency. He recalled how a new local group had started up in his area but he had made a conscious decision to avoid returning to his old level of participation:

> There was a local group that started up somewhere round here who actually wrote to me but I didn't get involved…I think there was something about not wanting to be able to get dragged into a group with wildly enthusiastic people…and there is the thing about not wanting to feel over committed or feeling obliged to do things…there is something about not wanting to get dragged in, and not wanting to feel that you are actually not doing enough.

Putting aside for the moment his feelings of obligation about participation, it is clear that he has deliberately curtailed the scope of his personal involvement with the local group structure of Amnesty. As he puts it 'I pay my sub and I am very clear that that is my contribution'. For him there was a distinct feeling that he had reached the limits of his involvement with Amnesty, and he no longer wished to engage in extensive processes of discourse. He continued:

> ….there is something about the energy and enthusiasm about Amnesty that for some people, and certainly for me, that it tends to run its course….I see many people doing it for a long time….one or two still have the energy to do it all brilliantly….but most of them become slightly removed. They back off sufficiently to defend themselves from it all.

Interestingly, he was keen to make it clear that this was not tied to a decline of support for the ideals and aims of Amnesty International. He was as enthusiastic about the importance of human rights as he had always been. Rather, he noted that his experience of the political participation that went on within the local group structures of Amnesty International UK had become largely negative and alienating:

> It is quite disillusioning . Even though I know it is the way organisations run I still find it disillusioning when you see that actually very few people are active. Far more people are just loosely connected than are active….I think I got fed up and annoyed because that was the way it was. At first it is not a problem. It is not an issue at all. I think it is when you find that the load on you is there, and you know it could be easily shared out.

It is also illuminating to note that this Amnesty International respondent alluded to aspects of participatory discourse that he felt would be more enabling for him as a potential participant. He felt that alternative structures could be developed if one was to hypothetically start afresh. In particular, he highlighted ways in which the tight control of group tasks amongst active members could be challenged:

> I think it is the opportunity to start off by maybe avoiding some of the errors that you have already seen in the more established groups. One of which is the overloading of specific individuals. And if I had been in on that group at an early stage and we were talking about jobs and who was going to do what, one of the things that I would have been heading for very, very heavily would have been a wide share out. Give everyone a little bit to do and it is easy. They can do it. Put it all on the heads of one or two individuals and they have got a real load. And of course some people embrace that, they think it is wonderful. But I don't think it is good for the group. Because they are either going to tire of it or they will move on....you get into habits as a group and you end up running things certain ways.

An experienced Labour Party member to whom I spoke had cultivated a similar concern about the distribution of tasks within the local branch. He felt that:

> Too many people in this party take on offices at branch level...we have got so many bloody offices, far more than there are people in the Party taking part. And they say I will do this, either knowing or not knowing that they will end up just not doing it. A position should be left vacant if no bugger wants it. There is no point in somebody saying I will be membership secretary if they won't be membership secretary or they haven't got the time or if they are already a councillor or whatever....it would be a lot better if there were a lot less positions and we possibly re-thought what they were all there. Officer of this, officer of that....I don't know.

A similar interest in developing alternative types of discourse was detectable during an interview with a Labour Party member of twenty-five years standing. He described how he had been involved in an effort to develop a more vibrant way of running meetings at the branch level:

> We would stop business at nine o'clock and have a discussion about some issue. And we would announce what that was, and we would have somebody who would act as the kind of initiator of it. They would either present their position or present a position or a range of positions. And then we would have a decent discussion. We would look at what we felt about Party policy in a particular area. And that is what I thought we should be doing rather than reading out endless letters.

Another experienced Party member noted how he had come to the conclusion that the style and tone of branch meetings needs to be changed:

> At branch meetings and other meetings you will always hear people wringing their hands and saying oh isn't it terrible people don't come to these meetings and we really ought to persuade them to do so. But I do think that at the end of the day you have got to get beyond guilt tripping people. You have got to make it worth coming to I'm afraid....they will only want to come to a meeting if it is worth coming to and where they feel they can actually do something.

He also felt that the problems associated with attracting new members could be addressed by developing more informal, enabling structures within the local branch:

> I don't know....perhaps we need a forum for some of the new members....maybe pick out half a dozen people who have turned up at one branch meeting and never come back. Socially down the pub or something. To chat about why they didn't come back and what they think we should do about it. And to almost take out the old guard who have been there since the dawn of time. Perhaps not even let them into the discussion almost, because I'm not sure they won't bring the orthodoxy back into it. It is an organisational thing. We have got ourselves stuck in a rut and we probably can't get ourselves out of it.

The aforementioned Amnesty International UK member also noted that if he was to ever become involved in a local group again he would make a conscious assessment of the characteristics of the group before becoming heavily involved. As he put it: 'I think I would go along to the meetings a few times and I would be looking to see what they did and how they did it'. Clearly, the nature of the discourse that takes place and the potential requirements of being involved are factors influencing his decision.

It is important that this decline of enthusiasm for traditional methods of taking part is not overstated. The Tenants' and Residents' Association members to whom I spoke did not express a similar disillusionment with traditional forms of participation. Nonetheless, it was clear from the interviews that a large portion of those who have been involved in participation for a number of years experience a waning of interest in taking part. It is also evident that this results in part from sustained experience of traditional structures that exist within the organisations. It is therefore crucial to note these revised attitudes toward participation had not developed in an abstract or theoretical fashion for these respondents. On the contrary, these respondents had cultivated these concepts directly from their own experience of political participation. One should also recall the ways in which Exodus has made a deliberate attempt to develop alternative models of deliberation in response to the perceived limitations of existing forms of participation.

9 Conclusions

This book has sought to build upon existing analysis of political participation by presenting a predominantly qualitative analysis of the nature of political participation in contemporary liberal democracy. From the outset, I have argued that the ways in which citizens become involved in political life is a crucial component of the current state of democracy. The quality of political participation can tell us a great deal about the limits of existing forms of democracy. In order to provide an adequate overview of the wide range of structures that sustain such political participation I have undertaken a comparative analysis of a major political party, a campaigning pressure group, several examples of state-citizen dialogue and an alternative lifestyle collective. This collection of examples of political participation is intended to represent the spectrum of political activity that stretches between the state and civil society.

Throughout this book I have argued that the testimonies of the respondents to whom I have spoken should form the basis of my understanding of how and why citizens engage in political life. I began my theoretical discussion in Chapter Two with a critique of reductionist tendencies within existing analysis of political participation of citizens. I argued that analysis of the political participation of citizens must concern itself not only with the levels and composition of patterns of political participation, but also with qualitative questions centred on the process of taking part in political life. I have consequently adopted a methodology that has allowed the analysis to focus on the experiences and perceptions of those who have taken part in various facets of political participation. Furthermore, I have sought to highlight the dialectical link between those who engage with the sphere of political participation and the various structures through which such activity is mediated. The intention has been to avoid both an overly voluntaristic and an overly deterministic reading of the nature of political participation. In Chapter Three, I next developed a wider theoretical perspective that would enable me to connect the actual practice of political participation to broader questions around the nature of political discourse, civil society and the political public sphere. This discussion drew primarily on the work of Jürgen Habermas. It was argued that a key aim of the analysis of political participation should be to uncover distortions of political discourse. Underlying this analytical imperative was an interest in the potential development of a rational and deliberative democratic process. The role of civil society and voluntary participation within such as process was identified as a source of some contention. I then used Habermas' typology, where appropriate, to analyse the data in Chapters Five, Six and Seven.

What lessons can be learnt from the responses of the interviewees and the analysis of the organisations about the scope and characteristics of voluntary political participation in the 1990s? And what does this tell us about the state of 'actually existing' democracy in Britain today? Underlying this book has been a commitment to the idea that the nature of the political activity of citizens is a key component of both the capabilities and limits of the functioning democratic process. The question of how citizens participate in politics can thus be seen as an index of the relationship that exists between citizens and the political process. In this concluding chapter, I seek to make a series of theoretical observations about the nature of the voluntary political participation discussed in this book. The chapter is structured around three main interrelated themes that have arisen from the primary research. Firstly, I will consider the experience of participation that informs the testimonies of the respondents. This, in turn, leads to a consideration of the factors that influence decisions to take part in aspects of political life. Secondly, I will assess the spectrum of participation that constitutes the typology of activism outlined in Chapter Six, and consider the extent to which there are certain 'habits' of political activity that inhabit the typology. Finally, I will present a broader discussion about the potential role that the political structures of civil society can play in facilitating the tendencies outlined by Habermas in his discussion of communicative action and discourse ethics.

The general argument of the conclusion will be that whilst voluntary modes of political participation continue to play a key role in the democratic process, the data presented in this book suggests that these forms of political discourse are limited in their potential for developing a discursively structured public sphere. In many respects, the data challenges the image of activism as an inherently deliberative phenomenon. I will therefore question the emphasis that Habermas and other theorists place on civil society as a site for the potential reinvigoration of a discursively structured public sphere. I will argue that the findings indicate that there are a series of tensions and a tangible sense of distortion that somewhat surprisingly cut across contemporary forums of voluntary political participation. These factors imply that new forms of democratic relationships and practice are increasingly crucial to debates around the role of citizens in political life. In conclusion, I make a series of tentative observations about the potential route that democratisation, in the sense proposed by Habermas, might take in light of the findings presented in this book.

Experiencing Political Participation

A central theme that has arisen out of the primary research relates to the question of the relationship between the nature of political participation and the inclination to take part in some aspect of political life. Habermas has recently argued that the normative framework of discourse theory needs to be supplemented by 'the critical investigation of the mechanisms that in democracies constituted as social-welfare states function to alienate citizens from the political process' (Habermas, 1992c, p. 450). A central finding of the book has indicated the extent to which involvement in different structures of political participation actually affects the skewed distribution of political activity throughout the population. I have argued in Chapter Two that much of the existing analysis of political participation makes only limited reference to the actual conditions in which political activity proceeds. When thinking about why so few people actively engage with the participatory sphere the research suggests that we need to be sensitive to the experience of participation itself. By grounding my analysis in the experiences of participants I have been able to explore the effects of involvement in political life upon participants. It has been shown that, in fact, this plays a key role in influencing the likelihood of the respondents becoming involved in political activity.

Rather than being passive or apathetic recipients of politics, the data presented in this book suggests that the respondents tended to make active judgements about the value of becoming more involved in a particular forum. If the opportunities for participation in political life remain limited and disillusioning, then it is perhaps little surprise that many citizens remain cautious about becoming involved in political participation. The assumption that citizens are passive or uninterested in politics overlooks the disabling tendencies of participatory cultures. The findings indicate that it is not uncommon for inexperienced participants to encounter a barrier when entering traditional participatory mechanisms, such as Labour Party local branch meetings. For many, this leads to a decline of enthusiasm. It has been shown that those who do proceed to take part to any great degree are often required to invest in a process of learning participatory norms. It is clearly a minority of participants who appear willing to invest time and individual effort in this manner. The data clearly demonstrates that there is a widespread cautiousness about active engagement within the political realm. The role of active participants has also been shown to have an alienating effect on less experienced political actors. If one of the reasons why levels of political participation remain limited is that there is little incentive for citizens to engage in activity with existing forms of political deliberation, then it is perhaps logical to question the potential role that cultures of voluntary participation can play in reinvigorating processes of political discourse. This, in turn, raises a series of deeper questions about the capacities of civil society in facilitating and maintaining the communicative tendencies to which Habermas has referred. However, before turning to this question, attention needs to be given to the typology of activism developed in Chapter Six. What can this typology tell us about the scope of political participation in advanced liberal democracies? And how does this develop our understandings of the nature of activism?

Assessing the Typology: Habits of Political Participation?

In Chapter Three, I highlighted the importance of uncovering and analysing established 'habits' of discourse that might exist within forums of political participation. In light of the findings presented in the previous chapters, is it possible to refer to key assumptions that contribute to the shaping of political cultures within the range of political groups examined in the course of this book? In other words, do the findings indicate that there is a specific culture of participation that has become established within the spectrum of political forums? And how do these forms of political practice relate to the framework developed by Habermas? These questions are particularly relevant in view of Chambers' (1995b, p. 176) observation that 'it is plausible that the most serious barrier to discourse can be found in the conversational habits that citizens have become used to'. In this book, I have sought to consider this question by analysing the 'styles of political communication' (Bohman, 1996, p. 115) that inhabit the 'real world' of political participation. Given that I have investigated a wide range of political structures, one might have anticipated that the analysis would uncover a correspondingly diverse range of political activity.

With this in mind, in Chapter Three I made reference to the different expectations that a Habermasian perspective might have about the different forms of political discourse to be found in each organisation. One might have expected the Exodus collective to foster the most communicative discourse, and in many respects this was the case. Nonetheless, given that I have examined a wide range of organisations it is somewhat surprising to discover that there are also a number of generic features of political participation that stretch across the various organisations. In Chapters Five and Six I made reference to a number of persistent characteristics that, to varying degrees, transcend the organisations I have studied. These included factors such as the development of expert cultures, the prevalence of informal coercion, self-perpetuating hierarchies and the control of participatory mechanisms. These have already been discussed in detail, and have been shown to be predominantly instrumental in character. One can thus question the traditional image of activism as indicative of qualities such as political deliberation and discussion. Given that there appears to be common aspects of political participation that are evident within all of the groups to varying degrees, it is somewhat misleading to overstate the differences that exist between the political cultures of each body. If we are to provide a more accurate image of activism then it may be useful to conceive the typology as representing various points on a continuum. In this sense, the overt differences that exist between Exodus and a Tenants' Association, for instance, can be seen as degrees of emphasis along a spectrum between the instrumental and communicative rationality to which Habermas refers. I will take this point up shortly when I consider the nature of the Exodus collective in more depth.

There are a number of additional features of voluntary participation that are also worthy of comment. In Chapter Six I identified a widespread reluctance to engage with what might be defined as broader 'political' issues. The fact that several long-term Party members referred to 'duty' as a key reason for their continuing attendance at meetings is telling. On the one hand this aversion to political issues might represent a retreat from political dogma and rhetoric, but I feel that there was often more of a sense of withdrawal from 'the political' *per se*. Whereas the former might perhaps contribute to a more open and deliberative format, the latter would tend to foster some form of political quietism. In the case of the Tenants' and Residents' Associations there was a particularly strong sense of excluding certain issues from the agenda of the Association.

In Chapter Six, I referred to the prominence of forms of participation built around administrative issues. The involvement of citizens in the political process is fundamentally important to notions of democracy because in a democratic polity citizens must be able to take part in the determination of social aims and objectives. From this perspective, the public sphere should provide an arena in which citizens are able to fulfill this role. This implies that political participation is limited if it is primarily concerned with the details and means by which pre-defined aims are put into place. If the various forms of participation that inhabit the contemporary political public sphere are shown to be structured primarily around issues of administration and management, then we can argue that democracy is limited. As McCarthy (1984, p. 383) notes, '[T]he transformation of practical into technical questions legitimizes [sic] their withdrawal from public discussion and deprives the public sphere of its critical function'. The nature of interaction and discourse within spaces of participation then becomes concerned with technical and administrative issues. As I have shown, this is often the case. This is especially important in view of the comments made in Chapter Seven about the process of learning to participate. Several respondents made reference to the necessity of having to familiarise oneself with established methods of participation in order to play a significant role in proceedings. The scope of discourse therefore often reduces from deliberation about political issues down to the minutia of implementing certain procedural norms. Whilst Habermas' account of discourse ethics is an inherently procedural concept, one can clearly detect in the findings a sense in which existing forms of discursive procedure tend to shift political interaction away from what might be defined as a communicative form of action. Procedure tends to become a source of control and exclusion rather then an enabling forum in which the force of the better argument can hold sway. This suggests that there is either little sense in pursuing Habermas' proceduralism or that there is an inherent malaise within existing forums of participation. I would suggest that the latter is the most viable conclusion, particularly if one is unwilling to reject the concept of increasing democratisation. The notion of discourse ethics suggest that it is the type of procedure that is key to the development of more communicative methods of political communication. The findings of this book suggest that one must also consider the types of political culture that currently hold sway within such procedures.

For those who are prepared to take a central role in traditional structures of voluntary political participation, a willingness to engage with this type of culture is often a prerequisite of becoming more involved. The main route for those who find such discourse disillusioning is invariably one of exit. The comments from Labour Party members who referred to the tendency for new participants to fail to return to meetings is indicative of this facet of participation. This feature of political participation has implications for those interested in the development of discourse ethics within the public sphere because, as Cohen and Arato (1995, p. 448) observe, '[A]cting subjects become subordinated to the imperatives of apparatus that have become autonomous and substitutes for communicative interaction'. These ways of working 'develop their own logic – the proper meaning of colonisation' (Cohen and Arato, 1995, p. 479).

My own feeling is that procedural norms are the spaces in which these respondents were able to exercise some form of 'political' agency. When the spaces available to participants for meaningful action are severely limited then it is perhaps no surprise that an interest in retaining control of small-scale mechanisms comes to the fore. It is also perhaps no coincidence that some structures are also keen to retain such a situation. For instance, in Chapter Five I highlighted the reluctance of Tenants' Participation Officers to question the persistency of minority participation. One might also raise the question of the extent to which the control of mechanisms by small groups actually reflects a wider reluctance to open up political organisations to wider input from the membership. If participation remains in the hands of small, self-replicating groups which reflect the policy direction of the Labour Party, for instance, then it becomes less necessary for the Party hierarchy to directly involve the wider membership in internal processes of policy deliberation. If small clusters of activism provide an appropriate level of legitimacy to an organisation then one could argue that the need for internal deliberation has been successfully closed off.

It is also important to note that several of the more experienced respondents within the Labour Party and Amnesty International had developed their own personal critique of traditional methods of 'conducting politics'. The fact that these respondents had begun to question the validity and efficacy of established norms of participation suggests that the range of rationality at work within political structures tends to limit the scope of political discourse. The more communicative approaches, which many identified as possible routes of alternative discourse, are invariably excluded from the formats with which they have become familiar. Clearly, political participation takes place within organisational and cultural constraints.

Radical Political Structures and Civil Society

A central theme of contemporary political thought concerns the potential that exists within advanced liberal democracies for the deepening and extension of democracy. In the past decade there has been increasing discussion about the potential for the development of political participation that sustains a more direct and deliberative role for citizens in political decision-making processes. As I have argued, this theme has become particularly acute in view of growing cynicism about the scope and degree of voluntary citizen engagement with the political process. In Chapter Three, I also identified a widespread trend for identifying civil society as a space in which political discourse and interaction may be strengthened. The current interest in the development of civil society has inspired a growing interest in the changing nature of established political forums such as political parties and pressure groups, and the emergence of 'new' modes of political participation such as the Exodus collective. These debates are central to the perspective developed by Habermas. He observes that, with regard to democratisation, '[T]he only way is to radicalize [sic] those institutions we have already established in Western countries, to direct them toward a form of radical democracy that makes it possible....to change or at least to affect administration' (Habermas, 1992d, p. 470). In order to address this theme, I will discuss two facets of political activity that I have identified, namely radical political structures and minimalist participation associated with pressure groups. Seemingly innovative bodies such as Exodus and campaign groups such as Amnesty International are often cited as examples of the ways in which citizens can play a more vibrant role in politics.

In recent years, there has been much discussion about the potential role that 'social movement' groups can play in the reinvigoration of the public sphere of advanced liberal democracies. In line with the notions of 'do-it-yourself' politics espoused by many analysts in recent years, political experiments epitomised by groups such as the Exodus collective have been described by McKay (1998b, p. 3) as 'spaces of protest, pleasure and living'. In a similar vein, McNeish (1999) has identified British anti-roads protest as a form of resistance to the processes of colonisation identified by Habermas. A crucial component of such bodies is a rejection of established, formal political structures. This was clearly evident in the comments of participants within Exodus. The crucial contribution of Exodus might thus be seen to lie in the way in which political alienation becomes configured into some form of action rather than political withdrawal or quietism. This tends to distinguish such forms of political action from 'more straightforwardly cultural moments of resistance' (McKay, 1998b, p. 4). Exodus might be regarded as particularly potent in this context, because it offers a space for those who feel themselves excluded by the political process, particularly young people.

The organisational characteristics of Exodus and the experience of participation do, in fact, go some way to showing how groups outside of the established policy process are able to create alternative 'discursive space' for themselves (Herbst, 1994). In many respects, Exodus appears to represent a counterpoint to the dominant modes of instrumental political activity critiqued by Habermas. Certainly, the internal decision-making structure of Exodus appears to embody aspects of what Chambers (1995b), following Habermas, describes as 'consensual will formation'. These procedures and mechanisms are seen to foster 'discursive' rather than strategic actors who are likely to respect other viewpoints and perspectives. These are factors that I have shown to be evident within Exodus. Central to this development has been the overt rejection of established political mores associated with bodies such as the Labour Party and Socialist Workers Party. Exodus is seen by its founding members primarily as an alternative to the discredited forms of Leftist activism that, it might be argued, have traditionally acted as a source of social and political change. Moreover, the Exodus collective is relatively unusual within 'do-it-yourself' political culture because it attempts to positively engage with cultural and racial diversity (McKay, 1998b, pp. 44-45).

However, it is not necessarily clear that the political activity of a group such as Exodus vindicates the processes of rationalisation identified by Habermas. As Phillips (1991, pp. 129-130) has shown, unstructured and seemingly deliberative formats intended to foster enfranchisement can in fact generate 'false unity' or exaggerated impressions of harmony. The comments from some members suggest that this may be the case with Exodus. One cannot overlook the fact that in reality certain key members dominate proceedings in a manner not unlike more traditional groups. We might also raise the broader question of how a group such as Exodus is actually able to fulfill the communicative potential described by Habermas. Ray (1993, p. 179) has argued that this depends on 'the extent to which proto-public spheres have matured within the former system and are institutionalized [sic] through social movements capable of sustaining a participatory rather than repressive outcome'. In recent writings, Habermas (1996b, p. 330) similarly argues that it is a question of 'whether civil society, through resonant and autonomous public spheres, develops impulses with enough vitality to bring conflicts from the periphery into the centre of the political system'. For Habermas, it is important that these bodies do not cross the boundary into the system and therefore resist integration into existing structures:

> Grassroots organizations [sic]....may not cross the threshold to the formal organization [sic] of independent systems. Otherwise they will pay for the indisputable gain in complexity by having organizational [sic] goals detached from the orientations and attitudes of their members and dependent

instead upon imperatives of maintaining and expanding organizational [sic] power (Habermas, 1996f, p. 362).

But at what point do such communicative impulses 'cross over' into the system? This question again raises the issue of the relationship between civil society structures and the policy making process. The experience of the Exodus collective provides some tentative insights into this theme. In many respects, Exodus is caught between a desire for autonomy, and a need to engage with the policy making process. The later strategy is particularly significant for our discussion because it raises the issue of how spontaneous and impromptu forms of political participation take on more formal features as they become more 'solid' and lay down foundations in civil society. This conundrum between withdrawal and engagement with the policy making process is likely to play a significant role in the future of the collective, particularly in relation to the question of the extent to which the activity of members takes on features of established local bodies within civil society.

The Exodus collective may not be unusual in this respect. As Offe (1990) demonstrates, a group which has emerged spontaneously from the terrain of civil society is likely to be subject to a dilemma between increased institutionalisation and the maintenance of independent, *ad hoc* forms of activity. The latter strategy asserts that 'any step toward formalization [sic] might involve the danger of bureaucratization [sic], centralization [sic], alienation and deradicalization [sic]' (Offe, 1990, p. 240), whilst the former recognises the increased opportunities offered by established channels of political communication such as the local policy process. In order for a group such as Exodus to acquire a status as a 'durable collective actor' (Offe, 1990, p. 240) it may need to become more heavily involved with the policy process and take on the characteristics of more formalised bodies. Furthermore, Offe argues that this may lead to the development of more structured membership roles and the gradual differentiation between leaders and rank-and-file members. In this sense, we can speculate that the current status and characteristics of Exodus may represent one stage on a life cycle of political organisations that emerge from the 'institutional vacuum' (Offe, 1990, p. 236) of civil society. Of course, one does not necessarily need to view this process as an inevitability. As Offe observes, the 'logic of institutional politics' (Offe, 1990, p. 246) is a pressure which some participants of a group such as Exodus may resist. What is important is the possible outcomes of such tensions over the next few years.

One might also gain some insight into this question by comparing Exodus with more firmly established groups such as the Residents' Association analysed in this book. This body has consciously adopted more formal elements of political communication. In many respects, this has enabled them to open up channels of communication with institutions of the local state such as the Housing Department. As I have shown this has implications for the forms of participation to be found in such bodies. It is perhaps somewhat ironic that the communicative tendencies to be found in Exodus are emerging within a structure that can be best described as a 'weak' public (Fraser, 1992). In this sense, the collective remains at some distant from the policy process and is likely to be subject to fundamental compromises if it is able to take on the features of a 'strong' public by engaging more fully with the local policy process. This conundrum raises deep concerns about the capabilities of a structure such as Exodus to fulfill the potential identified by Habermas.

Minimalist Participation and Pressure Groups: Generating Political 'Influence'?

Another aspect of the findings to which I wish to draw attention is the continuing growth of minimalist participation of the type epitomised by the 'protest businesses' to which Jordan and Maloney (1997) refer. In Chapter Five I demonstrated the influence of this dimension of the participatory typology on the Campaigns Department of Amnesty International UK and within the Labour Party. The need for high membership rates is a key feature of pressure groups such as Amnesty International UK because of the perceived legitimacy acquired within the broader political arena. The comments of recent recruits to the Labour Party members suggest that the Party may be gradually transforming into a political organisation reminiscent of groups such as Greenpeace and Amnesty International. By this, I mean that members subscribe to the Party but have little or no expectations about taking part in the internal life of the Party. The reformed Labour Party internal policy process has increasingly displaced the face-to-face structure of the local branch in favour of more direct forms of consultation such as the individual ballot or referendum. This institutional reform has important implications for the changing nature of Labour Party membership and clearly reflects the growing prevalence of this 'minimalist' form of participation.

It is thus important to note that the scope of what comes under the definition of 'activism' is currently broadening beyond the traditional image of intense involvement within a given political body. A far more minimalist notion of what it means to take part in political life has gained currency in recent years. In particular, one needs to question the tacit assumption that participation necessarily entails the face-to-face interaction associated with membership meetings and such like. According to Thompson (1993, p. 187; italics in original) 'the phenomenon of publicness has become detached from the sharing of a common locale. It has become *de-spatialized* [sic] and *non-dialogical*'. One might productively label this trend as the spread of a form of 'virtual participation' in the sense that it tends to rely on limited forms of contact between members and the organisation in question. Of course, large numbers of members have always chosen to take a limited role within the Labour Party, for instance. But the findings discussed in Chapters Five and Six suggest that the technologies of membership are undergoing significant change. Davey (1996, pp. 82-83) has echoed this by observing that the contemporary Labour Party is 'not simply a larger version of its former self. It's structures have been re-engineered to encourage growth based on national rather than a neighbourhood identification with its political project'. What came through strongly from the testimonies of respondents within Amnesty International UK and, to some extent, the Labour Party was a sense of signing up to a pre-ordained agenda. For many of these respondents, there was little desire to take part beyond the level of basic membership. Although one can point to the influence of negative perceptions of extensive involvement, it is also necessary to highlight the extent to which the very act of becoming a member is increasingly seen to represent a participatory action in itself. For these respondents, the deliberative and discursive dimension of such participation has been largely undertaken before the individual actually joins the organisation in question. One might therefore question the extent to which such respondents were actually seeking deliberation as part of their membership of Amnesty International. In some respects, it is quite feasible to suggest that it is not uncommon for members of a body such as Amnesty International to seek an instrumental focus within their participatory activity.

One could quite easily critique this aspect of the participatory typology as indicative of a decline of strong discourse within the realm of political participation. Warren (1995, pp. 189-191), for instance, argues that self-organised voluntary forms of participation are less likely to foster discourse than bodies in which people are formally required to interact with each other. He argues that the voluntary character of these groups and the ease of exit are likely to lead to self-selecting arrangements of participation. As he puts it, 'in the case of many political interest and pressure groups, the likelihood of critique and discourse is low....because goals are action-oriented' (Warren, 1995, p. 189). He goes on to note that '[T]his will tend to steer communication away from critique and discourse, and toward strategic concerns' (Warren, 1995, p. 189). However, one could similarly argue that the political public sphere of advanced liberal democracy is such that the minimalist participation offered by bodies such as Amnesty International UK is an increasingly attractive option for many citizens. Certainly, the periodic rise and subsequent fall of Labour Party membership during the General Election period of 1997 would seem to lend some support to this argument, as would the comments of the respondents discussed in Chapter Six.

It may well therefore be the case that the relationship between large-scale political organisations and the development of communicative rationality is a complex one. In Chapter Five I identified a number of key tensions that currently inform the membership policies of Amnesty International and the Labour Party. These structures can subsequently be best viewed as sites of often-conflicting tendencies rather than as enclosed vehicles of single aspects of rationality. For instance, I highlighted the sense in which Amnesty International UK makes a number of key concessions to the idea of deliberation and internal policy debate. At the same time, Amnesty International UK finds itself split between this commitment and more instrumental tendencies such as the need for funds. As I have shown, these tensions are often played out in the experiences and expectations of Amnesty International members. The comments from members who felt that Amnesty had become overly 'business like' in its dealings with members are of some relevance here. This dissatisfaction suggest that perhaps large-scale groups such as Amnesty International are invariably guided by the factors to which Warren (1995) observes. The relationship between such bodies and their members are often instrumental in nature, with both members and the organisation itself developing pre-defined agendas about what they want or expect from each other. Yet at the same time, there is a detectable feeling within the Campaigns Department of Amnesty International UK that the organisation is distinctive for the key role that members can play within the organisation. One cannot therefore necessarily assume that Amnesty International is, by virtue of its reliance on minimalist forms of membership, unlikely to foster discursive tendencies.

Perhaps a more useful index of the role played by minimalist participation can be developed by examining more closely Habermas' specific account of the part that such structures can play in the contemporary political public sphere. I have commented in Chapter Three on the scaling down of Habermas' account of the scope and capabilities of communicative action within advanced liberal democracies. This is perhaps reflective of a wider growing disenchantment with deliberative potential of voluntary political participation. According to Habermas' more recent writings, the public sphere 'can be best described as a network for communicating information and points of view....the streams of communication are, in the process, filtered and synthesized [sic] in such a way that they coalesce into bundles of topically specified public opinions' (Habermas, 1996b, p. 360). The links between citizens and policy process therefore remain at the level of influence rather than direct input. In this sense, it is not entirely clear how the flows of discourse that are generated within the structures of civil society are seen to feed into the policy making process. Bohman (1994, p. 181) observes that within Habermas' more recent writings discursive political structures 'do little more than create channels of public influence'. Others, such as Cohen (1995, p. 38), have conversely argued that 'the political role of civil society is not directly related to the conquest of power, but to the generation of influence, through the life of democratic associations and unconstrained discussion in a variety of cultural and informal public spheres'. However, I would argue that this approach requires a more explicit account of how the 'influence' to which Habermas refers is able to translate into a form of political communication capable of forging a closer relationship between citizens and the political process. Certainly, bodies such as Amnesty International and Greenpeace generate a reservoir of public interest in issues such as human rights and environmentalism. But the findings presented in this book suggest that the generation of such 'influence' is not a clear-cut process. These types of organisations are actually informed by a number of internal tensions, both at the organisational level and within the nature of membership itself.

Developing the Political Culture of Participation

Given that the structures inhabiting civil society are subject to a number of conflicting tendencies, one must question the emphasis placed on such forms of participation by Habermas and others. This book has shown that these tensions are reflected in the nature of participatory activism. This is not to deny that there should be a role for the political structures of civil society within the policy-making process. Pressure groups ensure that interests and issues are not easily marginalised or overlooked within the democratic process. Such groups are vital for pushing issues on to the wider political agenda. However, the role that voluntary political participation might play in an evolving polity remains ambiguous. The data presented in this book has gone some way to illustrating the range of dilemmas and tensions that continue to shape the voluntary activism to be found in the public sphere. Political participation has been shown to be a complex and multi-dimensional phenomenon. Sparks of communicative rationality have been shown to emerge across civil society but this has been shown to be a delicate and partial process. Those theorists concerned with the relationship between democratisation and the participation of citizens must be prepared to acknowledge the difficulties and complexities associated with strengthening democracy.

Existing forms of voluntary political participation have been shown, in very general terms, to be guided by instrumental tendencies. Civil society structures are invariably subject to external pressures that tend to limit the capacities of such political institutions to enable their members to contribute to internal discursive processes. With this in mind, it will be instructive to observe how the Exodus collective develops in the future and in particular if it is forced to adopt more conventional methods of organisation and forms of practice. It may be expecting too much of civil society structures to anticipate that they are able to overcome internal frailties and the external pressures to which they are subject. As Burns *et al* (1994, p. 247) observe, 'to recognise civil society as flawed is to admit….it lacks the internal capacity to transcend its own fragmentation'.

I would, however, argue that this does not close off possibilities for the development of more open and enabling forums of political discourse within the democratic process. It does, however, force us to question the role of civil society structures within such a process. I am therefore arguing that one should question the primary role that is often afforded to civil society in much contemporary political thought. At the same time, one cannot simply dismiss the question of discourse as an unrealistic ideal. A particularly interesting aspect of the typology pertains to the comments from respondents who emphasised the social dimension of involvement in the Labour Party. In some respects, I would assert that this dimension of participation appears far more discursive than the more formal aspect of local Party life. This aspect of participation functions free from the constraints imposed by political mechanisms such as meetings. Much of the positive feelings about the experience of participation tended to stem from this social side of political involvement. It is also relevant to note that many of the more experienced respondents had developed personal critiques of established 'habits' of participation. There is consequently some evidence to suggest that citizens may well be capable of acting in a discursive manner given the appropriate conditions. This observation raises the question of the directions which democratisation might consequently take and the potential that exists for the reinvigoration of the political public sphere.

The role of voluntary political participation within such a process is clearly of some importance. This book has demonstrated that the deliberative potential of voluntary citizen participation is ambiguous. This, in turn, has led to a questioning of the emphasis that is placed on civil society by Habermas. Given that such dilemmas persist, it may be necessary to look elsewhere for potential sources of 'communicative rationality'. I can only make limited comment on these issues. Nonetheless, the question of future directions of democratisation remains central to current debates about the role of citizen participation within political structures, and the limits of democracy in Britain. Two points are especially worthy of comment. Firstly, I would concur with Chambers (1995b) when she argues that the development of something akin to discourse ethics is ultimately tied to the growth of a political culture in which citizens are able to cultivate a positive commitment to the practice of deliberation. One cannot realistically conceive of a discursively structured public sphere if citizens are not willing or able to exercise competence in such forms of deliberation. By focusing on the importance of the process of participation I hope to have reinforced the idea that it is too simplistic to assume that more participation would lead to greater democracy. It may well be the case that political participation will invariably remain a minority endeavour. As Parry et al (1992, p. 431) note, '[O]ne should not....think in terms of increasing participation *per se* but of the directions in which political activity might grow and of the possible consequences of its developing along certain dimensions rather than others'. Particularly relevant to the development of a deliberative and rational form of politics is the nature of the political cultures to which citizens are acclimatised. As Chambers (1995b, p. 177) puts it:

> The ideal of a consensually steered society is the ideal of a society that is committed to a certain type of political culture. Implementing practical discourse, then, is not so much a matter of setting up a constitutionally empowered "body" of some sort as it is of engendering a practice. It involves fostering a political culture in which citizens actively participate in public debate and consciously adopt the discursive attitudes of responsibility, self-discipline, respect, cooperation, and productive struggle necessary to produce consensual agreements.

In the course of this book, I have highlighted the instrumental tendencies associated with the cultures of 'actually existing' voluntary political participation to be found across the political public sphere. The limited nature of the political cultures that I have discussed in this book is of some importance because, as Bohman (1996, p. 110) observes, 'political poverty' of this type is indicative of a lack of deliberative capacities. The findings of the present study suggest that the types of political culture identified by Chambers (1995b) are in limited supply within contemporary political spaces. When I have been able to identify such tendencies it has been shown that these are subject to a number of pressures and tensions.

Secondly, I would argue that whilst the nature of political culture is fundamental to the potential development of discourse ethics, attention also needs to be given to the institutional contexts that may allow for such deliberation to evolve. The findings discussed in this book have stressed the extent to which political cultures are in part shaped by the structures within which these forms of participation develop. As I have shown, the question of what organisations want from participants and the extent to which these bodies offer spaces for deliberation and discussion are of some importance in this respect. The question then arises of the extent to which one can realistically expect discourse ethics to develop within the political public sphere without appropriate resources underpinning such a delicate process. In the contemporary distorted public sphere identified by Habermas, deliberative tendencies are largely usurped by the forms of participation analysed in this book. Attention therefore needs to be given to institutional designs that are most likely to encourage deliberation.

In light of the data presented in this book, these two dimensions of 'discursive democracy' may appear somewhat fanciful. In many respects, the notion of a discursively mediated political sphere remains a highly utopian concept and Habermas is undoubtedly accurate when he argues that discourse cannot organise society as a whole. However, the question of discourse ethics is especially relevant to 'the political', particularly in complex, post-traditional societies. Political participation would thus represent the channel through which citizens are able to deliberate and come to some form of agreement over issues of common concern. As Warren (1995, p. 171) observes, 'this is also why discourse is central to democratic politics: What sets political relationships apart from social relations more generally is that they involve disruptions and conflicts that require explicit negotiation'. Although one might question the potential for such deliberative qualities, I would assert that the extent to which the existing democratic process is, at the very least, defined by support for a political culture of uncoerced discourse is surely a central feature of increased democratisation. As McCarthy (1994, p. 224) observes, the extent to which a society is committed to the concept of undistorted and rational argumentation is in itself an important consideration. The data presented in this book has indicated that there is clearly some evidence of such a tendency. However, the extent to which citizens are inclined to take part in such activity depends, at least in part, on the cultivation of a more deliberative political culture. In view of the data presented in this book, the capability of civil society to fulfill such a task remains ambiguous.

Participation and Deliberative Democracy: Forging New Democratic Relationships?

One possible route for strengthening democratisation and cultivating a more deliberative political culture may well therefore reside in the continued development of innovative structures of public involvement. This book has suggested that a major reason for the limited potential for the development of a discursively structured public sphere is the reliance on limited voluntary contributions of the politically active within instrumentally mediated structures. One might therefore propose that alternative spaces must be constructed in which increased opportunities for deliberation are supported and proliferated throughout the population. Structures of political communication would then seek to reach out to those citizens who remain wary of entering the political domain, and who exist beyond the active minority who are more predisposed to participation. Those voices that have traditionally remained largely excluded from the political process such as the young and ethnic minorities would then be more able to contribute to the democratic process. This, in turn, suggests a central role for local institutions of the state, and this is indeed a direction toward which policy makers are increasingly attracted.

This is a move that may appear to contradict elements of Habermas' theoretical perspective, particularly if one assumes that the institutions of the state necessarily represent instrumental tendencies. Part of the problem with Habermas' model may lie in the implicit way in which his perspective links instrumental rationality with the system, and communicative rationality with the lifeworld or civil society. As I have shown in this book, this is a distinction that does not necessarily hold water when it is overlaid on the 'real world' of political participation. To a certain extent, Habermas (1996b, p. 368) has acknowledged these problems by arguing that the political system is intertwined with civil society through organisations such as political parties. However, Ray (1993) has developed the criticism by arguing that Habermas overemphasises the distance between the system and the lifeworld. He suggests that these spheres do not exist in pristine isolation, but are actually interpenetrated: 'systems of regulation and the architecture of the lifeworld are co-determining' (Ray 1993, p. 74). This implies that power relations might exist within lifeworld settings, and that sites of political discursive activity within civil society are therefore likely to contain both communicative and instrumental tendencies. The data presented in this book gives some credence to this suggestion.

There are a number of developments in the field of democratic innovation that may well open up new possibilities for the reinvigoration of a public sphere built around 'the force of the better argument' and increasingly undistorted political debate. Examples might include citizens' juries and deliberative polls that are currently being developed by a number of local authorities within Britain (Stewart et al, 1994; Coote and Lenaghan, 1997). These developments are especially relevant in view of the tendency for experimental forms of deliberation such as citizens' juries to foster forms of public involvement in which participants often develop and overcome subjective attitudes through the open discussion of policy issues (Coote and Lenaghan, 1997, p. 65). These agencies might then act as a conduit for the development of a more collective or common interest amongst participants. Early findings from analysis of citizens' juries suggest that the experience of acting as a representative of the local population leads to most jurors behaving as if they are acting on behalf of the wider population (Coote and Lenaghan, 1997, p. 89). These structures are also distinctive in that they do not rely on voluntary contributions from seasoned political actors. Stewart et al (1994, p. 52) have argued that citizens' juries provide a valuable contribution to contemporary democracy because they 'extend public discourse enabling citizens to explore issues in depth'. It is suggested that these mechanisms foster a serious attitude amongst participants and contribute to the development of a habit of citizenship. It might be useful at this point to draw a distinction between voluntary political participation of the type described in this book and a more mandatory form of participation that might underpin the development of increased deliberation. Participants are selected at random and are therefore not self-selecting. This is a distinction that could perhaps provide a basis for future analysis of political participation of many types.

It is questionable, however, to what extent state structures are likely to facilitate forms of discourse that are able to both shape policy decisions and be critical of broader political issues. For these reforms to succeed to any great degree they must enable citizens to initiate political discussion rather than simply discuss the details of pre-defined policy decisions. It is this type of democratisation that would be most likely to develop the discourse ethics and deliberative political culture to which Habermas refers, but which may also be the least appealing to local state structures. As I have shown, traditional state structures of state-citizen dialogue such as Tenants' Associations are more likely to rely upon forms of participation which marginalise discursive tendencies. Local authorities would therefore need to shift their reliance on the limited responses of existing voluntary contributions and move toward new models of participation.

These experiments in a more deliberative form of democracy are also currently susceptible to manipulation by sponsors and policy makers. In order for citizens' juries and other similar experiments to contribute to the development of increasingly deliberative forums of citizen participation they may need to become a more permanent feature of the democratic process, and therefore compliment continually evolving structures such as political parties and pressure groups. Much will depend on the directions that such innovation takes and the uses to which these new forms of political participation are put. It will also be important to consider how citizens perceive such structures, and it may be instructive to make comparisons with the experiences of voluntary political participants analysed in this book. This would enable a wider assessment to be made of the future role of civil society and institutions of the state within processes of democratisation.

Concluding Remarks

Political participation remains at the heart of contemporary debates about the nature of democracy in Western European liberal democracies. In recent years, the existing democratic process has been subject to growing scrutiny and criticism. A common theme of current political analysis concerns the apparently limited nature of democracy within advanced liberal democracies such as Britain. It is widely argued that the role of citizens in the political process often fails to fulfill the requirements of a democratic polity. Increasingly it is being suggested that one solution to these dilemmas lies in the cultivation of a habit of 'active citizenship' (Stewart *et al*, 1994, pp. 4-5). Throughout this book I have argued that such discussion should not overlook the actual nature of existing forms of political participation. I have suggested that political participation is crucial to democracy because it reflects the ways in which citizens are currently able to play a part in the political process. With this book I have attempted to clarify the nature of the voluntary involvement of citizens in contemporary political life. This, in turn, has raised a series of theoretical questions about the capacities of the various bodies through which citizens engage with political issues and the types of activity which currently inhabit these arenas. These are themes that will continue to inspire debate and contention amongst political theorists and scientists. Perhaps all we can say with certainty is that in the coming decades the participation of citizens in political structures, be it voluntary or otherwise, is likely to become an increasingly visible feature of the British political landscape. It is hoped that this book has gone some way to illustrating both the limits and possibilities that will continue to inform the involvement of citizens in the political process of liberal democracy.

Bibliography

Alvesson, M. and Willmott, H. (1992b) 'Critical Theory and management studies: An introduction', in Alvesson, M. and Wilmott, H. (1992a) (eds), pp. 1-20.
Alvesson, M. and Wilmott, H. (1992a) (eds) *Critical Management Studies*, London, Sage.
Amnesty International UK (1989) *Activists for Amnesty*, London, Amnesty International UK.
Amnesty International UK (1994) *Annual Report*, London, Amnesty International UK.
Amnesty International UK (1995) *Report on Group Profiles*, London, Amnesty International UK.
Andrews, M. (1992) *Lifetimes of Commitment: A Study of Socialist Activists*, PhD thesis, Cambridge University.
Anon (1993) 'Rave new world', *The Guardian*, 12 November 1993.
Anon (1996) *The Independent*, 29 March 1996.
Anon (1997) *The Independent*, 17 February 1997.
Arnstein, S. R. (1971) 'A ladder of participation in the USA', *Journal of the Royal Town Planning Institute*, April, pp. 176-182.
Bagguley, P. (1995) 'Protest, poverty and power: A case study of the anti-poll tax movement', *The Sociological Review*, 43 (4), pp. 693-719.
Bagguley, P. and Hearn, J. (1999) *Transforming Politics: Power and Resistance*, London: Macmillan.
Baxter, H. (1987) 'System and life-world in Habermas' theory of communicative action', *Theory and Society*, 16, pp. 39-86.
Becker, H. and Geer, B. (1982) 'Participant observation: The analysis of qualitative field data', in Burgess, R. (1982) (ed), pp. 239-250.
Beetham, D. (1996) 'Theorising democracy and local government', in King, D. and Stoker, G. (1995a) (eds), pp. 28-49.
Bell, J. (1987) *Doing Your Research Project: A Guide For First-Time Researchers in Education and Social Sciences*, Milton Keynes, Open University Press.
Berg, B. L. (1989) *Qualitative Research Methods For The Social Sciences*, Massachusetts, Simon and Schuster.
Blair, T. (1996) 'Why we need a new morality for the nineties', *The Independent*, 27 April 1996.
Blaug, R. (1996) 'New developments in deliberative democracy', *Politics*, 16 (2), pp. 71-77.
Blaug, R. (1997) 'Between fear and disappointment: Critical, empirical and political uses of Habermas', *Political Studies*, 45 (1), pp. 100-117.

Boaden, N., Goldsmith, M., Hampton, Stringer, P. (1982) *Public Participation in Public Services*, Harlow, Longman.

Boggs, C. (1986) *Social Movements and Political Power: Emerging Forms of Radicalism in the West*, Philadelphia, Temple University Press.

Bohman, J. (1996) *Public Deliberation: Pluralism, Complexity and Democracy*, Massachusetts, MIT Press.

Braaten, J. (1995) 'From communicative rationality to communicative thinking: A basis for feminist theory and practice', in Meehan, J. (1995a) (ed), pp. 139-161.

Brand, A. (1990) *The Force of Reason: An Introduction to Habermas' Theory of Communicative Action*, North Sydney, Allen and Unwin.

Brehony, K. J. (1992) 'Active citizens: the case of school governors', *International Studies in Sociology of Education*, 2 (2), pp. 199-217.

Bryman, A. (1988a) *Quantity and Quality in Social Research*, London, Unwin Hyman.

Bryman, A. (1988b) (ed) *Doing Research in Organizations*, London, Routledge.

Buchanan, D., Boddy, D. and McCalnon, J. (1988) 'Getting in and getting out', in Bryman, A. (1988b) (ed), pp. 53-67.

Burgess, R. (1982) (ed) *Field Research: A Sourcebook and Field Manual*, London, Allen and Unwin.

Burns, D., Hambleton, R., and Hoggett, P. (1994) *The Politics of Decentralisation: Revitalising Local Democracy*, London, Macmillan.

Byrne, P. (1997) *Social Movements in Britain*, London, Routledge.

Calhoun, C. (1992a) (ed) *Habermas and the Public Sphere*, Massachusetts, MIT Press.

Calhoun, C. (1992b) 'Introduction: Habermas and the public sphere', in Calhoun, C. (1992a) (ed), pp. 1-48.

Calhoun, C. (1995) *Critical Social Theory: Culture, Theory and the Challenge of Difference*, Oxford, Blackwell.

Chambers, S. (1995a) 'Discourse and democratic practices', in White, S. K. (1995a) (ed), pp. 233-259.

Chambers, S. (1995b) 'Feminist discourse/practical discourse', in Meehan, J. (1995a) (ed), pp. 163-180.

Channel Four (1995) *Tribe Time*, Channel Four Television, 11 November 1995.

Chartered Institute of Housing (1994) *Tenant Participation in Housing Management*, Rochdale, Chartered Institute of Housing/Tenants Participation Advisory Service.

Christiansen, L. and Dowding, K. (1994) 'Pluralism or state autonomy? The case of Amnesty International: The insider/outsider group', *Political Studies*, 42 (1).

Cochrane, A. (1996) 'From theories to practice: Looking for local democracy in Britain', in King, D. and Stoker, G. (1996) (eds), pp. 193-213.

Cohen, A. (1993) *Masquerade politics: Explorations in the Structure of Urban Cultural Movements*, Oxford, Berg.

Cohen, J. L. (1995) 'Interpreting the notion of civil society', in Walzer, M. (1995a) (ed), pp. 35-40.
Cohen, J. L. and Arato, A. (1994) *Civil Society and Political Theory*, Massachusetts, MIT Press.
Connolly, W. E. (1991) *Identity/Difference: Democratic Negotiations of the Political Paradox*, New York, Cornell University Press.
Coote, A. and Lenaghan, J. (1997) *Citizens' Juries: Theory into Practice*, London, Institute for Public Policy Research.
Crabtree, B. F. and Miller, W. L. (1992a) (eds) *Doing Qualitative Research*, Newbury Park, Sage.
Crabtree, B. F. and Miller, W. L. (1992b) 'Primary care research: a multimethod typology and qualitative road map', in Crabtree, B. F. and Miller, W. L. (1992a) (eds), pp. 3-28.
Croft, S. and Beresford, P. (1992) 'The politics of participation', *Critical Social Policy*, 35, pp. 20-44.
Crossley, N. (1996) *Intersubjectivity: The Fabric of Social Becoming*, London, Sage.
Dalton, R. J. (1988) *Citizen Politics in Western Democracies: Public Opinion and Political Parties in the United States, Great Britain, West Germany and France*, Chatham, Chatham House.
Dalton, R. J. and Knelcher, M. (1990) (eds) *Challenging the Political Order: New Social and Political Movements in Western Democracies*, Cambridge, Polity Press.
Davey, K. (1996) 'The impermanence of New Labour', in Perryman, M. (1996a) (ed), pp. 76-99.
Department of the Environment, Transport and the Regions (1998) *Modern Local Government: In Touch with the People*, London, DETR.
Devine, F. (1995) 'Qualitative methods', in Marsh, D. and Stoker, G. (1995a) (eds), pp. 137-153.
Dey, I. (1993) *Qualitative Data Analysis: A User-Friendly Guide for Social Scientists*, London, Routledge.
Diani, M. (1992) 'The concept of social movement', *The Sociological Review*, 40 (1), pp. 1-25.
Donnison, D. and Maclennan, D. (1994) (eds) *The Housing Service of the Future*, Coventry, Longman.
Dryzek, J. S. (1990) *Discursive Democracy: Politics, Policy and Political Science*, Cambridge, Cambridge University Press.
Dryzek, J. S. (1995) 'Critical theory as a research program', in White, S. K. (1995a) (ed), pp. 97-119.
Eley, G. (1992) 'Nations, publics and political cultures: Placing Habermas in the nineteenth century', in Calhoun, C. (1992a) (ed), pp. 289-359.
Exodus Collective (1994) *The Exodus Collective: An Introduction*, Luton, Exodus Collective.
Exodus Collective (1996) *The Ark: A Proposal for the Exodus Community and Activity Centre*, Luton, Exodus Collective.

Exodus Collective (undated) *An Introduction to HAZ Manor*, Luton, Exodus Collective.

Fisher, J. (1996) *British Political Parties*, Hemel Hempstead, Harvester-Wheatsheaf.

Fishkin, J. S. (1991) *Democracy and Deliberation: New Directions for Democratic Reform*, New York, Yale University Press.

Fitzgerald, M. (1984) *Political Parties and Black People: Participation, Representation and Exploitation*, Nottingham, The Runnymede Trust.

Fleming, M. (1995) 'Women and the public use of reason', in Meehan, J. (1995a) (ed), pp. 117-137.

Forester, J. (1985a) (ed) *Critical Theory and Public Life*, Cambridge, MA, MIT Press.

Forester, J. (1985b) 'Introduction: The applied turn in contemporary critical theory', in Forester, J. (1985a) (ed), pp. ix-xix.

Forester, J. (1985c) 'Critical theory and planning practice' in Forester, J. (1985a) (ed), pp. 202-227.

Forester, J. (1992) 'Critical ethnography: Fieldwork in a Habermasian way', in Alvesson, M. and Wilmott, H. (1992a) (eds), pp. 46-65.

Fox, C. J. and Miller, H. T. (1995) *Postmodern Public Administration: Toward Discourse*, Thousand Oaks, Sage.

Fraser, N. (1992) 'Rethinking the public sphere', in Calhoun, C. (1992a) (ed), pp. 109-142.

Garner, R. and Kelly, R. (1994) *British Political Parties Today*, Manchester, Manchester University Press.

Geuss, R. (1981) *The Idea of a Critical Theory*, Cambridge, Cambridge University Press.

Giddens, A. (1994) 'Brave new world: The new context of politics', in Miliband, D. (1994) (ed), pp. 21-28.

Goodland, R. (1994) 'Tenant participation', in Donnison, D. and Maclennan, D. (1994) (eds), pp. 114-126.

Grayson, J. (1996) *Opening the Window: Revealing the Hidden History of Tenants' Organisations*, Salford, Tenants Participation Advisory Service.

Gyford, J. (1991) *Citizens, Consumers and Councils: Local Government and the Public*, London, Macmillan.

Habermas, J. (1971) *Knowledge and Human Interests*, Boston, Beacon Press.

Habermas, J. (1974) 'The public sphere: An encyclopedia article', *New German Critique*, 3, pp. 49-55.

Habermas, J. (1975) *Legitimation Crisis*, Boston, Beacon Press.

Habermas, J. (1979) *Communication and the Evolution of Society*, Boston, Beacon Press.

Habermas, J. (1981) 'New social movements', *Telos*, 49.

Habermas, J. (1984) *The Theory of Communicative Action Volume 1: Reason and Rationalization of Society*, Cambridge, Polity Press.

Habermas, J. (1987a) *The Philosophical Discourse of Modernity*, Cambridge, Polity Press.

Habermas, J. (1987b) *The Theory of Communicative Action Volume 2: Lifeworld and System: A Critique of Functionalist Reason*, Cambridge, Polity Press.

Habermas, J. (1989a) *The Structural Transformation of the Public Sphere: An Inquiry into a Category of Bourgeois Society*, Cambridge, Polity Press.

Habermas, J. (1989b) *Moral Consciousness and Communicative Action*, Cambridge, Polity Press.

Habermas, J. (1992a) *Autonomy and Solidarity: Interviews*, edited by Dews, P., London, Verso.

Habermas, J. (1992b) *Postmetaphysical Thinking: Philosophical Essays*, Cambridge, Polity Press.

Habermas, J. (1992c) 'Further reflections on the public sphere', in Calhoun (1992a) (ed), pp. 421-461.

Habermas, J. (1992d) 'Concluding remarks', in Calhoun (1992a) (ed), pp. 462-479.

Habermas, J. (1994a) 'Three normative models of democracy', *Constellations*, 1 (1), pp. 1-10.

Habermas, J. (1994b) *Past as Future*, Cambridge, Polity Press.

Habermas, J. (1996a) 'Modernity: An unfinished project', in Passerin D'entreves, M. and Benhabib, S. (1996) (eds), pp. 38-55.

Habermas, J. (1996b) *Between Facts and Norms: Contributions to a Discourse Theory of Law and Democracy*, Cambridge, Polity Press.

Habermas, J. (1996c) 'Discourse theory and the public sphere', in Outhewiate, W. (1996a) (ed), pp. 217-220.

Habermas, J. (1996d) 'Marx and the thesis of internal colonization', in Outhewaite, W. (1996a) (ed), pp. 283-304.

Habermas, J. (1996e) 'The tasks of a critical theory of society', in Outhewaite, W. (1996a) (ed), pp. 309-336.

Habermas, J. (1996f) 'The normative content of modernity', in Outhewaite, W. (1996a) (ed), pp. 341-365.

Hall, J. A. (1995) (ed) *Civil Society: Theory, History, Comparison*, Cambridge, Polity Press.

Hammersley, M. (1993) (ed) *Social Research: Philosophy, Politics and Practice*, London, Sage.

Hammersley, M. and Atkinson, P. (1983) *Ethnography: Principles in Practice*, London, Routledge.

Held, D. (1987) *Models of Democracy*, Cambridge, Polity Press.

Held, D. (1993) (ed) *Prospects for Democracy: North, South, East, West*, Cambridge, Polity Press.

Herbst, S. (1994) *Politics at the Margin: Historical Studies of Public Expression Outside the Mainstream*, Cambridge, Cambridge University Press.

Hill, D. M. (1994) *Citizens and Cities*, Hemel Hempstead, Harvester-Wheatsheaf.

Hirst, P. (1994) *Associative Democracy: New Forms of Economic and Social Governance*, Cambridge, Polity Press.

Holub, R. C. (1991) *Jurgen Habermas: Critic in the Public Sphere*, London, Routledge.

Horster, D. (1992) *Habermas: An Introduction*, Pennbridge Books, Philadelphia.
Jones, P. (1993) *Studying Society: Sociological Theories and Research Practices*, London, Harper Collins.
Jordan, G. and Maloney, W. (1997) *The Protest Business? Mobilizing Campaign Groups*, Manchester, Manchester University Press.
Joseph Rowntree Foundation (1990) 'Tenant participation in council housing', *Housing Research Findings*, 8.
Katz, R. S. and Mair, P. (1994) (eds) *How Parties Organize: Change and Adaption in Party Organizations in Western Democracies*, London, Sage.
Keane, J. (1988) *Democracy and Civil Society*, London, Verso.
Keat, R. and Urry, J. (1975) *Social Theory as Science*, London, Routledge and Kegan Paul.
Kemp, R. (1985) 'Planning, public hearings, and the politics of discourse', in Forester (1985a) (ed), pp. 177-201.
Khan, U. (1990) *Neighbourhood Forums and the 'New Left' in Local Government*, PhD Thesis, Sheffield University.
Khan, U. (1999) (ed) *Participation Beyond the Ballot Box*, London, UCL Press.
King, D. and Stoker, G. (1996) (eds) *Rethinking Local Democracy*, London, Unwin Hyman.
Labour Party (1996) *Renewing Democracy, Rebuilding Communities*, London, The Labour Party.
Labour Party (1997a) *Shaping Our Future*, Membership consultation survey, October 1997.
Leftwich, A. (1984a) (ed) *What is Politics?*, Oxford, Basil Blackwell.
Leftwich, A. (1984b) 'On the politics of politics', in Leftwich, A. (1984a) (ed), pp. 1-18.
Love, N. (1995) 'What's left of Marx?', in White, S. K. (1995a) (ed), pp. 46-66.
Lyotard, J. F. (1984) *The Postmodern Condition*, Minneapolis, University of Minnesota Press.
Lyotard, J. F. (1988) *The Differend: Phrases in Dispute*, Manchester, Manchester University Press.
MacAskill, E. (1998) 'Stuff that envelope, say the activists', *The Guardian*, 23 June 1998.
Maloney, W. (1996) 'Mobilization and participation in large-scale campaigning groups in the UK: The rise of the protest business', Paper presented to European Consortium of Political Research Joint Sessions, Oslo.
Mandelson, P. and Liddle, R. (1996) *The Blair Revolution: Can New Labour Deliver?*, London, Faber and Faber.
Marquand, D. and Wright, T. (1996) 'Commentary: Preparing for power', *The Political Quarterly*, 67 (4), pp. 287-289.
Marris, P. (1987) *Meaning and Action: Community Planning and Conceptions of Change*, London, Routledge and Kegan Paul.
Marsh, D. and Stoker, G. (1995a) (eds) *Theory and Methods in Political Science*, Basingstoke, Macmillan.

Marsh, D. and Stoker, G. (1995b) 'Conclusions', in Marsh, D. and Stoker, G. (1995a) (eds), pp. 288-297.
May, T. (1993) *Social Research: Issues, Methods and Process*, Buckingham, Open University Press.
McAdam, D. and Paulson, R. (1993) 'Specifying the relationship between social ties and activism', *American Journal of Sociology*, 99 (3), pp. 640-667.
McCarthy, J. D and Zald, M. N. (1976) 'Resource mobilization and social movements: A partial theory', *American Journal of Sociology*, 82, pp. 1212-1293.
McCarthy, T. (1984) *The Critical Theory of Jürgen Habermas*, Cambridge, Polity Press.
McCarthy, T. (1989) 'Introduction', in Habermas, J. (1989a), pp. xi-xiv.
McCarthy, T. (1994) 'Rejoinder to David Hoy', in McCarthy, T. and Hoy, D. (1994) (eds), pp. 217-248.
McCarthy, T. and Hoy, D. (1994) (eds) *Critical Theory*, Oxford, Basil Blackwell.
McKay, G. (1996) *Senseless Acts of Beauty: Cultures of Resistance Since the Sixties*, Verso, London.
McKay, G. (1998a) (ed) *DIY Culture: Party and Protest in Nineties Britain*, London, Verso.
McKay, G. (1998b) 'DiY culture: Notes toward an intro', in McKay, G. (1998a) (ed), pp. 1-53.
McKenny, G. P. (1991) 'From consensus to consent: A plea for a more communicative ethic', *Soundings*, 74 (3-4), pp. 427-457.
McLaverty, P. (1996) *The Politics of Empowerment?*, Aldershot, Dartmouth.
McNeish, W. (1999) 'Resisting colonisation: The politics of anti-roads protesting', in Bagguley, P. and Hearn, J. (1999) (eds), pp. 67-84.
McRobbie, A. (1994) 'Folk devils fight back', *New Left Review*, 203, pp. 107-116.
Meehan, J. (1995a) (ed) *Feminists Read Habermas: Gendering the Subject of Discourse*, London, Routledge.
Meehan, J. (1995b) 'Introduction', in Meehan, J. (1995a) (ed), pp. 1-20.
Mies, M. (1993) 'Towards a methodology for feminist research', in Hammersley M. (1993) (ed), pp. 64-82.
Miliband, D. (1994) (ed) *Reinventing the Left*, Cambridge, Polity Press.
Miller, D. (1993), 'Deliberative democracy and social choice', in Held D. (1993) (ed), pp. 74-92.
Miller, W. L. (1995) 'Quantitative methods', in Marsh, D. and Stoker, G. (1995a) (eds), pp. 154-172.
Miller, W. L. and Dickson, M. B. (1996), *Local Governance and Local Citizenship: A Report on Public and Elite Attitudes*, Local Governance Programme Working Paper no. 1, Glasgow, The Local Governance Programme of the European Social Research Council.
Mouffe, C. (1992) (ed) *Dimensions of Radical Democracy*, London, Verso.
Mowlam, M. (1996) 'New Labour: The world has changed, and so has Labour', *The Independent*, 7 July 1996.
Mulgan, G. (1994) *Politics in an Antipolitical Age*, Cambridge, Polity Press.

Myerson, G. (1994) *Rhetoric, Reason and Society: Rationality as Dialogue*, London, Sage.
National Council for Voluntary Organisations (1997) *The Voluntary Agencies Directory*, London, NCVO Publications.
National Council for Voluntary Organisations (1998) *The Voluntary Agencies Directory*, London, NCVO Publications.
Nicholson, N., Ursell, G., Blyton, P. (1981) *The Dynamics of White Collar Unionism: A Study of Local Union Participation*, London, Academic Press.
O'Mally, J. (1977) *The Politics of Community Action*, Nottingham, Bertrand Russell Peace Foundation for Spokesman Books.
Offe, C. (1990) 'Reflections on the institutional self-transformation of movement politics: A tentative stage model', in Dalton, R. J. and Knechler, M. (1990) (ed), pp. 232-250.
Olsen, M. E. (1972) 'Social participation and voting turnout: A multivariate analysis', *American Sociological Review*, 37, pp. 317-333.
Olson, M. (1965) *The Logic of Collective Action*, Cambridge, MA, Harvard University Press
Outhewaite, W. (1987) *New Philosophies of Social Science*, London, Macmillan.
Outhewaite, W. (1994) *Habermas: A Critical Introduction*, Cambridge, Polity Press.
Outhewaite, W. (1996a) (ed) *The Habermas Reader*, Cambridge, Polity Press.
Outhewaite, W. (1996b) 'General introduction', in Outhewaite, W. (1996a), pp. 3-22.
Parry, G., Moyser, G., Day, N. (1992) *Political Participation and Democracy in Britain*, Cambridge, Cambridge University Press.
Passerin D'Entreves, M. and Benhabib, S. (1996) (eds) *Habermas and the Unfinished Project of Modernity*, Cambridge, Polity Press.
Pateman, C. (1970) *Participation and Democratic Theory*, Cambridge, Cambridge University Press.
Perryman, M. (1996a) *The Blair Agenda*, London, Lawrence and Wishart.
Perryman, M. (1996b) 'Introduction: Coming up for air', in Perryman, M. (1996a), pp. 1-17.
Phillips, A. (1991) *Engendering Democracy*, Cambridge, Polity Press.
Puddifoot, J. (1996) 'Debate: Are community campaign groups representative?', *Community Development Journal*, 31 (4), pp. 351-353.
Rasmussen, D. M. (1990), *Reading Habermas*, Oxford, Basil Blackwell.
Ray, L. J. (1993) *Rethinking Critical Theory: Emancipation in the Age of Global Social Movements*, London, Sage.
Richardson, J. (1995) 'The market for political activism: Interest groups as a challenge to political parties', *West European Politics*, 18 (1), pp. 116-139.
Robson, C. (1993) *Real World Research: A Resource for Social Scientists and Practitioner-Researchers*, Oxford, Blackwell.
Sayer, A. (1984) *Method in Social Science*, London, Hutchinson.
Schlosberg, D. (1995) 'Communicative action in practice: Intersubjectivity and new social movements', *Political Studies*, 43 (2), pp. 291-311.

Schumpeter, J. A. (1952) *Capitalism, Socialism and Democracy*, London, Allen and Unwin

Scott, A. (1990) *Ideology and the New Social Movements*, London, Unwin Hyman.

Seidman, I. E. (1991) *Interviewing as Qualitative Research: A Guide for Researchers in Education and the Social Sciences*, New York, Teachers College Press.

Seyd, P. and Whiteley, P. (1992) *Labour's Grass Roots: The Politics of Party Membership*, Oxford, Clarendon Press.

Seyd, P. and Whiteley, P. (1996a) 'Social capital formation, party activism and participation in voluntary organisations in Britain', Paper presented to European Consortium of Political Research Joint Sessions, Oslo.

Seyd, P. and Whiteley, P. (1996b) 'Rationality and party activism: Encompassing tests of alternative models of political participation', *European Journal of Political Research*, 29, pp. 215-234.

Seyd, P. and Whiteley, P. (1998) 'Blair's armchair support', *The Guardian*, 7 April 1998.

Shaffir, W. B. and Stebbins, R. A. (1991) (eds) *Experiencing Fieldwork: An Inside View of Qualitative Research*, London, Sage.

Snow, D. A., Zurcher, L. A., Ekland-Olson, S. (1980) 'Social networks and social movements: A microstructural approach to differential recruitment', *American Sociological Review*, 45, pp. 787-801.

Staeheli, L. A. (1996) 'Publicity, privacy, and women's political action', *Society and Space*, 14, pp. 601-619.

Stewart, J. (1995) *Innovation in Democratic Practice*, Birmingham, Institute of Local Government Studies.

Stewart, J. (1996) *More Innovation in Democratic Practice*, Birmingham, Institute of Local Government Studies.

Stewart, J. (1997) *Further Innovation in Democratic Practice*, Birmingham, Institute of Local Government Studies.

Stewart, J., Kendall, E. and Coote, A. (1994) *Citizens' Juries*, London, Institute for Public Policy Research.

Stoker, G. (1995) 'Introduction', in Marsh, D. and Stoker, G. (1995a) (eds), pp. 1-18.

Strauss, A. and Corbin, J. (1990) *Basics of Qualitative Research: Grounded Theory Procedures and Techniques*, London, Sage.

Taylor, J. and Bentley, T. (1997) 'Tony's new model revolution', *New Statesman*, 25 July 1997, pp. 18-19.

Taylor, S. J. (1991) 'Leaving the field: Research, relationships and responsibilities', in Shaffir, W. B. and Stebbins, R. A. (1991) (eds), pp. 238-247.

Thompson, J. B. (1993) 'The theory of the public sphere', *Theory, Culture and Society*, 10 (3), pp. 173-189.

Tonge, J. (1994) 'The anti-poll tax movement: A pressure movement?', *Politics*, 14 (2), pp. 93-99.

Tucker, K. H. (1991) 'How new are the new social movements?', *Theory, Culture and Society*, 8 (2), pp. 75-98.

van Dijk, T. A. (1993) 'Principles of critical discourse analysis', *Discourse and Society*, 4 (2), pp. 249-283.

Verba, S. and Nie, N. (1972) *Participation in America: Political Democracy and Social Equality*, New York, Harper Row.

Walzer, M. (1992) 'The civil society argument', in Mouffe, C. (1992) (ed), pp. 89-107.

Walzer, M. (1995a) (ed) *Toward a Global Civil Society*, Providence, Berghahm Books.

Walzer, M. (1995b) 'The concept of civil society', in Walzer, M. (1995a) (ed), pp. 7-27.

Ward, H. (1995) 'Rational choice theory', in Marsh, D. and Stoker, G. (1995a) (eds), pp. 76-93.

Warren, M. E. (1995) 'The self in discursive democracy', in White, S. K. (1995a) (ed), pp. 167-200.

Warren, M. E. (1996) 'What should we expect from more democracy? Radically democratic responses to politics', *Political Theory*, 24 (2), pp. 241-270.

Webb, P. D. (1994) 'Party organizational change in Britain: The iron law of centralization?', in Katz, R. S. and Mair, P. (1994) (eds), pp. 109-133.

White, S. K. (1995a) (ed), *The Cambridge Companion to Habermas*, Cambridge, Cambridge University Press.

White, S. K. (1995b) 'Introduction: Reason, modernity and democracy', in White, S. K. (1995a) (ed), pp. 3-16.

Whiteley, P., Seyd, P. and Richardson, J. (1994) *True Blues: The Politics of Conservative Party Membership*, Oxford, Clarendon Press.

Woliver, L. R. (1993) *From Outrage to Action: The Politics of Grass-Roots Dissent*, Chicago, University of Illinois Press.

Woodward, R. (1991) 'Mobilising opposition: The campaign against housing action trusts in Tower Hamlets', *Housing Studies*, 6 (1), pp. 44-56.

Yin, R. K. (1984) *Case Study Research: Design and Methods*, London, Sage.

Name Index

Alvesson, M. 64, 67
Andrews, M. 27
Arato, A. 49, 177, 178
Arnstein, S. 90
Atkinson, P. 76, 78, 80, 83, 85

Bagguley, P. 32
Baxter, H. 57
Becker, H. 86
Beetham, D. 4
Bell, J. 77
Bentley, T. 107
Beresford, P. 22
Berg, B. 87
Blair, T. 10, 94, 104, 107
Blaug, R. 42, 64
Boaden, N. *et al* 26
Boggs, C. 18
Bohman, J. 8, 42, 43, 175, 185, 188
Braaten, J. 48
Brand, A. 10, 55
Brehony, K. 25, 28, 33, 34, 37, 38
Bryman, A. 78
Buchanan, D. *et al* 79
Burgess, R. 76
Burns, D. *et al* 4, 6, 22, 26, 29, 33, 41, 63, 90, 186
Byrne, P. 18, 19, 23

Calhoun, C. 50, 59, 62, 64
Chambers, S. 49, 50, 57, 67, 159, 175, 180, 187, 188, 194
Christiansen, L. 92
Cochrane, A. 9
Cohen, A. 18
Cohen, J. 49, 177, 178, 185
Connolly, W. 48

Coote, A. 7
Corbin, J. 76, 77
Crabtree, B. 73
Croft, S. 22
Crossley, N. 46, 48

Dalton, R. 6, 17, 23, 29, 31, 38
Davey, K. 183
Devine, F. 73, 77, 81, 82, 84, 86
Dey, I. 74, 86
Diani, M. 18
Dickson, M. 7
Dowding, K. 92
Dryzek, J. 30, 42, 54, 64, 66, 67, 157, 159

Eley, G. 51

Fisher, J. 25, 35, 94
Fishkin, J. 42
Fitzgerald, M. 26
Fleming, M. 51
Forester, J. 50, 58, 64, 65, 68, 159
Fox, C. 43
Fraser, N. 13, 53, 59, 61, 67, 182

Garner, R. 94
Geer, B. 86
Geuss, R. 45, 68
Giddens, A. 42
Goodland, K. 22, 91
Grayson, J. 90
Gyford, J. 4, 20

Habermas, J. 8, 10, 11, 15, 18, 30, 42-70, 98, 100, 101, 113, 139-142, 157, 159, 173-191

Hall, J. 60, 63
Hammersley, M. 76, 78, 80, 83, 85
Held, D. 6, 8
Hill, D. 9, 22, 29
Holub, R. 44
Horster, D. 10

Jones, P. 72
Jordan, G. 13, 19, 20, 21, 25, 28, 30, 35, 36, 37, 92, 109, 114, 115, 182

Kant, E. 46
Keane, J. 4, 48, 60, 101
Keat, R. 74
Kelly, R. 94
Kemp, R. 47, 48, 49, 64
Khan, U. 9, 22, 26, 33

Leftwich, A. 3
Lenaghan, J. 7, 190
Liddle, R. 10, 107, 108
Love, N. 45, 58
Lyotard, J. 48

MacAskill, E. 19
Maloney, W. 13, 20, 21, 25, 28, 30, 35, 36, 37, 92, 109, 114, 115, 182
Mandelson, P. 10, 107
Marquand, D. 101
Marris, P. 34, 38
Marx, K. 45, 46, 56
May, T. 77, 78
McAdam, D. 32
McCarthy, J. 31
McCarthy, T. 10, 52, 177, 189
McKay, G. 19, 179, 180
McKenny, G. 46
McLaverty, P. 22, 94
McNeish, W. 179
McRobbie, A. 60
Meehan, J. 66
Mies, M. 77
Miller, D. 42, 53
Miller, H. 43
Miller, W. 7, 72, 73

Mowlam, M. 107
Mulgan, G. 7
Myerson, G. 48

Nicholson N. *et al* 37
Nie, N. 5, 31

O'Mally, J. 33, 34
Offe, C. 18, 181
Olsen, M. 5
Olson, M. 29
Outhewaite, W. 10, 44, 45, 48, 51, 52, 57, 61, 74, 75

Parry, G. *et al* 2, 3, 6, 14, 17, 18, 23, 24, 25, 26, 27, 28, 29, 31, 32, 38, 39
Pateman, C. 49
Paulsen, R. 32
Perryman, M. 94
Phillips, A. 152, 180
Puddifoot, H. 29

Rasmussen, D. 45
Ray, L. 10, 46, 58, 60, 62, 63, 157, 180, 189, 190
Robson, C. 76

Sawyer, T. 107
Sayer, A. 72, 74, 75, 76
Scholsberg, D. 66
Schumpeter, J. 8
Scott, A. 18
Seidman, I. 87, 88
Seyd, P. 9, 19, 21, 24, 28, 29, 30, 35
Snow, D. *et al* 32
Staeheli, L. 63
Stewart, J. 9, 190, 191
Stoker, G. 3, 71, 72, 76
Strauss, A. 76, 77

Taylor, J. 107
Taylor, S. 88
Thompson, J. 52, 183

Tonge, J. 18
Tucker, K. 18

Urry, J. 74

van Dijk, T. 67
Verba, S. 5, 31

Walzer, M. 7, 59, 61, 63
Ward, H. 30
Warren, M. 49, 54, 57, 62, 184, 188
Webb, P. 20, 21, 94

White, S. 26, 49, 59
Whiteley, P. 9, 19, 20, 21, 24, 25, 28, 35
Wilmott, H. 64, 67
Woliver, L. 9
Woodward, R. 34
Wright, I. 101

Yin, R. 89

Zald, M. 31